MARTIAL

EPIGRAMS V

Edited with an Introduction, Translation & Commentary

by

Peter Howell

ARIS & PHILLIPS LTD – WARMINSTER – ENGLAND

British Library Cataloguing-in-Publication Data
A catalogue record for this book is available from the British Library.

ISBNs cloth   0 85668 589 5
      limp   0 85668 590 9

Printed and published in England by Aris & Phillips Ltd. Teddington House, Warminster, Wiltshire BA12 8PQ

Contents

Preface & Acknowledgments

This commentary had its origin in a request made by the Joint Association of Classical Teachers. They asked if I would edit an anthology of Martial, but I consider it so important to read his poems in the books in which he arranged them that I proposed instead an edition of Book V. This book has several advantages: it is comparatively short (647 lines, as against 850 in Book I), it contains some of Martial's best-known poems, and it is one of the only two books, out of the regular series of I–XII, which contain no 'obscene' poems.

The JACT accepted my suggestion. However, after I had already worked for some time to their specification, it turned out that they would not be able to publish the work themselves. I am grateful to Aris and Phillips for taking it on: this meant that I had to adapt the book to suit the style of their series. It has also meant that I have not aimed it so specifically at the requirements of schools, although I hope that they will still find it useful.

It will be readily apparent that I have striven for clarity and concision. I have tried not to waste space on refuting (or even, in most cases, mentioning) interpretations which I consider to be mistaken. I hope that this will not be taken as arrogance. I have not attempted to pile up lists of references to sources ancient and modern. On the other hand, I have translated both Greek and Latin passages cited. My own translations are not intended to be taken as 'literature' in their own right: their point is to assist understanding of the Latin. I do not doubt that many people will find the commentary wanting in various aspects: it is the inescapable fate of the commentator to be unable to satisfy all his users.

I have not attempted to analyse the structure of every epigram, but have done this for a limited number of what I consider to be particularly interesting examples. I hope that this will help readers to appreciate Martial's artistry elsewhere.

I have tried not to weary the reader by constant reference back to my own earlier and more ample commentary on Book I, but assume that those who have access to it will realise that it contains fuller discussions of common matters.

Abbreviations are based on the practice of the *Oxford Latin Dictionary* and *L'Année Philologique.*

I owe a particular debt of gratitude to Professor R.G.M. Nisbet, who first guided me in the study of Martial, and instilled in me such merits as a commentator as I may possess. This commentary has benefited, in its earlier stages, from the criticism of Mr Ken Hughes, of JACT, and later from that of Professor M.M. Willcock, editor of the series for Aris and Phillips. I have gained a great deal from acting as examiner for the PhD theses of five commentators on Martial. The only one whose thesis has been published so far is Nigel Kay (Book XI), but that of T.J. Leary (Book XIV) is forthcoming. Those still unpublished include Richard George (Book III, 1-68); John Jenkins (a selection from Book X); and Michael Bowie (Book XII). Among those who have helped with advice on specific matters are Miss Lesley Fitton; Dr Nigel Kay; Dr. C. Perrin; and Dr Boris Rankov.

Peter Howell   November 1995

Introduction

1. THE LIFE OF MARTIAL

Marcus Valerius Martialis was born at Bilbilis in Hispania Tarraconensis. This little town stood on a rocky hill near the modern town of Calatayud, on the road from Zaragoza to Madrid. He was given the *cognomen* Martialis because he was born on March 1st. He must have been born in about AD 40, since X 24 celebrates his 57th birthday, and that book was published in about 95–98. His parents were called Fronto and Flaccilla (V 34). They ensured that he received the usual Roman education, in 'grammar' and oratory, which was no doubt already widely available in Spain at this time: Tarraco (Tarragona) would be the obvious place. We know nothing of his parents' background, but, from what he says about himself, he would appear to have been a native Spaniard, with bristly hair and hirsute legs and cheeks.

We know nothing about the first forty years of his life, except that in about AD 64 he settled at Rome (at X 103 – which must be among the latest poems in that book, and so date from about 98 – he says that he has been in Rome for thirty-four years). This was the natural course for any talented and ambitious provincial, and he was following in the footsteps of his literary compatriots the Senecas, Lucan, Columella, and Quintilian. No doubt he was already composing poetry: he refers to youthful works at I 113. His livelihood was probably obtained entirely through the benefactions of rich friends, and there is reason to suppose that these included the younger Seneca, and perhaps other members of the same family, together with L. Calpurnius Piso. It is possible that it was either Seneca or his heirs who gave him his estate at Nomentum, which he owned by at least c. 83 (see on V 62).

The failure of the conspiracy in AD 65 which aimed to replace Nero with Piso must have deprived Martial of some of his most generous benefactors (including Seneca), and one suspects that in the aftermath distinguished senators must have become less ostentatious in their generosity. It was open to Martial to take up the profession of rhetoric, whether by pleading in the courts or by teaching. Friends urged him to earn an honest living by doing so, including Quintilian (II 90). But he preferred a quiet life devoted to poetry and friendship (see e.g. V 20). In the absence of copyright laws, literature could bring no direct reward, but Martial provides plenty of clues to the less direct rewards available to an author who pleased his readers.

The earliest surviving work of Martial is the so-called *Liber de Spectaculis*, written to celebrate the opening of the Flavian Amphitheatre (the Colosseum) in AD 80. He seems to have enjoyed the favour of Titus (emperor 79–81), who gave him the *ius trium liberorum* (the privileges of a father of three children), despite the fact that he never even married. The honour was later confirmed by Domitian. It may also have been Titus who gave Martial his titular tribunate, a sinecure army commission which brought with it equestrian rank. To qualify as an *eques* (knight), he must have possessed at least 400,000 sesterces, a sum which would have produced enough income to enable a man to live respectably at Rome.

His next works appeared under Domitian (emperor 81–96). These were the two books of (mostly) two-line poems intended to be sent along with all sorts of presents, called the *Xenia* and *Apophoreta* (misleadingly known as Books XIII and XIV). These seem to have been published in 83 or soon after.

It was the publication of his 'Book I', probably in 86, which was the decisive stage in Martial's career. From then on his books appeared with remarkable regularity, at intervals of one or two years, up to the publication of Book XI in 96 (followed in 98 by the publication of a second edition of Book X). Meanwhile, his personal circumstances had improved. Sometime before 94 he had exchanged his third-floor flat for a small house, probably in the same part of Rome, the Quirinal (see on V 22). He also owned a pair of mules, and he mentions several slaves (I 88; 101; V 34 and 37, and X 61; also perhaps XI 91).

Nevertheless, he often found life at Rome irksome: it was noisy and expensive, and its tedious social duties interfered with his writing. He had already, in about 87, gone off for a stay at Forum Cornelii (the modern Imola, between Bologna and Ravenna): Book III was sent back from there. At last, in 98, or soon after, he decided to return to the homeland for which he had long yearned nostalgically. The younger Pliny gave him money to help with the journey. At first he found life at Bilbilis idyllic, not least because he had there a generous benefactress called Marcella, who provided him with a house and small estate (XII 31). He wrote a rapturous poem to his friend Juvenal (almost certainly the satirist), teasing him about the tiresome client's life he was still living at Rome (XII 18). But before long he became disillusioned with provincial life, with people pestering him for help, and small-town scandal-mongering – and there was nothing to write about. He sent back Book XII from there in 101 or 102 (an enlarged version of it appeared later, possibly after his death). However, within a few years of his return to Bilbilis (certainly by AD 104), he was dead. His loss was mourned by Pliny in a letter (III 21 – see pp. 12–13), which provides our only substantial piece of external evidence for Martial's life and character.

From his works, one can reach certain unprovable, but probable conclusions. As already mentioned, he never married (despite poems like XI 104 where he writes in the person of a husband). Although by no means blind to the attractions of the opposite sex, he seems to have had a preference for his own. Friendship was something which mattered greatly to him. Warm-hearted and quarrelsome, he was eternally inquisitive, but not malicious. He liked nothing so much as a quiet and sociable life, enjoying the sights, the gossip, and the luxuries of Rome. He never ceases to encourage his friends and readers to enjoy life while they can, and not take things too seriously.

2. THE DATE OF BOOK V

It is impossible to fix the date of this book with absolute certainty. It must have been published after Degis (or Diegis), brother of the Dacian king Decebalus, was sent to

Rome (V 3), and this must have taken place after Domitian had returned from his visit, in early 89, to Mainz, following the revolt of Saturninus, and to the Danube, where he came to terms with Decebalus. Domitian was certainly back in Rome by November, when he celebrated his double triumph over the Chatti and the Dacians (Jones, *Domitian*, 151).

The reference to 'triumphs', in the plural, at V 19.3, can be taken to refer to those of 83 and 86 (assuming that the latter really existed – see Jones, *Domitian*, 139), but it could also, of course, include the double triumph of 89.[1]

The book contains several references to the Saturnalia (18; 30; 59; and especially the last poem, 84), and these suggest that it was published at that time of the year (as Books XIII, XIV, VII, and XI were – also possibly IV). So December 89 would seem to be the earliest likely date. However, since Book VII was not published until December 92, and there is also, apart from that, no definite *terminus ante quem* for Book VI, December 90 would also be possible.[2]

3. MARTIAL AND DOMITIAN

Books V and VIII are the only ones, out of the series of twelve numbered books, which contain no 'improper' poems. The second poem in the book, which 'dedicates' it to matrons, boys, and girls, explains that this is done as a tribute to the emperor, so as to spare his blushes when he reads it. The prose preface and the first poem of Book VIII give a similar explanation. However, only books XI and XII were published after the death of Domitian. So why should these two have a different character from the others?

Elsewhere, Martial had been at pains to justify his outspokenness. The most important example of this is in the prose preface to Book I, where he explains that 'playful frankness' is 'the language of epigram', and is what Catullus and other Latin predecessors of Martial used. He returns to the subject at I 35, where he argues that it is the rule [*lex*] established for humorous poems 'that they cannot entertain unless they titillate', and urges the man he is addressing (possibly fictitious) not to 'castrate my books'. But, if Martial genuinely considered that obscenity was a defining characteristic of epigram, how could he 'castrate' two of his own books? It is worth noting that the only book which is shorter than V is VIII.[3]

The decision is usually related to Domitian's assumption of the perpetual censorship in AD 85. However, at I 4.7, addressed to the emperor, Martial had explicitly claimed that 'censorship can permit harmless fun'. Furthermore, although Book VI has near the beginning several poems specifically referring to the emperor's

---

1 It may seem surprising that Martial does not write more about this triumph, but then neither does he do so in Book VI, which must postdate it.

2 This is the date suggested (without argument) by Sullivan (*Martial*, 35). The most recent discussion of the date is by M. Citroni, *ICS* 14 (1989), 220–222; see also *Maia* 40 (1988), 21–2.

3 There are 82 poems in VIII; 84 in V. The longest book is I (118): the others vary between 89 and 108.

censorship (2; 4 – NB line 5; 7), it nevertheless contains a fair share of 'obscene' poems. So there must have been some particular reason why Book V differed in this respect from its four predecessors, and its two successors – to look no further ahead.

In order to find a possible explanation, one needs to consider Martial's relationship with Domitian. It has already been argued (above, page 1) that the emperor Titus had shown his favour in practical ways. Since no love was lost between the two brothers, this would not in itself have recommended Martial to Domitian. Books XIII and XIV, published perhaps two and three years after the accession of Domitian, contain compliments to the emperor (XIII 4; 127; XIV 1). In Book I he plays a greater role. At I 4 (see above), Martial asks that, if the emperor should 'happen upon his books by chance', he should read them with a relaxed state of mind, and in the succeeding poem he puts a humorous reply into the emperor's mouth (a liberty which he never repeated). The book contains a 'cycle' of seven poems dealing with a spectacle put on by the emperor, at which a lion allowed a hare to jump in and out of its jaws: this is the occasion for flattery of Domitian which (as often) compares him to Jupiter.

The second book also contains a tribute to him near the beginning (II 2), and at the end (91) he asks him, if his poems have pleased him, to give him the privileges of a father of three children (or rather – to judge from III 95.5 and IX 97.5 – to confirm the grant made by Titus). The next poem (92) humorously reports the granting of this request, as 'a reward for my poetry'. In the third book, the only reference to the emperor appears at 95, where, in comparing himself with a superior man, he says that 'both Caesars' have praised and rewarded him (see above), and also refers to his tribunate, and to the fact that he has 'made many citizens by the bounty of Caesar' (in other words on Martial's recommendation). The absence of any poems directly flattering the emperor may be explained by the circumstance that the book was written at Forum Cornelii: Martial may have thought it less important to seek imperial favour when he was out of the capital. By contrast, the fourth book opens with a poem lavishly praising Domitian, and see also 3, 8, 11, 74, and especially 27, where he addresses the emperor, saying that he is accustomed to praise his books, and has rewarded him with gifts (which must refer in particular to the *ius trium liberorum*), and humorously suggests that the best way to punish those who are jealous is to give him even more.

This would seem to indicate a renewed eagerness to ingratiate himself with Domitian, and this is the most likely explanation for the character of Book V. Presumably the experiment had no obvious result, and so in his next book Martial reverted to his usual practice. The explanation for the character of the eighth book must be its formal dedication to Domitian.

Martial's flattery of the emperor has been a stumbling block for readers in recent times. However, there is no reason to suppose that he was particularly close to him. At IX 18 he asks for a private water-supply, but the fact that he never published an epigram thanking the emperor for it indicates that (unlike Statius) he never got it. Nor does he ever record other such signs of favour as does Statius – for example, an invitation to dinner (Stat. *Silv*. IV 2). Two other factors have been emphasised by recent scholarship. The first is the partial rehabilitation of the character of

Domitian.[4] He was intolerant of any opposition, and was loathed by the established members of the senatorial class, but he was conspicuously efficient and successful at ensuring the peace and good government of the Empire. The second point – which, however, lacks all plausibility – is the suggestion that Martial's apparent flattery of the emperor actually conceals criticism. N. Holzberg even argues that Domitian must have realised what Martial was up to, but tolerated it.[5]

There is no good reason to doubt Domitian's interest in literature, despite Suetonius's denial (*Dom.* 20). A limit to his appreciation of Martial would seem to be set by Jones's description of him as 'completely lacking a sense of humour' (*Domitian*, 198). On the other hand, his ability to turn a witty phrase is shown by the remarks quoted by Suetonius in the passage referred to – for example, his complaint that no-one ever believed that a conspiracy had been formed against a ruler unless he had been assassinated.[6]

It cannot be denied that Martial's abuse of Domitian once he had been got rid of does him no credit. But he can hardly be blamed for flattering him while he was alive. He owed to his deceased brother and to him his prized status as a member of the equestrian order – his pride in which is clearly revealed in Book V by the series of epigrams rejoicing in the imperial edict which reinstated the law guaranteeing the knights reserved seats in the theatre. The emperor was the ultimate source of all patronage (as even Juvenal would emphasise at the beginning of his seventh satire), and Martial was bound to direct his efforts towards securing his generosity.

4. WHAT IS AN EPIGRAM?

The word 'epigram' comes from the Greek ἐπιγράφειν, 'to write on' something.[7] Its earliest uses were practical – for example, to record who was buried under a stone, or who had dedicated an object, and to which god, or who had made it, or to whom it belonged. Naturally such an inscription would be brief, and the earliest known are in verse, which makes them more memorable. Eventually the word came to be used only for verse. By the fifth century this was usually the elegiac couplet, which remained the most common metre throughout antiquity. Fictitious epigrams were being written by the fourth century, and by the third its range had extended to include sympotic and erotic poetry.

This was the work of the Alexandrian poets, and it is not surprising that, with their insistence on brevity and neatness, they should have had a special liking for the genre of epigram. Martial considered that Callimachus himself was the greatest Greek epigrammatist (IV 23). Epigrams at this period were often comparatively long (up to sixteen lines – the length of Callimachus's longest) and in a variety of metres.

---

4   See especially B.W. Jones, *The Emperor Domitian* (London, 1992).
5   *Martial* (Heidelberg, 1988). See my review in *CR* 40(1990), 36.
6   See K.M. Coleman, *ANRW* 2.32.5, 3091–2.
7   This account is based on that of Alan Cameron, *The Greek Anthology* (Oxford, 1993), 1–18.

The compilation of anthologies, containing poems by one or by several authors, may go back at least to the early third century, when epigrams by Asclepiades, Posidippus and Hedylus may have been put together in the so-called *Soros*, possibly by Hedylus himself. In about 100 BC Meleager, himself an accomplished epigrammatist, compiled his *Garland*, possibly of as many as 1,000 epigrams. His selection was based on principles which have shaped our concept of the genre, with a substantial proportion consisting of erotic poems – the type for which he himself was best known. By Meleager's time the elegiac couplet was virtually standard for the genre.

It is not certain whether the genre of satirical epigram existed as such before the time of the later Greek epigrammatists whose work was collected by Philip of Thessalonica in his *Garland*, published under Nero. This collection reveals the pervasive influence of rhetoric, and the satirical epigram looms large. Its most striking exponent in Greek was Lucillius, who wrote at Rome in the generation after Philip: he was an important model for Martial.[8]

Meanwhile, the Latin epigram had a history of its own, going back to the epitaphs in the Saturnian metre from the Tomb of the Scipios (mid-3rd century BC).[9] Obviously these already show Greek influence. Other early examples were also intended as epitaphs or inscriptions, but the literary epigram can be said to go back as far as Ennius. His epitaph for himself (whether or not intended for actual use) is a masterpiece of epigrammatic structure and concision. A number of other specimens exist, of which the most celebrated are the two on the subject of boy-love by Q. Lutatius Catulus and Porcius Licinus which are preserved by Aulus Gellius (*NA* XIX 9.13).

Much the most important Latin model for Martial was Catullus, and he makes it clear that his dearest wish would be to be ranked second after him (X 78). Catullus is not generally thought of as an epigrammatist, but for Martial all his shorter poems, in whatever metre, served as models, and there is no reason why they should not be so classified.[10] It is conceivable that their original arrangement was similar to that found in Martial, with metre serving for variety. Of the other epigrammatists mentioned by Martial as his particular models, Marsus and Pedo (see on V 5), we know regrettably little.

If one attempts a definition of the epigram, as practised up to the time of Martial, it is impossible to be more specific than 'a short poem, generally of six lines or less, most commonly in elegiac couplets, on any conceivable subject'. There is evidence, not least from Martial himself, that doctrinaire theorists attempted to restrict the genre in length and in metre, but this was probably a comparatively recent development.

How then does one account for the modern definition of epigram? The *Concise Oxford Dictionary* has 'Short poem ending in witty turn of thought'. In fact, it was

---

8   W. Burnikel, *Untersuchungen zur Struktur des Witzepigramms bei Lukillios und Martial* (Wiesbaden, 1980).

9   For the Latin epigram before Martial, see N.M. Kay, *Martial Book XI* (London, 1985), 9–13.

10   Bruce W. Swann, *Martial's Catullus* (Hildesheim, 1994).

Martial himself who was chiefly responsible, since he brought this type of epigram to such a pitch of perfection that it has shaped the concept for later ages – regardless of the fact that such a definition will fit only a limited number of his poems.

5. MARTIAL AND THE EPIGRAM

It was a bold decision for Martial to concentrate on the genre of epigram alone. There were a number of reasons for doing so, the most important of which stem from his own character. It is obvious that he had a particular hatred for all forms of pretentiousness and hypocrisy, and he detested the current fashion for following the risky precedent set by Virgil and writing stale mythological epics – a fashion made all the more attractive by the political and social harmlessness of such subject-matter (Juv. 1.162–4). As he himself says, he is not interested in Gorgons or Harpies, but in real people (X 4), and it is his acute perception of human nature, and boundless interest in the life going on around him, that make him so permanently fascinating.

His concern with mankind, however, is not malicious: he never attacks real people, even under fictitious names (see I *Praef.*). In this, he differed conspicuously from Catullus. To some extent, it was imposed on him by the circumstances of the Early Empire, when personal attacks were likely to incur punishment.[11] However, Martial's temperament was averse to any such abuse of the writer's power, as he makes clear in the Preface to his first book (already referred to). He would have approved of the rule laid down by his fellow-Spaniard Quintilian: *nimium enim risus pretium est, si probitatis impendio constat (Inst. Or., Praef.–* 'a laugh is won at too high a price if it costs the loss of good character'). In avoiding personal attack, Martial's work may have lost, for his contemporary readers, a certain amount of topicality and fire. But it gained in return a timelessness and breadth of application which doubtless helped it to survive. Attacks on real people naturally tend to lose their interest when the victims are unfamiliar to the readers.[12]

The knottiest problem faced by an epigrammatist is that of preventing the reader from becoming wearied by so many short poems. The principal way in which Martial countered this was by taking great pains over the arrangement of his poems within each book. Variety was the chief aim, although inter-relationships could also play a significant role. Variety might be achieved in subject-matter, in length, and in metre. Inter-relationships might be established in a number of different ways. There are five poems in which the emperor is directly addressed, including the first of all: the others are put in third, fifteenth, and nineteenth places, with the last at sixtyfifth – two thirds of the way through. Five other poems refer to the emperor, and these are placed within the first eight. Obviously the opening of the book – the part most likely to be read by the casual browser, and to be read with closest attention – was the most complimentary position. So two of these poems address important freedmen of Domitian (5 and 6), and most of the poems addressing important friends

---

11   See M. Coffey, *Roman Satire* (London, 1976), 98–9.
12   Some modern critics have been unwilling to take Martial at his word on this subject. See V 15.2, and especially VII 12 – and *Honi soit qui mal y pense.*

of the poet are also placed near the beginning (10, to Regulus; 11, to Severus, concerning Stella; 12, to Stella; 20, to Iulius Martialis; 30, to Varro; and note also 28), though others are set at wider intervals (48, to Pudens; 59, to Stella; 71, to Faustinus). Severus is addressed again, along with Secundus, at 80, where the subject dictates the poem's position near the end of the book. The eight poems dealing with the theatre edict are placed at intervals within the first half of the book (8, 14, 22, 25, 27, 35, 38, 41), as is Martial's practice with such 'cycles'.[13] In this way, the reader is not wearied by an uninterrupted series, but can still perceive the interconnections. Similarly the two poems on Erotion are not placed side by side, but are separated by two poems of quite different character. Sometimes, however, two poems have to be set together, for the meaning of the second to be comprehensible, e.g. 11 and 12.

Some inter-relationships are distinctly subtle. V 64 refers to imperial mausolea, which might seem a trifle tactless, but the next poem specifically asks the gods to grant Domitian long life. The first poem on the theatre edict (8) follows a poem praising the emperor for the splendid new physical aspect of the city, thus implying that improved social regulation is an added blessing. Poem 13, in which Martial speaks proudly of his status as a knight, precedes one of the poems on the theatre edict, and so hints at Martial's vested interest in its operation. Poem 18, which cleverly justifies Martial's apparent meanness, as a *pauper*, in not sending expensive Saturnalia presents, precedes a poem in which he regrets the failure of richer men to support their *pauper* friend. Similarly poem 15, where he claims to the emperor that the lack of profitable return for his poems is unimportant, is followed by a longer poem addressed to the reader which jokingly complains about the lack of return. This recurring theme turns up again at the end of the book, where 81, 82, and 84 all drop hints. Sometimes a short, humorous poem is used to interrupt a more solemn sequence: obvious examples are 4 and 9.

A conspicuous example of variety in length appears at 77–79, near the end of the book, where the longest poem in it (78, with 32 lines) is flanked by one of two lines and one of six. It will be noticed that the next longest poem (37, with 24 lines), set towards the middle of the book, also follows a distich.

6. METRE[14]

In Book V Martial uses only three metres – elegiac couplets (58 poems); hendecasyllables (16); and scazons (10).[15] Metre was one of the ways in which he achieved variety (see above), and it is not surprising that the poems in different metres tend to alternate. It is noteworthy that at no point do a poem in hendecasyllables and a poem in scazons appear side by side, nor do two poems in

---

13   K. Barwick, 'Zyklen bei Martial und in den kleinen Gedichten von Catull', *Philologus* 102 (1958), 284–318.

14   For a detailed account of Martial's metres see Friedlaender, 26–50 (the section on the elegiac couplet is by T. Birt). Sullivan (227–230) follows that account closely.

15   In other books, Martial occasionally uses other metres (Friedlaender, 27).

either of these two metres. On the other hand, the higher proportion of poems in elegiac couplets makes it inevitable that they often occur in 'runs', of which the longest consists of the nine poems 61–69 (the next longest consists of six – 29–34).

In the elegiac couplet, Martial's practice is less strict than that of Ovid, but nevertheless observes certain rules. At the end of the pentameter, he allows polysyllables, including (at V 50.2 – cf. XIV 201.2) a word of six syllables. He also allows monosyllables, though these are always preceded by a word of one or two syllables (e.g. V 61.2 *quis est*; 62.8 *minus est*). In some respects, his practice in Book V is stricter than in some other books: for example, here a word of three syllables at the end of the pentameter is always preceded by a monosyllable (e.g. 7.6; 9.4), and there is no elision in the second half of a pentameter. His use of elision in hexameters is also judicious. At the end of the hexameter, he sometimes uses two monosyllables, but only if closely connected (e.g. 9.1 *protinus ad me*; 13.3 *dicitur hic est*; 33.1). When a line ends with a disyllable preceded by another of two shorts, this is always preceded by a monosyllable (e.g. 13.9; 19.7; 29.3; 61.7; 76.3). Words of five syllables are placed at the end (e.g. 81.1 *Aemiliane*). In spondaic lines, the fourth foot is always a dactyl, and a final word is usually of four syllables (e.g. 64.5). Martial's practice with regard to caesuras also shows care. For example, the type of line (found in Ovid) in which there are caesuras in the second and fourth, but not in the third, feet, is rare in Martial (e.g. 7.7 *parce, pater: sic Lemniacis lasciva catenis*). In Book V, there are only two examples of a word of three syllables before a final trisyllable.

The hendecasyllable was (as the name implies) a line of eleven syllables. It was a favourite metre of Catullus, which is sufficient to account for Martial's fondness for it. In this metre, Martial always uses a spondee at the opening of the line, unlike Catullus, whose practice seemed harsh to later authors (Plin., *HN Praef.* 1). He rarely allows the words in a line to correspond with the feet: an example is 20.9 *campus, porticus, umbra, Virgo, thermae*, where he obviously intends the special effect to emphasise the list ('counting the elements of the happy life piece by piece' – Friedlaender). Where Martial has a monosyllable at the end of a line it is always preceded by another monosyllable (e.g. 80.8 *hic est*), or an elided word.

The third metre used in the book is the scazon (or choliambus). The name means 'limping', and the distinguishing feature of this type of iambic trimeter is that the last foot is always a spondee or a trochee: the penultimate long syllable, together with the inevitably preceding long syllable, makes the line drag. Martial rarely uses a 'pure' scazon, and usually has a spondee in the first or third feet, or in both, though never in the fifth. He often uses a dactyl in the first or third foot; the only line where he has dactyls in both is V 37.5 *nec modo politum pecudis Indicae dentem*. The first foot is the only place where an anapaest is permitted, and he rarely uses a tribrach here. On the rare occasions when he places a monosyllable before the caesura, he usually precedes it with another (e.g. 37.20 *deflere non te*).

To sum up, Martial in his use of metre avoids the extremes of either rigidity or license: he pursues the middle course that one would expect of so well-tempered a writer.

7. THE TEXT

The division of the MSS into three families (deriving from a common source in antiquity, rather than in the Middle Ages) was first made by Schneidewin. They are as follows:

α : represented only by three *florilegia* of the 9th–10th centuries.

β : this edition goes back to a recension made in AD 401 by Torquatus Gennadius. Its archetype may have been a MS recorded in Florence by Politian.

γ : represented by the largest number of surviving MSS.

On the whole it may be said that the text of Martial is in a comparatively healthy state. It has been fortunate in receiving the attention of editors of the calibre of Lindsay, Heraeus, and Shackleton Bailey, and among scholars who have contributed to the solution of individual problems Housman occupies a notable place.

One question which has aroused a good deal of discussion is that of whether some of the variant readings of the MSS might go back to the author himself. It is most unlikely that this is so: see W. Schmid, 'Spätantike Textdepravationen in den Epigrammen Martials', *Ausgewählte philologische Schriften* (Berlin, 1984), 400–444.

In the matter of orthography, Lindsay tended to follow the MS tradition, even when it was inconsistent. Heraeus, however, was probably right to adopt a more systematic approach, and this has been done also by Shackleton Bailey and in this edition.

8. CONCLUSION

Martial has always been valued for the extraordinarily vivid insights which he gives into the life of imperial Rome. His infinite curiosity, and fascination with the humorous and bizarre, are immediately attractive. The satirical element in his work (which was a vital influence on Rome's greatest satirist, Juvenal) appeals strongly to an age which revels in this type of irreverence. Martial's chief enemy is always the hypocrite, and the obverse of this is his preference for plain talking and straightforward living. In an age when priggish philosophising was fashionable, his commonsense humanity must have been refreshing: no wonder his readers loved him.

The idea that writers like Martial and Juvenal were trapped in a system where their social position deprived them of any chance of honourably earning a living, and left them dependent on the charity of mean 'patrons', is one which they themselves cultivate, but it is a fiction. As mentioned above, the obvious way for them to earn a living, as Martial several times makes clear, was by practising in the law-courts, or by teaching, but these professions were distasteful and impossible to combine with the sort of writing to which they wanted to devote themselves. One may then criticise Martial for his more or less blatant begging, but one has to allow for a difference in attitudes. His contemporaries would not have found the idea of a literary man hoping for support from his wealthy friends any more reprehensible than it would have seemed in England up to the eighteenth century.

Above all we must value Martial as a poet. Our conception of the poet in the twentieth century has widened sufficiently for us to have no problem in appreciating a poet for whom verbal dexterity and wit are more important than romantic effusion. And it would in any case be sadly mistaken to see Martial as a poet without a heart: for all that romantic love is not one of his professed themes, he can write movingly of human affection and warm friendship.

His work may not be classed as 'great literature', but there is a good deal to be said for a writer who perceives with a steady eye the genre for which his talents best suit him, and pursues his chosen course with a success that rewards the diligence and conscientiousness which his artistry conceals.

Testimonium

Pliny, *Epistles* III.21, quoting Martial X.20.12–21:

C. PLINIVS CORNELIO PRISCO SVO S.

Audio Valerium Martialem decessisse et moleste fero. erat homo ingeniosus, acutus, acer, et qui plurimum in scribendo et salis haberet et fellis nec candoris minus. prosecutus eram viatico secedentem: dederam hoc amicitiae, dederam etiam versiculis, quos de me composuit. fuit moris antiqui eos, qui vel singulorum laudes vel urbium scripserant, aut honoribus aut pecunia ornare; nostris vero temporibus ut alia speciosa et egregia ita hoc in primis exolevit. nam, postquam desiimus facere laudanda, laudari quoque ineptum putamus.

Quaeris, qui sint versiculi, quibus gratiam rettuli? remitterem te ad ipsum volumen, nisi quosdam tenerem; tu, si placuerint hi, ceteros in libro requires. adloquitur Musam, mandat, ut domum meam Esquiliis quaerat, adeat reverenter:

> Sed ne tempore non tuo disertam
> pulses ebria ianuam, videto:
> totos dat tetricae dies Minervae,
> dum centum studet auribus virorum
> hoc, quod saecula posterique possint
> Arpinis quoque comparare chartis.
> seras tutior ibis ad lucernas;
> haec hora est tua, cum furit Lyaeus,
> cum regnat rosa, cum madent capilli:
> tunc me vel rigidi legant Catones!

Meritone eum, qui haec de me scripsit, et tunc dimisi amicissime et nunc ut amicissimum defunctum esse doleo? dedit enim mihi, quantum maximum potuit, daturus amplius, si potuisset. tametsi quid homini potest dari maius quam gloria et laus et aeternitas? 'at non erunt aeterna, quae scripsit'; non erunt fortasse, ille tamen scripsit, tamquam essent futura. vale.

Pliny, *Epistles* III.21, quoting Martial X.20.12–21:

I hear that Valerius Martialis has died, and I am sorry. He was talented, sharp, and passionate, and in his writing he had a great deal of wit and gall and an equal amount of frankness. When he left Rome, I helped him with a contribution for his journey: this was in return for his friendship, and also for the verses which he wrote about me. It was an old custom to reward those who had written eulogies of individuals or of cities with either honours or money; however, in our times, along with many other attractive and admirable practices, this one likewise has been conspicuous in becoming obsolete. For, since we have ceased to do things worthy of praise, we consider it bad form also to be praised.

Do you ask which are the verses for which I showed my gratitude? I should refer you to the volume itself, if I did not know some of them by heart; if these please you, you will look out the rest in the book. He addresses his Muse, and bids her seek out my house on the Esquiline, and approach it reverently:

> 'But take care not to beat on his eloquent door at a time which does not belong to you: he gives up his whole days to stern Minerva, while he works to please the ears of the hundred men [the centumviral court] with work which later ages may compare even with Cicero's pages. It will be safer for you to go when the late lamps are lit: this is your hour, when the god of relaxation raves, when the rose rules, when hair drips with perfume. Then let even stiff Catos read me!'

Was I justified both in giving a most friendly send–off to the man who wrote these things about me, and in grieving now for the death of an excellent friend? For he gave me the greatest gift he could, and would have given more if he had been able. And yet what greater gift can be given to a man than glory and praise and eternity? 'But what he wrote will not last for eternity': perhaps it will not, but he wrote as if it would. Farewell.

Bibliography

Editions of Martial

T. Farnaby, London 1605 (with commentary)

K. Schrevel, Amsterdam 1656 (*cum notis Farnabii et variorum* – later editions in 1661 and 1670 incorporate notes by J.F. Gronov)

V. Collesson, Paris 1680 (*ad usum Delphini* – *cum notis variorum*)

F. G Schneidewin, Grimma 1842; 2nd edition, Leipzig 1853

F.A. Paley and W.H. Stone, London 1868 (selection – with commentary)

W. Gilbert, Leipzig 1886 (*Bibliotheca Teubneriana*; 2nd edition, 1896)

L. Friedlaender, Leipzig 1886 (with commentary)

W.M. Lindsay, Oxford 1903 (*Oxford Classical Texts*; 2nd edition 1929)

R.T. Bridge and E.D.C. Lake, Oxford 1908 (selection – with commentary)

W.C.A. Ker, London 1919–20 (*Loeb Classical Library*)

W. Heraeus, Leipzig 1925 (*Bibliotheca Teubneriana*; '*editio correctior*' by I. Borovskij,1976)

H.J. Izaac, Paris 1930–33 (*Collection Budé*)

M. Citroni, Florence 1975 (Book I – with commentary)

P. Howell, London 1980 (Book I – with commentary)

U. Carratello, Rome 1981 (*Liber Spectaculorum*)

N.M. Kay, London 1985 (Book XI – with commentary)

D.R. Shackleton Bailey, Stuttgart 1990 (*Bibliotheca Teubneriana*)

D.R Shackleton Bailey, Cambridge, Mass., 1993 (*Loeb Classical Library*)

T.J. Leary (forthcoming), (Book XIV – with commentary)

Works Referred to by Abbreviations

J. André, *L'Alimentation et la Cuisine à Rome*, Paris 1961

J.P.V.D. Balsdon, *Life and Leisure in Ancient Rome*, London 1969

H. Blümner, *Die römischen Privataltertümer*, München 1911

CIL = *Corpus Inscriptionum Latinarum*

S. Demougin, *L'Ordre Équestre sous les Julio-Claudiens*, Paris 1988

L. Friedlaender, *SG* = *Darstellungen aus der Sittengeschichte Roms*, 10th edition, ed. G. Wissowa, Leipzig 1921–3

J.B. Hofmann, *Lateinische Umgangssprache*, 3rd edition, Heidelberg 1951

Brian W. Jones, *The Emperor Domitian*, London 1992

C. Marot, *Les Épigrammes*, ed. C.A. Mayer, London 1970

R. Meiggs, *Roman Ostia*, 2nd edition, Oxford 1973

E. Nash, *Pictorial Dictionary of Rome*, revised edition, London 1968

OLD = *Oxford Latin Dictionary*

L. Richardson, *A New Topographical Dictionary of Ancient Rome*, Baltimore 1992

J.P. Sullivan, *Martial: The Unexpected Classic*, Cambridge 1991

TLL = *Thesaurus Linguae Latinae*

Books and Articles about Martial

This is merely a personal selection. Fuller bibliographies may be found in M. Citroni's edition of Book I; in J.P. Sullivan's *Martial: The Unexpected Classic* (Cambridge 1991); and, covering the years 1901–70, by G.W.M. Harrison in *Lustrum* 18 (1975), 300–337.

Amos, Andrew   *Martial and the Moderns*   Cambridge 1858

Barwick, Karl   *Martial und die zeitgenössische Rhetorik*   Leipzig 1959

Citroni, Mario   'Pubblicazione e dediche dei libri in Marziale', *Maia* 40 (1988), 3–39

Dolç, Miguel   *Hispania y Marçial*   Barcelona 1949

Hausmann, F.–R.   'Martial in Italien', *Studi medievali* 17 (1976), 173–218

Holzberg, Niklas   *Martial*   Heidelberg 1988

Laurens, Pierre   *L'Abeille dans l'Ambre: Célébration de l'Épigramme*   Paris 1989

Lindsay, W.M.   *The Ancient Editions of Martial*   Oxford 1903

Mason, H.A.   'Is Martial a Classic?', *The Cambridge Quarterly* 17 (1988), 297–368

Mehnert, K.–H.   *Sal Romanus und Esprit Français: Studien zur Martialrezeption in Frankreich des sechzehnten und siebzehnten Jahrhunderts*   Bonn, 1970

Nixon, Paul   *Martial and the Modern Epigram*   New York 1927

Prinz, S.   *Martial und die griechische Epigrammatik*   Vienna 1911

Reeve. M.D.   'Martial' in *Texts and Transmission*, ed. L. D. Reynolds   Oxford 1983, 239–244

Schmid, Wolfgang   'Spätantike Textdepravationen in den Epigrammen Martials', in *Ausgewählte philologische Schriften*,   Berlin 1984, 400–444

Siedschlag, Edgar   *Zur Form von Martials Epigrammen*   Berlin 1977

Siedschlag, Edgar   *Martial Konkordanz*   Hildesheim 1979

Sullivan, J.P.   *Martial: The Unexpected Classic*   Cambridge 1991

Sullivan, J.P. and Whigham, Peter   *Epigrams of Martial Englished by Divers Hands*   Berkeley 1987

Swann, Bruce W.   *Martial's Catullus*   Hildesheim 1994

Weinreich, Otto   *Studien zu Martial*   Stuttgart 1928

Whipple, T.K.   *Martial and the English Epigram from Sir Thomas Wyatt to Ben Jonson*   Berkeley 1925

Sigla

α	=	archetypum codicum HTR
β	=	archetypum codicum LPQf
γ	=	archetypum codicum EXAVBGC
A	=	Vossianus Leidensis primus (Q 56), saec. XI
B	=	Vossianus Leidensis secundus (Q 121), saec. XII
Bonon.	=	Bononiensis 2221, saec. XIV
C	=	Vossianus Leidensis tertius (F 89), saec. XIV
E	=	Edinburgensis bibliothecae Facultatis Advocatorum, saec. X in.
F	=	Florentinus membranaceus bibliothecae Laurentianae (XXXV, 38), saec. XV
f	=	Florentinus chartaceus bibliothecae Laurentianae (XXXV, 39), saec. XV
Fris.	=	Frisingensia excerpta bibliothecae Monacensis (6292), saec. XI
G	=	Gudianus Wolfenbuttelensis (157), saec. XII
H	=	Hauptii florilegium Vindobonense (277), saec. IX in.
It.	=	Italorum doctorum coniecturas codices et libri impressi qui exhibent
L	=	Lucensis, nunc Berolinensis (fol. 612), saec. XII
M	=	Marginalia Bongarsii in libro impresso bibliothecae publicae Bernensis
N	=	Nostrodamensia excerpta Parisina (188), saec. XIII
P	=	Palatinus Vaticanus (1696), saec. XV
Q	=	Arondellianus Musei Britannici (136), saec. XV
R	=	Vossianum florilegium Leidense (Q 86), saec. IX
T	=	Thuaneum florilegium Parisinum (8071), saec. IX–X
V	=	Vaticanus (3294), saec. X
Vindob. 3	=	Vindobonensis Lat. 316, saec. XV
W	=	Westmonasteriensis 15, saec. XIII
X	=	Puteaneus Parisinus (8067), saec. X

MARTIAL V

Epigrammata
Liber V

1

Hoc tibi, Palladiae seu collibus uteris Albae,
    Caesar, et hinc Triviam prospicis, inde Thetin,
seu tua veridicae discunt responsa sorores,
    plana suburbani qua cubat unda freti,
seu placet Aeneae nutrix seu filia Solis   5
    sive salutiferis candidus Anxur aquis,
mittimus, o rerum felix tutela salusque,
    sospite quo gratum credimus esse Iovem.
tu tantum accipias: ego te legisse putabo
    et tumidus Galla credulitate fruar.   10

2

Matronae puerique virginesque,
vobis pagina nostra dedicatur.
tu, quem nequitiae procaciores
delectant nimium salesque nudi,
lascivos lege quattuor libellos: 5
quintus cum domino liber iocatur;
quem Germanicus ore non rubenti
coram Cecropia legat puella.

1   (T; R 7–8)   **1 hoc** βγ : **haec** T   **8 credimus** β: **quaerimus** γ
2   **6 iocatur** It. : **vo**–γ : **iocetur** β

Epigrams
Book V

1

We send this to you, Caesar, whether you are enjoying the hills of Palladian
Alba, and looking out on one side at Trivia, on the other at Thetis, whether
the truth-telling sisters are learning their responses from you, where the wave
of the suburban strait reclines, whether the nurse of Aeneas pleases you, or
the daughter of the Sun, or white-gleaming Anxur with its health-giving
waters; to you, O happy protector and saviour of the world, whose own
safety leads us to believe that Jupiter is grateful. May you just accept it: I
shall imagine that you have read it, and, swollen with pride, enjoy my Gallic
credulity.

2

Matrons, boys, and girls, our page is dedicated to you. As for you, who take
excessive delight in ruder naughtiness and naked jokes, you should read the
four playful books: the fifth book has its fun in the company of its lord.
This book Germanicus may read without a blush in the presence of the
Cecropian girl.

MARTIAL

3

Accola iam nostrae Degis, Germanice, ripae,
    a famulis Histri qui tibi venit aquis,
laetus et attonitus viso modo praeside mundi
    affatus comites dicitur esse suos:
'sors mea quam fratris melior, cui tam prope fas est   5
    cernere tam longe quem colit ille deum.'

4

Fetere multo Myrtale solet vino,
sed fallat ut nos, folia devorat lauri
merumque cauta fronde, non aqua miscet.
hanc tu rubentem prominentibus venis
quotiens venire, Paule, videris contra,   5
dicas licebit 'Myrtale bibit laurum.'

5

Sexte, Palatinae cultor facunde Minervae,
    ingenio frueris qui propiore dei –
nam tibi nascentes domini cognoscere curas
    et secreta ducis pectora nosse licet–,
sit locus et nostris aliqua tibi parte libellis,   5
    qua Pedo, qua Marsus quaque Catullus erit.
ad Capitolini caelestia carmina belli
    grande cothurnati pone Maronis opus.

4   1 **myrtale** vel sim. β : **tuccius** γ (sed v.4 **hanc** et v.6 **Myrtale**)

3

Degis, the inhabitant of a river-bank which is now ours, who has come to you, Germanicus, from the subject waters of the Ister, was filled with joy and amazement when he had lately seen the ruler of the world, and is said to have addressed his companions thus: 'My fortune is better than that of my brother, for I am privileged to see at close quarters him whom he reveres at such a distance as a god'.

4

Myrtale usually stinks of a lot of wine, but, to trick us, she gobbles up laurel leaves, and mixes her wine not with water but with the protective leaf. Whenever, Paulus, you see her coming along with red face and bulging veins, you may say: 'Myrtale has drunk laurel'.

5

Sextus, eloquent worshipper of Palatine Minerva, you who enjoy the god's genius at closer quarters – for you are permitted to become familiar with the literary efforts of our master as they come to birth, and to know the secrets of our leader's heart – may you find a place somewhere for my little books too, where Pedo, where Marsus, and where Catullus will be. Beside the heavenly poems of the Capitoline War set the great work of buskined Virgil.

6

Si non est grave nec nimis molestum,
Musae, Parthenium rogate vestrum:
sic te serior et beata quondam
salvo Caesare finiat senectus
et sis invidia favente felix,   5
sic Burrus cito sentiat parentem:
admittas timidam brevemque chartam
intra limina sanctioris aulae.
nosti tempora tu Iovis sereni,
cum fulget placido suoque vultu,   10
quo nil supplicibus solet negare.
non est quod metuas preces iniquas:
numquam grandia nec molesta poscit
quae cedro decorata purpuraque
nigris pagina crevit umbilicis.   15
nec porrexeris ista, sed teneto
sic tamquam nihil offeras agasque.
si novi dominum novem sororum,
ultro purpureum petet libellum.

7

Qualiter Assyrios renovant incendia nidos,
    una decem quotiens saecula vixit avis,
taliter exuta est veterem nova Roma senectam
    et sumpsit vultus praesidis ipsa sui.
iam precor oblitus notae, Vulcane, querelae   5
    parce: sumus Martis turba sed et Veneris.
parce, pater: sic Lemniacis lasciva catenis
    ignoscat coniunx et patienter amet.

7   (TR 1–4)

6

If it is not troublesome, or too much of a nuisance, Muses, make this request to your Parthenius: may a more extended and a happy old age bring your life to an end at a far-off date, while Caesar is still in good health; may you be fortunate, as envy smiles upon you; and may Burrus soon learn to appreciate his father, should you admit my fearful and brief book within the doors of the more sacred part of the palace. You know the times when Jupiter is peaceful, when he glows with the placid expression which is natural to him, and wearing which he is accustomed to refuse nothing to those who approach him. There is no reason why you should be afraid of unreasonable requests: great and tiresome demands are never made by my page, which is decorated with cedar-oil and purple, and has grown longer with its black knobs. You should not stretch out to hand over my poems, but hold onto them as if you were offering nothing and doing nothing. If I know the master of the nine sisters, he will ask for the purple book of his own accord.

7

Just as fires renew Assyrian nests, as often as the one bird has lived ten ages, so has the new Rome stripped itself of its former old age and itself taken on the appearance of its ruler. I beg you now, Vulcan, to forget your well-known complaint and spare us: we are the crowd of Mars, but also of Venus. Spare us, father: so may your playful wife forgive you for the Lemnian chains and show moderation in her love.

8

Edictum domini deique nostri,
quo subsellia certiora fiunt
et puros eques ordines recepit,
dum laudat modo Phasis in theatro,
Phasis purpureis ruber lacernis,   5
et iactat tumido superbus ore:
'tandem commodius licet sedere,
nunc est reddita dignitas equestris;
turba non premimur, nec inquinamur' –
haec et talia dum refert supinus,   10
illas purpureas et arrogantes
iussit surgere Leitus lacernas.

9

Languebam: sed tu comitatus protinus ad me
   venisti centum, Symmache, discipulis.
centum me tetigere manus Aquilone gelatae:
   non habui febrem, Symmache, nunc habeo.

10

'Esse quid hoc dicam vivis quod fama negatur
   et sua quod rarus tempora lector amat?'
hi sunt invidiae nimirum, Regule, mores,
   praeferat antiquos semper ut illa novis.
sic veterem ingrati Pompei quaerimus umbram,   5
   sic laudant Catuli vilia templa senes.
Ennius est lectus salvo tibi, Roma, Marone,
   et sua riserunt saecula Maeoniden,
rara coronato plausere theatra Menandro,
   norat Nasonem sola Corinna suum.   10
vos tamen o nostri ne festinate libelli:
   si post fata venit gloria, non propero.

8   5 **ruber** γ : –**ens** β   12 **leitus** E ex corr. : **lelius** β : **lectus** γ
9   (TR)
10   (T.R 3–4)

8

While Phasis was recently praising the edict of our lord and god, as a result of which the benches become more definitely allocated and the knights have recovered their unsullied rows, Phasis scarlet with his purple cloak, and while he proudly boasts with overweening face, 'At last we may sit more comfortably, now the equestrian dignity has been restored; we are not squeezed or befouled by a crowd' – while he goes on in this kind of way, with his head thrown back, Leitus ordered that arrogant purple cloak to get up.

9

I was ill, but you came to me at once accompanied by a hundred pupils, Symmachus. A hundred hands made cold by the north wind touched me. I didn't have a fever, Symmachus, but I have one now.

10

'What am I to say about the fact that fame is denied to the living, and that few readers love their own times?' To be sure, Regulus, these are the habits of envy, that it should always prefer the old men to the new ones. Thus we ungratefully seek the old shade of Pompey, thus do old men praise the worthless temple of Catulus. Ennius was read by you, Rome, while Maro was still alive, and his own age laughed at Maeonides; few theatres applauded the crowned Menander; Corinna alone was familiar with her Ovid. But as for you, my books, do not hasten: if glory comes after death, I am in no hurry.

11

Sardonychas, zmaragdos, adamantas, iaspidas uno
    versat in articulo Stella, Severe, meus.
multas in digitis, plures in carmine gemmas
    invenies: inde est haec, puto, culta manus.

12

Quod nutantia fronte perticata
gestat pondera Masclion superbus,
aut grandis Ninus omnibus lacertis
septem quod pueros levat vel octo,
res non difficilis mihi videtur,   5
uno cum digito vel hoc vel illo
portet Stella meus decem puellas.

13

Sum, fateor, semperque fui, Callistrate, pauper,
    sed non obscurus nec male notus eques,
sed toto legor orbe frequens et dicitur 'hic est',
    quodque cinis paucis hoc mihi vita dedit.
at tua centenis incumbunt tecta columnis,   5
    et libertinas arca flagellat opes,
magnaque Niliacae servit tibi gleba Syenes,
    tondet et innumeros Gallica Parma greges.
hoc ego tuque sumus: sed quod sum, non potes esse:
    tu quod es, e populo quilibet esse potest.   10

11   (T) 2 **versat** β : **portat** Tγ
12   1 **perticata** β : –**inaci** γ   2 **maschlion** It. 3 **ninus** γ : **li–** β
13   (T.R 1–4)

11

My friend Stella twists sardonyxes, emeralds, diamonds, and jaspers all on
one finger-joint, Severus. You will find many gems on his fingers, but even
more in his poetry: that is the real source, I think, of his hand's elegance.

12

As for the fact that Masclion carries tottering weights on his pole-bearing
forehead, or that stout Ninus lifts up seven or eight boys with the whole force
of his arms, this does not seem to me to be a difficult feat, when my friend
Stella carries on one finger – either this one or that – ten girls.

13

I am poor – I admit it – and I always have been, Callistratus, but I am a
knight who is not obscure or of ill repute, and I am much read throughout the
whole world, and people say 'It's him!', and what death has given to few, life
has given to me. On the other hand, your roofs rest on a hundred columns,
and your cash-box whips up the wealth of a freedman, and a great estate in
Egyptian Syene is your slave, and Gallic Parma shears innumerable flocks of
yours. This is what I and you are, but, what I am, you cannot be; what you
are, any person can be.

MARTIAL

14

Sedere primo solitus in gradu semper
tunc cum liceret occupare Nanneius
bis excitatus terque transtulit castra,
et inter ipsas paene tertius sellas
post Gaiumque Luciumque consedit.   5
illinc cucullo prospicit caput tectus
oculoque ludos spectat indecens uno.
et hinc miser deiectus in viam transit,
subsellioque semifultus extremo
et male receptus altero genu iactat   10
equiti sedere Leitoque se stare.

15

Quintus nostrorum liber est, Auguste, iocorum
    et queritur laesus carmine nemo meo,
gaudet honorato sed multus nomine lector,
    cui victura meo munere fama datur.
'quid tamen haec prosunt quamvis venerantia multos?'   5
    non prosint sane, me tamen ista iuvant.

14   2 **tunc cum** γ : **cum** β : **hunc cum** Housman (JPh 30 (1907), 236) 3 **terque** γ : **t–
     quaterque** β   11 **sedere** Scriverius: **se dedere** βγ
15   (T)   3 **honorato** Tγ : **–tus** β **nomine** Tβ : **carm–** γ

14

Nanneius, who was always accustomed to sit in the front row at the time when it was permitted to occupy it, after being turned out two or three times has moved camp, and between the very seats of the senators has sat down behind Gaius and Lucius, almost making a third. From there he looks out, hiding his head with his hood, and shamefully watches the shows with one eye. Thrown out of here too, the wretched man crosses into the gangway, and, half-propped up on the end of a bench and grudgingly allowed there,with one knee he boasts to the knight that he is sitting, and with the other to Leitus that he is standing.

15

This is the fifth book, Augustus, of my jokes, and no one complains that he has been harmed by my verse, but instead many a reader rejoices that his name has been honoured since a fame that will live is given through my gift. 'But what profit do these bring, even though they address many with respect?' Granted that they may bring no profit, nevertheless they please me.

16

Seria cum possim, quod delectantia malo
    scribere, tu causa es, lector amice, mihi,
qui legis et tota cantas mea carmina Roma:
    sed nescis quanti stet mihi talis amor.
nam si falciferi defendere templa Tonantis   5
    sollicitisque velim vendere verba reis,
plurimus Hispanas mittet mihi nauta metretas
    et fiet vario sordidus aere sinus.
at nunc conviva est comissatorque libellus
    et tantum gratis pagina nostra placet.   10
sed non et veteres contenti laude fuerunt,
    cum minimum vati munus Alexis erat.
'belle' inquis 'dixti: iuvat et laudabimus usque.'
    dissimulas? facies me, puto, causidicum.

17

Dum proavos atavosque refers et nomina magna,
    dum tibi noster eques sordida condicio est,
dum te posse negas nisi lato, Gellia, clavo
    nubere, nupsisti, Gellia, cistibero.

18

Quod tibi Decembri mense, quo volant mappae
gracilesque ligulae cereique chartaeque
et acuta senibus testa cum Damascenis,
praeter libellos vernulas nihil misi,
fortasse avarus videor aut inhumanus.   5
odi dolosas munerum et malas artes:
imitantur hamos dona: namque quis nescit
avidum vorata decipi scarum musca?
quotiens amico diviti nihil donat,
o Quintiane, liberalis est pauper.   10

---

16   (T) 2 **causa es** Tγ : −**sas** β 6 **que** Tγ : om.β 13 **inquis** T : −**it** βγ   **iuvat et** T : **satis**
est β : **satis** γ **laudabimus** T : −**mur** β : −**mus** vel −**mur** γ

17   (T) 4 **cistibero** γ : −**ifero** Tβ

18   5 **videor** PQF: −**ear** γ Lf

16

As for the fact that, although I could write serious works, I prefer to write entertaining ones, you, friend reader, are my reason, you who read and chant my verses throughout the whole of Rome; but you do not know how much such affection costs me. For if I should wish to defend the temple of the sickle-bearing Thunderer, and to sell words to anxious defendants, very many sailors would send me Spanish oil-jars, and my pocket would become dirty with all sorts of coins. But as it is now my book is a dinner-guest and fellow-reveller, and my page only pleases free of cost. But men of old were not equally content with praise, when the very least present for a bard was an Alexis. 'Nicely put', you say: 'it pleases us and we shall go on praising you'. Are you pretending not to understand? I think you'll make me a reader.

17

While you go on about your great-grandfathers and great-great-great-grandfathers and mighty names, while considering knights like myself a lowly match, while you say that you can only marry a broad stripe, Gellia, you have married a police sergeant.

18

Because I have sent to you in the month of December, when napkins and slender spoons and wax candles and sheets of papyrus and pointed jars of aged damsons fly about, nothing but home-born little books, perhaps I seem mean or uncivil. I hate the deceitful and evil tricks of gifts: presents are like hooks. For who is unaware that the gaudy wrasse is deceived by the fly it has devoured? As often as a poor man gives nothing to his rich friend, Quintianus, he is being generous.

19

Si qua fides veris, praeferri, maxime Caesar,
    temporibus possunt saecula nulla tuis.
quando magis dignos licuit spectare triumphos?
    quando Palatini plus meruere dei?
pulchrior et maior quo sub duce Martia Roma?   5
    sub quo libertas principe tanta fuit?
est tamen hoc vitium sed non leve, sit licet unum,
    quod colit ingratas pauper amicitias.
quis largitur opes veteri fidoque sodali,
    aut quem prosequitur non alienus eques?   10
Saturnaliciae ligulam misisse selibrae
    †flammaris†ve togae scripula tota decem
luxuria est, tumidique vocant haec munera reges:
    qui crepet aureolos forsitan unus erit.
quatenus hi non sunt, esto tu, Caesar, amicus: 15
    nulla ducis virtus dulcior esse potest.
iam dudum tacito rides, Germanice, naso
    utile quod nobis do tibi consilium.

20

Si tecum mihi, care Martialis,
securis liceat frui diebus,
si disponere tempus otiosum
et verae pariter vacare vitae,
nec nos atria nec domos potentum   5
nec litis tetricas forumque triste
nossemus nec imagines superbas;
sed gestatio, fabulae, libelli,
campus, porticus, umbra, Virgo, thermae,
haec essent loca semper, hi labores.   10
nunc vivit necuter sibi, bonosque
soles effugere atque abire sentit,
qui nobis pereunt et imputantur.
quisquam, vivere cum sciat, moratur?

---

19 (T.R 15–19) 1 **veris** Tβ : –i γ   12 **flammaris**] damnatis Housman   **togae** Tβ : **tol(a)e** γ
20   11 **necuter sibi** Schneidewin : **nec ut eius ibo** γ: **neuter sibi** β

19

If the truth can be trusted, greatest Caesar, no ages can be preferred to your times. When were men allowed to watch more deserved triumphs? When did the Palatine gods deserve more thanks? Under what leader was Martian Rome more beautiful and greater? Under what emperor was there such complete liberty? However, there is this defect, and not a trifling one at that, even though it is the only one, namely that the poor man cultivates ungrateful friendships. Who bestows wealth on an old and faithful companion, or who is escorted by a knight of his own making? It is regarded as extravagance to have sent one spoon out of a Saturnalian halfpound, or the whole ten scruples of a flaming coat [?], and the puffed-up patrons call these gifts: there will perhaps be just one of them who jingles gold coins. Since these are not real friends, may you, Caesar, be a friend: no virtue on the part of a ruler can be more attractive. For some time now, Germanicus, you have been laughing, quietly wrinkling up your nose, because I am giving you advice which is to my own advantage.

20

If I were permitted, dear Martialis, to enjoy carefree days in your company, and to dispose of my leisure-time, and to be at liberty for a truly full life, we should have no acquaintance with the entrance-halls or houses of potentates, or grim lawsuits and the dismal forum, or proud ancestral images; but instead exercise, stories, light literature, the Campus, the portico, the shade, the Aqua Virgo, the baths – these would always be the scenes of our labours. As it is now, neither of us lives his life for his own benefit, and we feel that good sunny days are slipping away and disappearing, those days which are lost to us, but are reckoned up all the same. Does anyone, when he knows how to live life to the full, hang about waiting?

21

Quintum pro Decimo, pro Crasso, Regule, Macrum
    ante salutabat rhetor Apollodotus.
nunc utrumque suo resalutat nomine. quantum
    cura laborque potest! scripsit et edidicit.

22

Mane domi nisi te volui meruique videre,
    sint mihi, Paule, tuae longius Esquiliae.
sed Tiburtinae sum proximus accola pilae,
    qua videt anticum rustica Flora Iovem:
alta Suburani vincenda est semita clivi   5
    et numquam sicco sordida saxa gradu,
vixque datur longas mulorum rumpere mandras
    quaeque trahi multo marmora fune vides.
illud adhuc gravius, quod te post mille labores,
    Paule, negat lasso ianitor esse domi.   10
exitus hic operis vani togulaeque madentis:
    vix tanti Paulum mane videre fuit.
semper inhumanos habet officiosus amicos?
    rex, nisi dormieris, non potes esse meus.

23

Herbarum fueras indutus, Basse, colores,
    iura theatralis dum siluere loci.
quae postquam placidi censoris cura renasci
    iussit et Oceanum certior audit eques,
non nisi vel cocco madida vel murice tincta   5
    veste nites et te sic dare verba putas.
quadringentorum nullae sunt, Basse, lacernae,
    aut meus ante omnis Cordus haberet equum.

---

21   (T) 1 **macrum** Tγ : **marcum** β   2 **Apollodotus** Heinsius: –odorus codd.
    4 **scripsit et edidicit** βγ : –**erat et didicit** T
22   5 **Suburani** It.: –**rbani** βγ 7 **rumpere** β : **vincere** γ   13 interrog. fecit Shackleton
    Bailey (AJPh 110 (1989), 278) **colet** Shackleton Bailey : **habet** βγ

21

The rhetorician Apollodotus used previously, Regulus, to greet Decimus as Quintus, and Crassus as Macer. Now he returns each man's greeting by his correct name. The power of trouble and effort! He wrote them down and learned them by heart.

22

If I have not both wished and deserved to see you at home in the morning, Paulus, may your Esquiline residence be even further away from me. But I live right beside the Tiburtine Pillar, where rustic Flora looks at ancient Jupiter: I have to surmount the steep path of the Suburan hill, and dirty stones which never offer a dry foothold, and I am scarcely allowed to push through the lengthy herds of mules, and the loads of marble which you see dragged on many ropes. Still more burdensome is the fact that after my endless labours, Paulus, your porter says that you are not at home. This is the outcome of my vain effort and my soaking little toga. It would hardly have been worth all this to see Paulus in the morning. Does a dutiful man always have discourteous friends? You cannot be my patron unless you sleep.

23

You were dressed in the colour of grass, Bassus, while the laws of the theatre remained silent. Since the discipline of the placid Caesar has ordered them to be reborn, and the more definite knight listens to Oceanus, you dazzle in clothing dyed only in scarlet or purple and think that in this way you can trick him. No cloaks, Bassus, are worth 400,000 – otherwise my friend Cordus would, above all others, own a horse.

24

Hermes Martia saeculi voluptas,
Hermes omnibus eruditus armis,
Hermes et gladiator et magister,
Hermes turbo sui tremorque ludi,
Hermes, quem timet Helius, sed unum,   5
Hermes, cui cadit Advolans, sed uni,
Hermes vincere nec ferire doctus,
Hermes suppositicius sibi ipse,
Hermes divitiae locariorum,
Hermes cura laborque ludiarum,   10
Hermes belligera superbus hasta,
Hermes aequoreo minax tridente,
Hermes casside languida timendus,
Hermes gloria Martis universi,
Hermes omnia solus et ter unus.   15

25

'Quadringenta tibi non sunt, Chaerestrate: surge,
   Leitus ecce venit: sta, fuge, curre, late.'
ecquis, io, revocat discedentemque reducit?
   ecquis, io, largas pandit amicus opes?
quem chartis famaeque damus populisque loquendum ?   5
   quis Stygios non vult totus adire lacus?
hoc, rogo, non melius quam rubro pulpita nimbo
   spargere et effuso permaduisse croco?
quam non sensuro dare quadringenta caballo,
   aureus ut Scorpi nasus ubique micet?   10
o frustra locuples, o dissimulator amici,
   haec legis et laudas? quae tibi fama perit!

---

24   4 **turbo** Heinsius: –**ba** βγ 8 **ipse** γ: **ipsi** β
25   11 **amici** β: –**ce** γ

24

Hermes, martial sweetheart of the age, Hermes, skilled in every sort of weapon, Hermes, both gladiator and trainer, Hermes, whirlwind and terror of his own school, Hermes, whom Helius fears – and him alone, Hermes, to whom Advolans falls – and to him alone, Hermes, skilled at winning without wounding, Hermes, himself his own substitute, Hermes, wealth of the seat-touts, Hermes, anxiety and torment of the female fans, Hermes, proud with his warlike spear, Hermes, menacing with his marine trident, Hermes, fearsome in his drooping helmet, Hermes, glory of the whole of Mars, Hermes, who alone is everything and thrice unique.

25

'You haven't got 400,000, Chaerestratus: get up – look, Leitus is coming. Stand up, escape, run, hide.' Hey! Who calls him back and brings him back as he goes off? Hey! What friend displays generous wealth? Whom do we give to our page and to fame, and to be spoken of by peoples? Who wishes not completely to approach the Stygian lakes? I ask you, is this not better than to spray the stage with a red cloud, and be soaked in the poured-out saffron? Than to give 400,000 to a horse which will not appreciate it, so that the golden nose of Scorpus may gleam on every side? O uselessly rich man, you who put on a false pretence of being a friend, do you read these words and praise them? What a reputation you are losing!

26

Quod alpha dixi, Corde, paenulatorum
te nuper, aliqua cum iocarer in charta,
si forte bilem movit hic tibi versus,
dicas licebit beta me togatorum.

27

Ingenium studiumque tibi moresque genusque
sunt equitis, fateor: cetera plebis habes.
* * * * * *
bis septena tibi non sint subsellia tanti,
ut sedeas viso pallidus Oceano.

28

Ut bene loquatur sentiatque Mamercus,
efficere nullis, Aule, moribus possis:
pietate fratres Curvios licet vincas,
quiete Nervas, comitate Rusones,
probitate Macros, aequitate Mauricos,   5
oratione Regulos, iocis Paulos:
robiginosis cuncta dentibus rodit.
hominem malignum forsan esse tu credas:
· ego esse miserum credo, cui placet nemo.

26   (T)
27   **ad Paulum** lemm. α   post 2 lacunam statuit Schneidewin   3 **sint** β : **sunt** γ
28   (T)   3 **Curvios** Friedlaender: **curios** codd.   4 **rusones** Tγ : **dr**– β

26

As for the fact that I recently called you, Cordus, 'A1 among coat-wearers', when I was making a joke in some piece or other, if this verse perhaps made you cross, you may call me 'B2 among toga-wearers'.

27

You have the intellect and learning and character and birth of a knight, I agree: as for the rest, you have those of the people ... Let not the fourteen rows be worth so much to you that you should sit pale with fear when you have sighted Oceanus.

28

You cannot cause Mamercus to speak well or have a good opinion of you, Aulus, by any virtues. Even though you surpass the brothers Curvius in family feeling, men like Nerva in gentleness, men like Ruso in civility, men like Macer in uprightness, men like Mauricus in fairness, men like Regulus in oratory, men like Paulus in humour, he grinds away at everything with his rusty teeth. Perhaps you think he is a spiteful man: I think a man whom no-one pleases is a miserable wretch.

29

Si quando leporem mittis mihi, Gellia, dicis
    'formosus septem, Marce, diebus eris.'
si non derides, si verum, lux mea, narras,
    edisti numquam, Gellia, tu leporem.

30

Varro, Sophocleo non infitiande cothurno
    nec minus in Calabra suspiciende lyra,
differ opus nec te facundi scaena Catulli
    detineat cultis aut elegia comis;
sed lege fumoso non aspernanda Decembri   5
    carmina, mittuntur quae tibi mense suo:
commodius nisi forte tibi potiusque videtur
    Saturnalicias perdere, Varro, nuces.

31

Aspice quam placidis insultet turba iuvencis
    et sua quam facilis pondera taurus amet.
cornibus hic pendet summis, vagus ille per armos
    currit et in toto ventilat arma bove.
at feritas immota riget: non esset harena   5
    tutior et poterant fallere plana magis.
nec trepidat gestus nisi de discrimine palmae;
    securus puer est sollicitumque pecus.

---

29   (TR) 1 et 4 **gellia** βγ, Hist. Aug. 18.38.2, codd. plurimi: **gal–** α
30   2 **suspic–** γ : **suscip–** β
31   (T)7 **trepidat** Shackleton Bailey: **–ant** codd. **nisi de** Shackleton Bailey: **sed de** Tβ: **et ne**
    γ **palmae** Tβ : **parmas** γ

29

Whenever you send me a hare, Gellia, you say, 'You will be handsome, Marcus, for seven days'. If you are not making fun of me, if you are telling the truth, light of my life, you, Gellia, have never eaten hare.

30

Varro, you who would not be disowned by the Sophoclean buskin, and are not less to be looked up to on the Calabrian lyre, postpone your labours, and let neither the stage of eloquent Catullus nor elegy with her elegant hair detain you. Read instead poems which should not be despised in smoky December, and which are being sent to you in the month which is theirs – unless perhaps it seems more appropriate and preferable to you, Varro, to lose Saturnalian nuts.

31

See how the troupe leaps upon the placid steers, and how each obliging bull loves its own burden. One hangs from the tips of the horns, another roams running along the shoulders, and shakes about weapons over the whole ox. But its unmoved ferocity remains still: the sand would not be safer, and level ground could more readily cause him to slip. The one who is carried has no fear, except about the chance of victory; the boy is free from worry, but the bull is anxious.

32

Quadrantem Crispus tabulis, Faustine, supremis
    non dedit uxori. 'cui dedit ergo?' sibi.

33

Carpere causidicus fertur mea carmina: qui sit
    nescio. si sciero, vae tibi, causidice!

34

Hanc tibi, Fronto pater, genetrix Flaccilla, puellam
    oscula commendo deliciasque meas,
parvula ne nigras horrescat Erotion umbras
    oraque Tartarei prodigiosa canis.
impletura fuit sextae modo frigora brumae,   5
    vixisset totidem ni minus illa dies.
inter tam veteres ludat lasciva patronos
    et nomen blaeso garriat ore meum.
mollia non rigidus caespes tegat ossa, nec illi,
    terra, gravis fueris: non fuit illa tibi.   10

35

Dum sibi redire de Patrensibus fundis
ducena clamat coccinatus Euclides
Corinthioque plura de suburbano
longumque pulchra stemma repetit a Leda
et suscitanti Leito reluctatur,   5
equiti superbo, nobili, locupleti
cecidit repente magna de sinu clavis.
numquam, Fabulle, nequior fuit clavis.

33 (TR) 1 **quis** CG
34 (TR) 3 **parvula** (**–vola**) **ne** αγ : **pallida nec** β 6 **ni** β : **ne** αγ 7 **inter tam** αβ :
     interim γ : **inter iam** Heinsius 9 **non** αγ : **nec** β
35 1 **Patre–** It.: **patruen–** βγ

32

Crispus did not give his wife a quarter of his estate in his will, Faustinus. 'To whom then did he give it?' To himself.

33

A lawyer is said to be criticising my poems. I don't know who he is. If I find out, woe on you, lawyer!

34

Father Fronto and mother Flaccilla, I commend to you this girl, the pet I love to kiss, lest the poor little Erotion should shudder at the black shades and the prodigious mouths of the Tartarean dog. She would just now have completed her sixth cold winter, had she not lived the same number of days less. May the frolicsome creature play among such old patrons, and chatter my name with lisping lips. May a stiff turf not cover her soft bones, and may you, earth, not be heavy on her: she was not heavy on you.

35

While the scarlet-clad Euclides was crying out that his estates at Patras bring him 200,000 sesterces a year, and his suburban property at Corinth more, and tracing his long lineage back to lovely Leda, and struggling with Leitus who was trying to get him to move, from the pocket of this proud, noble and rich knight suddenly fell a big key. Never, Fabullus, was there a more wicked key.

36

Laudatus nostro quidam, Faustine, libello
dissimulat, quasi nil debeat: imposuit.

37

Puella senibus voce dulcior cycnis,
agna Galaesi mollior Phalantini,
concha Lucrini delicatior stagni,
cui nec lapillos praeferas Erythraeos
nec modo politum pecudis Indicae dentem   5
nivesque primas liliumque non tactum;
quae crine vicit Baetici gregis vellus
Rhenique nodos aureamque nitelam;
fragravit ore quod rosarium Paesti,
quod Atticarum prima mella cerarum,   10
quod sucinorum rapta de manu gleba;
cui comparatus indecens erat pavo,
inamabilis sciurus et frequens phoenix:
adhuc recenti tepet Erotion busto,
quam pessimorum lex amara fatorum   15
sexta peregit hieme, nec tamen tota,
nostros amores gaudiumque lususque.
et esse tristem me meus vetat Paetus,
pectusque pulsans pariter et comam vellens:
'deflere non te vernulae pudet mortem ?   20
ego coniugem' inquit 'extuli et tamen vivo,
notam, superbam, nobilem, locupletem.'
quid esse nostro fortius potest Paeto?
ducentiens accepit et tamen vivit.

---

37   (T 1–7, 9–14)   1 **voce dulcior** Shackleton Bailey: **dulcior mihi** codd.   **5 indicae dentem**
(**ge**–γ)βγ : **indicentem** T   8 **nitelam** LPfEAX, Heraeus: –**llam** QVF   12 **pavo** β : **pano**
T: **pavus** γ   13 **sciurus** T: (s)**cyrus** γ : **chy**– β   22 **notam** β : **noram** γ

A man who was praised in my little book, Faustinus, is trying to pretend that he owes me nothing: he has cheated me.

37

Girl sweeter in voice than aged swans, softer than the lamb of Phalanthine Galaesus, more delicate than the shell of the Lucrine pool, girl to whom you would prefer neither Erythraean jewels nor the freshly polished tooth of the Indian beast, first snows or the untouched lily; who with her hair has outdone the fleece of the Baetic flock and the knots of the Rhine and the golden dormouse; whose mouth was as fragrant as the rose-garden of Paestum, as the first honey from Attic combs, as a lump of amber snatched from the hand; to whom compared a peacock would have been ugly, a squirrel unlovable, and a phoenix commonplace: Erotion is still warm in her fresh tomb, she whom the bitter law of the most evil fates carried off in her sixth, but as yet incomplete, winter, my love and joy and plaything. And yet my friend Paetus forbids me to be sad, as he likewise beats his breast and tears his hair: 'Are you not ashamed to grieve heavily for the death of a little home-born slave? I have buried my wife', he says, 'and yet I remain alive, a woman who was well-known, proud, noble, wealthy'. What can be braver than our Paetus? He has received twenty million sesterces, and yet remains alive.

38

Calliodorus habet censum – quis nescit? – equestrem,
    Sexte, sed et fratrem Calliodorus habet.
'quadringenta seca' qui dicit, σῦκα μερίζει:
    uno credis equo posse sedere duos?
quid cum fratre tibi, quid cum Polluce molesto?   5
    non esset Pollux si tibi, Castor eras.
unus cum sitis, duo, Calliodore, sedebis?
    surge: σολοικισμόν, Calliodore, facis.
aut imitare genus Ledae: cum fratre sedere
    non potes: alternis, Calliodore, sede.   10

39

Supremas tibi triciens in anno
signanti tabulas, Charine, misi
Hyblaeis madidas thymis placentas.
defeci: miserere iam, Charine:
signa rarius, aut semel fac illud,   5
mentitur tua quod subinde tussis.
excussi loculosque sacculumque:
Croeso divitior licet fuissem,
Iro pauperior forem, Charine,
si conchem totiens meam comesses.   10

40

Pinxisti Venerem, colis, Artemidore, Minervam:
    et miraris opus displicuisse tuum?

---

38   3 **seca** Rutgers: –**at** βγ **dicis** Postgate μερίζει Paley: **merize** βγ: μέριζε Postgate
     7 **sedebis** Markland: **sedetis** βγ
39   10 **conchem** γ : –**en** β

38

Calliodorus has the equestrian property qualification, Sextus – who does not know this? – but Calliodorus also has a brother. The man who says 'Split up four hundred thousand sesterces' divides up figs: do you think that two men can sit on one horse? What business have you with a brother, with a troublesome Pollux? If you had no Pollux, you would be Castor. Since you two are one, will you alone sit as two, Calliodorus? Get up: you are committing a solecism, Calliodorus. Or imitate the offspring of Leda – for you cannot sit together with your brother – and take turns to sit, Calliodorus.

39

When you were signing your will thirty times in the year, Charinus, I sent you cakes soaked in Hyblaean honey. I have given up: pity me now, Charinus. Sign more rarely, or else just once do that thing which your cough often fakes. I have shaken out my money-boxes and my purse. Even though I had been richer than Croesus, I should be poorer than Irus, Charinus, if you had eaten my beans so often.

40

You have painted Venus, Artemidorus, but you cultivate Minerva. Are you then surprised that your work has not found favour?

41

Spadone cum sis eviratior fluxo,
et concubino mollior Celaenaeo,
quem sectus ululat matris entheae Gallus,
theatra loqueris et gradus et edicta
trabeasque et Idus fibulasque censusque,   5
et pumicata pauperes manu monstras.
sedere in equitum liceat an tibi scamnis
videbo, Didyme: non licet maritorum.

42

Callidus effracta nummos fur auferet arca,
   prosternet patrios impia flamma lares:
debitor usuram pariter sortemque negabit,
   non reddet sterilis semina iacta seges:
dispensatorem fallax spoliabit amica,   5
   mercibus extructas obruet unda rates.
extra fortunam est quidquid donatur amicis:
   quas dederis, solas semper habebis opes.

43

Thais habet nigros, niveos Laecania dentes.
   quae ratio est? emptos haec habet, illa suos.

42   3–4 et 5–8 separatim βγ : corr. It.   7 **quidquid** β : **siquid** γ

41

Although you are more emasculated than a flabby eunuch, and more effeminate than the Celaenaean concubine, for whom the castrated Gallus of the divinely inspiring mother wails, you talk of theatres and rows and edicts, and knights' uniforms and the Ides and buckles and property qualifications, and you point out the poor with pumice-smoothed hand. I shall see whether you are allowed to sit in the seats of the knights, Didymus; you are not allowed to sit in the seats of the married men.

42

The skilful thief will break open your safe and take away your money; impious flame will flatten your ancestral home; your creditor will refuse to return both interest and capital; the barren field will fail to return the seeds you have sown; the treacherous girl-friend will clean out the steward; the wave will overwhelm the ships piled high with merchandise. Whatever is given to friends is outside the power of fortune: the only wealth you will always possess is what you have given away.

43

Thais has black teeth; Laecania has snow-white ones. What's the reason? The latter has bought teeth, the former has her own.

44

Quid factum est, rogo, quid repente factum est,
ad cenam mihi, Dento, quod vocanti—
quis credat? – quater ausus es negare?
sed nec respicis et fugis sequentem,
quem thermis modo quaerere et theatris   5
et conclavibus omnibus solebas.
sic est, captus es unctiore mensa
et maior rapuit canem culina.
iam te, sed cito, cognitum et relictum
cum fastidierit popina dives,   10
antiquae venies ad ossa cenae.

45

Dicis formosam, dicis te, Bassa, puellam.
   istud quae non est dicere, Bassa, solet.

46

Basia dum nolo nisi quae luctantia carpsi
   et placet ira mihi plus tua quam facies,
ut te saepe rogem, caedo, Diadumene, saepe:
   consequor hoc, ut me nec timeas nec ames.

47

Numquam se cenasse domi Philo iurat, et hoc est:
   non cenat, quotiens nemo vocavit eum.

44   1 **est** (alt.)β : om. γ
45   (TR) 2 **quae ... solet** βγ : **quod ... soles** R : **quod ... solet** T¹
46   (TR) 1 **carpsi** β : **–pis** γ 3 **caedo** γ : **credo** αβ 4 **consequor** αγ : **–uar** β

44

What has happened, I ask you, what has suddenly happened, Dento, so that when I have invited you to dinner – who'd believe it? – you have dared four times to refuse? But you don't look back, and you run away from me when I follow you – me, whom you used recently to seek out at all the baths and theatres and public conveniences, That's it – you've been caught by a smarter dinner-table, and a greater kitchen has snatched away the dog. Any time now, and soon too, when the wealthy tavern has spurned you, found out and abandoned, you will come back to the bones of the old dinner.

45

You say that you are beautiful, Bassa, you say that you're just a girl. The person who goes around saying that is usually a person who is neither.

46

So long as I don't want any kisses except those I have snatched with a struggle, and so long as your anger gives me more pleasure than your looks, in order to ask you for them often, I often beat you, Diadumenos: what I achieve by this is that you neither fear nor love me.

47

Philo swears that he has never dined at home, and it's true: whenever no–one has invited him out, he doesn't dine.

48

Quid non cogit amor? secuit nolente capillos
    Encolpos domino, non prohibente tamen.
permisit flevitque Pudens: sic cessit habenis
    audaci questus de Phaethonte pater:
talis raptus Hylas, talis deprensus Achilles   5
    deposuit gaudens, matre dolente, comas.
sed tu ne propera – brevibus ne crede capillis –
    tardaque pro tanto munere, barba, veni.

49

Vidissem modo forte cum sedentem
solum te, Labiene, tres putavi.
calvae me numerus tuae fefellit:
sunt illinc tibi, sunt et hinc capilli
quales vel puerum decere possint;   5
nudum est in medio caput nec ullus
in longa pilus area notatur.
hic error tibi profuit Decembri,
tunc cum prandia misit Imperator:
cum panariolis tribus redisti.   10
talem Geryonen fuisse credo.
vites censeo porticum Philippi:
si te viderit Hercules, peristi.

48   7 **ne** (alt.) βCG : **nec** γ : **neu** Hand
49   (T)   5 **possint** γ : **–sunt** Tβ   9 **tunc** βγ : **tum** T   11 **Geryonen** It.: **–nem** codd.

48

What is there that love does not force a man to do? Encolpos has cut off his
hair against the will of his master Pudens, but not against his orders. Pudens
permitted it and wept: thus did Phaethon's father yield the reins,
complaining about his son's boldness; so did the ravished Hylas lay aside his
hair, so did the caught-out Achilles, happy while his mother grieved. But do
not hurry – put no faith in his short hair – and, in return for so great a reward,
come, beard, slowly.

49

When I had by chance seen you recently sitting on your own, Labienus, I
thought there were three of you. The total of your scalp deceived me: you
have hair on one side, and hair on the other side, such as could suit even a
boy; in the middle your head is bare, and no hair is spotted in a wide area.
This mistake was to your benefit in December, at the time when the emperor
sent out meals: you came back with three little picnic baskets. I imagine
that Geryon was like this. I advise you to avoid the portico of Philippus: if
Hercules sees you, you are done for.

50

Ceno domi quotiens, nisi te, Charopine, vocavi,
    protinus ingentes sunt inimicitiae,
meque potes stricto medium transfigere ferro,
    si nostrum sine te scis caluisse focum.
nec semel ergo mihi furtum fecisse licebit?   5
    improbius nihil est hac, Charopine, gula.
desine iam nostram, precor, observare culinam,
    atque aliquando meus det tibi verba cocus.

51

Hic, qui libellis praegravem gerit laevam,
notariorum quem premit chorus levis,
qui codicillis hinc et inde prolatis
epistulisque commodat gravem vultum
similis Catoni Tullioque Brutoque,   5
exprimere, Rufe, fidiculae licet cogant,
have Latinum, χαῖρε non potest Graecum.
si fingere istud me putas, salutemus.

52

Quae mihi praestiteris memini semperque tenebo.
    cur igitur taceo, Postume? tu loqueris.
incipio quotiens alicui tua dona referre,
    protinus exclamat 'dixerat ipse mihi.'
non belle quaedam faciunt duo: sufficit unus   5
    huic operi: si vis ut loquar, ipse tace.
crede mihi, quamvis ingentia, Postume, dona
    auctoris pereunt garrulitate sui.

50   (T) 3 **potes** γ : **putes** β: **uelis** T   8 **cocus** βγ : **fo–** T
51   (T)
52   (TR) 7 **dona** β : **dones** γ

50

Whenever I dine at home, unless I have invited you, Charopinus, straightaway there is tremendous hostility, and you are capable of piercing me through in the middle with a drawn sword, if you become aware that my hearth has grown warm without your presence. So I shan't be allowed to have committed a theft even once? Nothing is more wicked, Charopinus, than this gluttony. Cease now, I beg you, to watch my kitchen, and let my cook sometimes deceive you.

51

This man, who wields a left hand weighed down with books, whom a smooth-cheeked chorus of shorthand-writers hems in, who lends a solemn face to notebooks offered on this side and that and to letters, looking like Cato and Tullius and Brutus, even though the rack were to force him, cannot manage to utter 'Greetings' in either Latin or Greek. If you think I'm making this up, let's greet him.

52

I remember, and shall always bear in mind, those things with which you have provided me. So why am I silent, Postumus? Because you speak. Whenever I begin to tell someone about your gifts, he exclaims at once 'He himself has told me'. There are some things which it's not nice to have two people doing: one is enough for this job. If you want me to speak, keep quiet yourself. Believe me, however huge gifts are, Postumus, they are wasted by the talkativeness of the giver.

53

Colchida quid scribis, quid scribis, amice, Thyesten?
  quo tibi vel Nioben, Basse, vel Andromachen ?
materia est, mihi crede, tuis aptissima chartis
  Deucalion vel, si non placet hic, Phaethon.

54

Extemporalis factus est meus rhetor:
Calpurnium non scripsit, et salutavit.

55

Dic mihi, quem portas, volucrum regina? 'Tonantem.'
  nulla manu quare fulmina gestat? 'amat.'
quo calet igne deus? 'pueri.' cur mitis aperto
  respicis ore Iovem? 'de Ganymede loquor.'

56

Cui tradas, Lupe, filium magistro
quaeris sollicitus diu rogasque.
omnes grammaticosque rhetorasque
devites moneo: nihil sit illi
cum libris Ciceronis aut Maronis,   5
famae Tutilium suae relinquat;
si versus facit, abdices poetam.
artes discere vult pecuniosas ?
fac discat citharoedus aut choraules;
si duri puer ingeni videtur,   10
praeconem facias vel architectum.

---

53   (T) 4 **vel** Tγ : **aut** β
55   1 **portas** β: **–tes** γ
56   6 **relinquat** β : **–as** γ

53

Why do you write about Colchis, why, my friend, do you write about Thyestes? What use to you are either Niobe, Bassus, or Andromache? Believe me, the most appropriate subject for your pages is Deucalion, or, if he doesn't suit you, Phaethon.

54

My rhetorician friend has become an extempore speaker: he did not write down the name of Calpurnius, but greeted him correctly.

55

Tell me, whom are you carrying, queen of birds? 'The Thunderer.' Why does he bear no thunderbolts in his hand? 'He is in love.' With what kind of fire does the god burn? 'For a boy.' Why do you look mildly at Jupiter with open mouth? 'I am speaking about Ganymede'.

56

For a long time, Lupus, you have been anxiously asking and enquiring to which master you should entrust your son. I advise you to avoid all teachers of grammar and rhetoric; let him have nothing to do with the books of Cicero or Virgil, and let him leave Tutilius to his reputation; if he writes verses you should disinherit the poet. Does he want to learn skills that make money? Make him learn to be a lyre-singer or a pipe-playing choir accompanist; if the boy seems to be of a thick disposition, you should make him an auctioneer or an architect.

57

Cum voco te dominum, noli tibi, Cinna, placere:
saepe etiam servum sic resaluto tuum.

58

Cras te victurum, cras dicis, Postume, semper.
    dic mihi, cras istud, Postume, quando venit?
quam longe cras istud, ubi est? aut unde petendum?
    numquid apud Parthos Armeniosque latet?
iam cras istud habet Priami vel Nestoris annos.   5
    cras istud quanti, dic mihi, possit emi?
cras vives? hodie iam vivere, Postume, serum est:
    ille sapit quisquis, Postume, vixit heri.

59

Quod non argentum, quod non tibi mittimus aurum,
    hoc facimus causa, Stella diserte, tua.
quisquis magna dedit, voluit sibi magna remitti;
    fictilibus nostris exoneratus eris.

57   (TR) 2 **tuum** αγ : **meum** ante corr., ut vid., β
58   3 **longe** γ : −**e est** β   4 **que** βγ : **ve** Fris., ed. Rom.   6 **possit** γ : −**set** β   7 **vives** γ : **vivis** β
serum γ: **tardum** β, Fris.

When I call you 'master', Cinna, don't be pleased with yourself: I often
return even your slave's greeting like this.

58

Tomorrow, Postumus, you are always saying that you will live properly
tomorrow. Tell me, Postumus, when does that 'tomorrow' come? How far
off is that 'tomorrow', where is it? Or from where must it be sought? Surely
it isn't hidden among the Parthians and Armenians? That 'tomorrow' is
already as old as Priam or Nestor. Tell me, for how much could that
'tomorrow' be bought? Will you live properly tomorrow? Today is already
too late, Postumus, for living properly: that man is wise, Postumus, who
lived properly yesterday.

59

As for the fact that I am sending you neither silver nor gold, I am doing this
for your sake, eloquent Stella. Whoever has given great gifts, has wished for
great gifts to be sent back in return; by means of my pots you will have been
freed from a burden.

60

Allatres licet usque nos et usque
et gannitibus improbis lacessas,
certum est hanc tibi pernegare famam,
olim quam petis, in meis libellis
qualiscumque legaris ut per orbem.   5
nam te cur aliquis sciat fuisse?
ignotus pereas, miser, necesse est.
non deerunt tamen hac in urbe forsan
unus vel duo tresve quattuorve
pellem rodere qui velint caninam: 10
nos hac a scabie tenemus ungues.

61

Crispulus iste quis est, uxori semper adhaeret
    qui, Mariane, tuae? crispulus iste quis est,
nescio quid dominae teneram qui garrit in aurem
    et sellam cubito dexteriore premit?
per cuius digitos currit levis anulus omnis,   5
    crura gerit nullo qui violata pilo?
nil mihi respondes? 'uxoris res agit' inquis
    'iste meae.' sane certus et asper homo est,
procuratorem vultu qui praeferat ipso:
    acrior hoc Chius non erit Aufidius.   10
o quam dignus eras alapis, Mariane, Latini:
    te successurum credo ego Panniculo.
res uxoris agit? res ullas crispulus iste?
    res non uxoris, res agit iste tuas.

60   4 in γ : a β   5 orbem γ: ur‑ β
61   7 inquis γ : ‑it β   9 praeferat β : prof‑ γ

Although you may keep on constantly barking at me, and provoking me with your awful yappings, I am determined to continue to deny you the reputation, which you have for so long been seeking, of being read about in my books, in whatever way, throughout the world. For why should anyone know that you existed? It is essential that you should perish unknown, wretch! However, perhaps there will not be lacking in this city one or two or three or at most four who may wish to bite the dog's skin: I keep my nails away from this itch.

61

Who is that curly chap who always sticks close to your wife, Marianus? Who is that curly chap, who chatters something into the tender ear of the mistress and leans on her sedan-chair with his right elbow? Over all of whose fingers runs the light ring, and who has legs spoiled by no hair? Do you make no reply to me? 'He looks after my wife's affairs', you say. To be sure, he is a reliable and fierce-looking man, such as to reveal the steward by his very appearance: Aufidius Chius will not be sharper than him. O, how much you deserve the slaps of Latinus, Marianus: I believe you will be Panniculus's successor. Does he look after your wife's affairs? Does that curly chap look after any affairs? He looks after, not your wife's affairs, but yours.

62

Iure tuo nostris maneas licet hospes in hortis,
    si potes in nudo ponere membra solo,
aut si portatur tecum tibi magna supellex:
    nam mea iam digitum sustulit hospitibus.
nulla tegit fractos – nec inanis – culcita lectos,   5
    putris et abrupta fascia reste iacet.
sit tamen hospitium nobis commune duobus:
    emi hortos; plus est: instrue tu; minus est.

63

'Quid sentis' inquis 'de nostris, Marce, libellis?'
    sic me sollicitus, Pontice, saepe rogas.
admiror, stupeo: nihil est perfectius illis,
    ipse tuo cedet Regulus ingenio.
'hoc sentis?' inquis 'faciat tibi sic bene Caesar,   5
    sic Capitolinus Iuppiter.' immo tibi.

64

Sextantes, Calliste, duos infunde Falerni,
    tu super aestivas, Alcime, solve nives,
pinguescat nimio madidus mihi crinis amomo
    lassenturque rosis tempora sutilibus.
tam vicina iubent nos vivere Mausolea,   5
    cum doceant ipsos posse perire deos.

64   5 **tam** β: **iam** γ

You may stay as a guest in my suburban villa as a matter of right, if you can rest your limbs on the bare ground, or if a great quantity of furnishings is brought with you for your use; for my own have already asked for mercy from the guests. No cushion – not even an empty one – covers the broken couches, and the rotten webbing lies collapsed after the rope has broken. But let it be a common lodging for both of us: I bought the villa, which is the greater expense; why don't you furnish it? – it costs less.

63

'What is your opinion, Marcus', you ask, 'about my books?' You often question me anxiously like this, Ponticus. I admire them, I am amazed by them; nothing is more perfect. Regulus himself will give way to your talent. 'Is this your opinion?', you say. 'If so, then may Caesar be kind to you, and Capitoline Jupiter.' No, to *you*.

64

Pour in four ladles-full of Falernian wine, Callistus, and you, Alcimus, melt summer snows on top; let my damp hair grow rich with excessive balsam, and let my temples be wearied by woven roses. The Mausolea which are so close by bid us live life to the full, since they teach us that the very gods can die.

65

Astra polumque dedit quamvis obstante noverca
    Alcidae Nemees terror et Arcas aper
et castigatum Libycae ceroma palaestrae
    et gravis in Siculo pulvere fusus Eryx,
silvarumque tremor, tacita qui fraude solebat   5
    ducere non rectas Cacus in antra boves.
ista tuae, Caesar, quota pars spectatur harenae !
    dat maiora novus proelia mane dies.
quot graviora cadunt Nemeaeo pondera monstro!
    quot tua Maenalios collocat hasta sues!   10
reddatur si pugna triplex pastoris Hiberi,
    est tibi qui possit vincere Geryonen.
saepe licet Graiae numeretur belua Lernae,
    improba Niliacis quid facit Hydra feris?
pro meritis caelum tantis, Auguste, dederunt   15
    Alcidae cito di, sed tibi sero dabunt.

66

Saepe salutatus numquam prior ipse salutas:
    sic eris? aeternum, Pontiliane, vale.

67

Hibernos peterent solito cum more recessus
    Atthides, in nidis una remansit avis.
deprendere nefas ad tempora verna reversae
    et profugam volucres diripuere suae.
sero dedit poenas; discerpi noxia mater   5
    debuerat, sed tunc cum laceravit Ityn.

65   4 **siculo** γ : **–la** β   **fusus** γ : **tu–** β   6 **non** β : **nec** γ   9 **graviora** γ : **maiora** β
        12 **geryonen** E : **–nem** cett.   13 **licet** γ : **quidem** β
66   (TR) 2 **erit** It.
67   (T) 4 **suae** βγ: **suam** TN

Despite his stepmother's opposition, Alcides was given the stars and the sky by the terror of Nemea and the Arcadian boar and the punished mud of the Libyan wrestling-ring, and heavy Eryx flattened on the Sicilian dust, and the scare of the woods Cacus, who was accustomed with silent deceit to lead back-to-front oxen into caves. How small a part of your arena is provided by these spectacles, Caesar! Each new day gives us greater battles in the morning. How many beasts heavier than the Nemean monster fall! How many Maenalian boars does your spear lay out! If the triple fight of the Iberian ox-herd were repeated, you have someone who could defeat Geryon. Although the beast of Grecian Lerna may often be counted, what can the evil Hydra do against the wild animals of the Nile? For such great merits, Augustus, the gods gave Alcides heaven quickly, but to you they will give it late.

66

Although you have often been greeted, you yourself never greet me first. Is this how you will behave? Farewell for ever, Pontilianus.

67

When the Attic birds, according to their usual custom, were seeking their winter retreats, one bird remained in the nests. When they came back in springtime, its fellow-birds found out the crime, and tore apart the deserter. It paid the penalty too late: the guilty mother ought to have been ripped apart, but at the time when she mangled Itys.

68

Arctoa de gente comam tibi, Lesbia, misi,
    ut scires quanto sit tua flava magis.

69

Antoni, Phario nihil obiecture Pothino
    et levius tabula quam Cicerone nocens,
quid gladium demens Romana stringis in ora?
    hoc admisisset nec Catilina nefas.
impius infando miles corrumpitur auro,   5
    et tantis opibus vox tacet una tibi.
quid prosunt sacrae pretiosa silentia linguae?
    incipient omnes pro Cicerone loqui.

70

Infusum sibi nuper a patrono
plenum, Maxime, centiens Syriscus
in sellariolis vagus popinis
circa balnea quattuor peregit.
o quanta est gula, centiens comesse!   5
quanto maior adhuc, nec accubare!

71

Umida qua gelidas summittit Trebula valles
    et viridis cancri mensibus alget ager,
rura Cleonaeo numquam temerata leone
    et domus Aeolio semper amica Noto
te, Faustine, vocant: longas his exige messes   5
    collibus; hibernum iam tibi Tibur erit.

68   (T)
71   1 **qua** γ : **quae** β

68

I have sent you hair from a northern tribe, Lesbia, so that you might know how much more blond is your own.

69

Antony, you who will have no reproach to make to Egyptian Pothinus, and who are less guilty because of your proscription-list than because of Cicero, why do you insanely draw your sword against the mouth of Rome? Not even Catiline would have committed this crime. The impious soldier is bribed with unspeakable gold, and for such great wealth one voice is silent for you. What is the benefit of the costly silence of the sacred tongue? All will begin instead to speak of Cicero.

70

Syriscus recently had a windfall of a whole ten million sesterces from his patron, Maximus, and, by roaming about in sit-down bars, got through the lot round four bath-establishments. Oh, what great greed, to eat up ten million! But how much greater still, not even to do it reclining!

71

Where damp Trebula drops down its cool valleys and the green field is cold in the months of the Crab, your country estate, never desecrated by the Cleonaean Lion, and your house which is always friendly to the Aeolian south wind summon you, Faustinus: pass the long harvest-times on these hills. Tivoli will now be your winter resort.

72

Qui potuit Bacchi matrem dixisse Tonantem,
    ille potest Semelen dicere, Rufe, patrem.

73

Non donem tibi cur meos libellos
oranti totiens et exigenti
miraris, Theodore? magna causa est:
dones tu mihi ne tuos libellos.

74

Pompeios iuvenes Asia atque Europa, sed ipsum
    terra tegit Libyes, si tamen ulla tegit.
quid mirum toto si spargitur orbe? iacere
    uno non poterat tanta ruina loco.

75

Quae legis causa nupsit tibi Laelia, Quinte,
    uxorem potes hanc dicere legitimam.

76

Profecit poto Mithridates saepe veneno
    toxica ne possent saeva nocere sibi.
tu quoque cavisti cenando tam male semper
    ne posses umquam, Cinna, perire fame.

77

Narratur belle quidam dixisse, Marulle,
    qui te ferre oleum dixit in auricula.

---

74   (TR) 2 **libyes** βγ : −**y(a)e** α
76   (TR) 2 **possent** γ : −**sint** αβ   4 **posses** βγ : −**sis** α

72

The man who was able to call Jupiter the mother of Bacchus can call Semele, Rufus, his father.

73

Do you wonder, Theodorus, why I do not give you my little books, although you so often request and demand them? There is an important reason – I'm afraid that you may give me your books.

74

Asia and Europe cover the young Pompeii, but the earth of Libya covers the man himself – that is, if any earth covers him. What surprise is there if he is scattered over the whole world? So great a fall could not lie in one single place.

75

Laelia has married you, Quintus, for the sake of the law: you can call her your legitimate wife.

76

By often drinking poison, Mithridates ensured that fierce toxins could do him no harm. You too have taken precautions, by always dining so badly, Cinna, so as never to be able to die of starvation.

77

Someone is reported to have made a neat remark, Marullus, when he said that you carried oil in your ear.

78

Si tristi domicenio laboras,
Torani, potes esurire mecum.
non deerunt tibi, si soles προπίνειν,
viles Cappadocae gravesque porri,
divisis cybium latebit ovis. 　　　　　　　　　　5
ponetur digitis tenendus unctis
nigra coliculus virens patella,
algentem modo qui reliquit hortum,
et pultem niveam premens botellus,
et pallens faba cum rubente lardo. 　　　　　　　10
mensae munera si voles secundae,
marcentes tibi porrigentur uvae
et nomen pira quae ferunt Syrorum,
et quas docta Neapolis creavit
lento castaneae vapore tostae: 　　　　　　　　15
vinum tu facies bonum bibendo.
post haec omnia forte si movebit
Bacchus quam solet esuritionem,
succurrent tibi nobiles olivae,
Piceni modo quas tulere rami, 　　　　　　　　20
et fervens cicer et tepens lupinus.
parva est cenula, – quis potest negare? –
sed finges nihil audiesve fictum
et vultu placidus tuo recumbes;
nec crassum dominus leget volumen, 　　　　　25
nec de Gadibus improbis puellae
vibrabunt sine fine prurientes
lascivos docili tremore lumbos;
sed quod non grave sit nec infacetum,
parvi tibia Condyli sonabit. 　　　　　　　　30
haec est cenula. Claudiam sequeris.
quam nobis cupis esse tu priorem?

78　　6 **unctis** Lipsius et Heinsius: **ustis** βγ　　24 **placidus** β(?): **–do** L: **–dis** γ　　29 **quod non** γ :
quo nec β

If you are suffering from a sad bout of eating at home, Toranius, you can starve with me. If you are in the habit of taking an apéritif, you will not lack cheap Cappadocian lettuces and overpowering leeks, and pickled tunny will lie hid among chopped eggs. A small cabbage, green on the black dish, will be set before you, to be held with greasy fingers, which has only recently left the cool garden, and a little sausage squashing snow-white polenta, and pale beans with red bacon. If you want the rewards of the second course, shrivelling grapes will be offered to you, and the pears which bear the name of Syrian, and chestnuts, roasted in slow steam, which learned Naples produced. You will make the wine good by drinking it. After all these things, if perhaps Bacchus shall arouse the usual hunger, noble olives which Picenian branches lately bore will come to your aid, and boiling chickpeas and warm lupins. It's a little dinner – who can deny it? – but you will make nothing up, nor will you hear anything made-up, and you will recline peacefully wearing your genuine expression. Neither will the master of the house read a thick volume, nor will girls from naughty Cadiz wobble their lascivious loins with skilled trembling, itching with endless desire; instead, the reedpipe of little Condylus will play something which is neither oppressive nor lacking in finesse. This is the little meal. You will come after Claudia. What woman do you want to be in front of me?

79

Undecies una surrexti, Zoile, cena,
   et mutata tibi est synthesis undecies,
sudor inhaereret madida ne veste retentus
   et laxam tenuis laederet aura cutem.
quare ego non sudo, qui tecum, Zoile, ceno?   5
   frigus enim magnum synthesis una facit.

80

Non totam mihi, si vacabis, horam
dones, et licet imputes, Severe,
dum nostras legis exigisque nugas.
'durum est perdere ferias': rogamus
iacturam patiaris hanc ferasque.   5
quod si legeris ista cum diserto
—sed numquid sumus improbi ? – Secundo,
plus multo tibi debiturus hic est
quam debet domino suo libellus.
nam securus erit, nec inquieta   10
lassi marmora Sisyphi videbit,
quem censoria cum meo Severo
docti lima momorderit Secundi.

81

Semper pauper eris, si pauper es, Aemiliane.
   dantur opes nullis nunc nisi divitibus.

79   (T.R 5–6) 1 **surrexti** TQ: **–xit** βγ
80   1 **vacabit** BC   6 **ista** β : **ipsam** (**–a** A)γ : **ipse** Schneidewin
81   (TR) 2 **nullis** βγ : **–i** TDX : **–ius** R

79

You have got up eleven times, Zoilus, at one dinner-party, and your dinner-suit has been changed eleven times, for fear that sweat might be kept in and adhere to the damp clothing, and the slight breeze injure your relaxed skin. Why do I not sweat, Zoilus, who am dining with you? To be sure, a single dinnersuit produces great coolness.

80

Please give me not even a whole hour, if you have any free time, Severus – and you may charge it to my account – while you read and try out my odds and ends. 'It's a hard thing to lose one's holidays': I beg you to suffer and endure this loss. If you read these along with the eloquent Secundus – but am I not being importunate? – this little book will owe much more to you than it owes to its master. For it will be free from anxiety, and it will not see the unquiet marble of the weary Sisyphus, this book which the critical file of learned Secundus, helped by my friend Severus, will have rasped.

81

You will always be poor, if you are poor, Aemilianus. Wealth is now given to none except the rich.

MARTIAL

82

Quid promittebas mihi milia, Gaure, ducenta,
    si dare non poteras milia, Gaure, decem?
an potes et non vis? rogo, non est turpius istud?
    i tibi, dispereas, Gaure: pusillus homo es.

83

Insequeris, fugio; fugis, insequor; haec mihi mens est:
    velle tuum nolo, Dindyme, nolle volo.

84

Iam tristis nucibus puer relictis
clamoso revocatur a magistro,
et blando male proditus fritillo,
arcana modo raptus e popina
aedilem rogat udus aleator.   5
Saturnalia transiere tota,
nec munuscula parva, nec minora
misisti mihi, Galla, quam solebas.
sane sic abeat meus December:
scis certe, puto, vestra iam venire   10
Saturnalia, Martias Kalendas;
tunc reddam tibi, Galla, quod dedisti.

82   (TR) 4 **i** (**si** αX) **tibi dispereas** codd.: **i, tibi d–** edd.: **vae t–, d–** Heinsius: **di t–, d–** Gruter
83   (TR)
84   9 **abeat** QF: **hab–** βγ

82

Why used you to promise me two hundred thousand, Gaurus, if you weren't able to give me ten thousand, Gaurus? Or is it that you are able to but don't want to? I ask you, is that not more disgraceful? Get along with you, Gaurus, and go to blazes: you're a weedy fellow.

83

You chase, I run away; you run away, I chase. This is my state of mind: I don't want your desire, Dindymus, I want your refusal.

84

Now the boy, gloomy at leaving behind his nuts, is being called back by the loud-voiced schoolmaster, and the drunken gambler, treacherously betrayed by the seductive dice-box, and just dragged out of the secret drinking-joint, asks the aedile for mercy. The whole of the Saturnalia is past, and you have sent me, Galla, no tiny presents, not even smaller ones than you used to send. Well, let my own December finish like this: you know for sure, I think, that your own Saturnalia is approaching – the Kalends of March. Then I shall give back to you, Galla, what you gave.

Commentary

1

Martial begins his book with an epigram addressed to Domitian, and written to accompany the gift of a copy of it. In effect, it serves as a 'dedication' to him (but see also on V 2).

Five of Martial's books have prefaces in prose, so as to distinguish them from the rest of the book: one of these (Book VIII) is addressed to Domitian. In earlier books, such as this one, Martial's approach is more discreet. On his relationship with the emperor, see the Introduction.

In the long first sentence, which takes up no fewer than eight lines, Martial speculates as to which of his four favourite villas Domitian may be staying at. He spent much of his time outside Rome, where he felt more secure.

The epigram flatteringly recalls the form of the type of hymn in which the deity is asked to leave its regular homes, which are listed, in order to come and bless the subject of the poem with his or her presence: see Nisbet and Hubbard on Hor. *Carm.* I 30. Furthermore, in listing the different names by which the deity might prefer to be addressed, the use of *sive* or *seu* is often found in hymns, e.g. at Hor. *Carm. Saec.* 15–16; Apul. *Met.* XI 2. The fact that each place mentioned here is associated with named divinities adds to the religious tone.

1   **Palladian Alba:** the Alban Hills provide the striking skyline to the south of Rome. They take their name from Alba Longa (site of modern Castel Gandolfo), traditionally said to have been founded by Ascanius. *Palladian* refers to the Palladium brought by the Trojans from Troy, but also to Domitian's cult of Minerva, whose festival he used to keep at the Alban villa. This was situated near the modern Albano Laziale (2 km S) between the Via Appia and the beautiful Lago Albano, which fills the crater of an extinct volcano. Juvenal refers to it (*Sat.* 4.145) as 'the Alban citadel' (*Albana arx*). See G. Lugli, *La Villa di Domiziano sui Colli Albani* (Rome, 1920).

2   **Trivia:** a cult title of Diana (identified with Artemis/Hecate as goddess of crossroads). There was a famous temple of Diana beside the Lago di Nemi, another volcanic lake 4 km SE of the Alban villa. Martial must be referring to the lake, to contrast with *Thetis* (the name of the sea-nymph, mother of Achilles, used by metonymy for the sea), which could not in fact be seen from the villa itself.
    Thetin: Martial regularly declines Greek words, including proper names, in their Greek forms.

3   **the truth-telling sisters:** Domitian had another villa at Antium (modern Anzio), on a promontory 61 km SSE of Rome. Nero also had a villa there. There was a famous temple at Antium where the Fortunae Antiates were worshipped, under the form of two female figures, identified as Fortuna Victrix and Fortuna Felix (compare Hor. *Carm.* I 35 *0 diva gratum quae regis Antium*

('O goddess who rules over pleasant Antium'), and see Nisbet and Hubbard's note). There was also an oracle, which warned Caligula to beware of a man called Cassius (Suet. *Cal.* 57.3 – the name of his assassin). Martial flatteringly suggests that Domitian, as a higher divinity, teaches the goddesses what to say.

4   **suburban:** close to the town of Antium.

5   **the nurse of Aeneas:** the town of Caieta (modern Gaeta) also occupied a promontory on the coast of Latium, some 50 km ESE of Anzio. It was reputed to have taken its name from the nurse of Aeneas, who had been buried there (Virg. *Aen.* VII 1–4).

    the daughter of the Sun: the town of Circeii (modern S. Felice Circeo) was supposed to have taken its name from Circe, daughter of the Sun (Virg. *Aen.* VII 10–14). It is situated on the east side of Monte Circeo, a mountainous promontory on the coast between Antium and Caieta. Domitian's villa has been identified with one on the shore of the Lago di Sabaudia, a long lagoon which runs parallel with the sea NW of Monte Circeo, whose extensive remains have been excavated. Numerous sculptures, including the famous staue of Apollo now at Kassel, were found here. See G. Lugli, *Forma Italiae: Regio I, Latium et Campania; Vol. I, Ager Pomptinus; Pars II, Circeii* (Rome, 1928), 66–76; S. Aurigemma, A. Bianchini, A. de Santis, *Circeo-Terracina-Fondi* (Rome, 1960).

6   **Anxur:** Tarracina (modern Terracina), also on the coast of Latium, between Circeii and Caieta. At this point the mountains come right down to the sea, and the ancient town was perched on the hillside. The white cliffs above led Horace to describe it as *impositum saxis late candentibus Anxur* ('Anxur set upon far-gleaming rocks' – *Serm.* I 5.26). Anxur is the old Volscian name, used by Horace and Martial for metrical reasons. In Horace and Livy it is neuter, but in Martial masculine: he refers to the mountain rather than to the town.

    health-giving waters: the position of Terracina would make it a healthy summer resort, but the reference here is more specifically to hot springs for bathing in, referred to again by Martial at VI 42.6. Magnesiac and sulphur springs still exist near the sea at the east end of the town.

8   Domitian's good health is regarded as proof of Jupiter's gratitude for his defence of the Capitolium when he and his uncle Flavius Sabinus were besieged there by Vitellius in December 69, and for the rebuilding of his temple (burnt in the siege), as well as for the founding of the Agon Capitolinus.

9   Martial modestly suggests that he will not go so far as to assume that Domitian will actually read the poems, though he will satisfy his own vanity (*tumidus*) by thinking that he has. This is mere politeness: Martial had earlier taken it for granted that Domitian would read his poems (e.g. I 4).

10   Caesar (*B. Gall.* IV 5) had described the Gauls as being ready to believe anything they heard from travellers, to the extent of basing important decisions on mere rumour. Martial's phrase suggests that this trait had by his time become proverbial.

2

Martial 'dedicates' this book to respectable matrons, and to boys and girls, for it contains no poems which will shock them – unlike its four predecessors. But the ending of the epigram suggests that this was done chiefly to please Domitian, who had assumed the censorship in 85 and was much concerned with public morals. The fact that Martial was anxious about Domitian's attitude towards his less proper poems is shown by, for example, I 4, where he uses the stock defence *lasciva est nobis pagina, vita proba* ('my page is mischievous, but my life is honourable'). The only other book (not counting the *Liber de Spectaculis, Xenia* or *Apophoreta*) which includes no improper poems is Book VIII, which Martial dedicates to Domitian with a preface explaining that this is a tribute to the emperor's sacred majesty.

1 **matrons:** at III 68 Martial addresses the 'matron', saying that the previous poems in the book have been written for her, but the rest will be more explicit. At III 86 he teases the 'chaste woman' for the fact that despite his warning, she is still reading

3 **nequitiae:** 'naughtiness' rather than 'wickedness'.

6 This book is being sent to the emperor for his amusement. The term *dominus* became common under the Empire as a polite form of address, so that it is not so gross a piece of flattery for Martial to use it of Domitian as one might suppose. However, the word's associations with slavery were not forgotten: cf. X 72.8, where Martial says of Trajan *non est hic dominus, sed imperator* ('this is not a master, but a general'). (However, in Book X of his *Epistles* Pliny regularly addresses Trajan as *domine*).

7 **Germanicus:** Caligula, Claudius, and Nero had all used this name, but in their cases it was because of their descent from the first Germanicus. Domitian assumed it in 83, after his triumph over the Chatti in Germany. Hence his pride in it: he even renamed October *Germanicus* (as well as renaming September *Domitianus*). See R Merkelbach, *ZPE* 34(1979), 62–4; Jones, *Domitian*, 129.

8 **the Cecropian girl:** for Domitian's devotion to the chaste virgin goddess Minerva, see on V 1.1. Cecrops was the mythical first king of Athens.

3

The Romans had been at war since 85 with the Dacians (whose territory more or less corresponded to the modern Romania). In 86 they had defeated the Romans under the command of Cornelius Fuscus, Prefect of the Praetorian Guard. While Domitian was in Germany in 89, he heard the news of the revolt of the Suebian Germans, and met Decebalus, king of the Dacians, on the Danube, in order to come to terms with him. Decebalus sent his brother Degis (or Diegis, as Dio calls him) to Rome to receive a diadem (see also VI 10.7). Dio (LXVII 7) interprets this as symbolising Domitian's specious claim to have conquered the Dacians and to have the right to give them a king.

B.W. Jones (*Domitian*, 151) describes Domitian's settlement with Decebalus as 'tactically very sensible', and 'consistent with Roman diplomatic practice'. The exaggeration in which Martial here indulges can indeed be compared with Augustus's boastful claims about the Parthians in his *Res Gestae*.

At VI 76 Martial writes an epitaph for Fuscus, whose death, he says, has been avenged.

1   **now ours:** it was in fact Trajan who subdued Dacia and made it a Roman province.
2   **river-bank:** the frontier of the Roman Empire on the Danube.
2   **Histri:** the Greeks called the lower Danube the Ister. Although Sallust had pointed out that it and the *Danuvius* were the same river, poets still used the name where convenient.
        famulis ... aquis: similarly at VI 76 the tomb of Fuscus (see above) is described as being in a *famulum ... nemus.*
6   **a god:** Domitian liked to be referred to as a god, and Martial was happy to oblige (from *Spect.* 17.4 onwards). See also on V 8.1.

4

An attack on a woman who chews scented leaves to disguise the fact that she drinks too much. Martial often attacks hypocrites who attempt to cover up their faults.

At I 87 a woman called Fescennia eats expensive pastilles for the same purpose, but Martial points out that when she belches the smell is twice as bad as it would have been without them.

1   **Myrtale:** the name identifies her as a prostitute, for whom it would be appropriate because myrtle is sacred to Venus. It is used in an erotic context at Hor. *Carm.* I 33.14.
2   **laurel leaves:** one ancient remedy for bad breath was to chew 'leaves of Malabar', the leaves from which *malabrathum* was made (*Laurus Malabrathum L.*). This was an expensive scented oil (Hor. *Carm.* II 7.8, with Nisbet and Hubbard's note). But there is also a humorous reference to the fact that the Delphic priestess chewed laurel leaves in order to gain inspiration for her oracular utterances.
3   Myrtale drinks *merum*, neat wine, not mixing it with water, as was the Roman custom. This was always a sign of a heavy drinker. Wine was sometimes spiced with myrtle-berries, for medicinal purposes (Columella *Rust.* XII 38), but the use of bay-leaves is a novelty (see S. Lilja, *The Treatment of Odours in the Poetry of Antiquity* (Helsinki, 1972), 130).
5   **Paulus:** as so often, Martial introduces an addressee, for dramatic purposes. The name is a very common one.

5

Martial addresses Sextus, Domitian's librarian, and asks him to put his epigrams beside the works of authors whom he claims as his models. He combines a request intended to flatter Sextus with a restatement of his own literary position, and a compliment to Domitian.

1   **Sextus:** probably a freedman, he presumably held the post of *a studiis*, having responsibility for the emperor's literary pursuits. The post was probably created

by Claudius. It appears that Sextus was also in charge of the library, dedicated to Apollo, which Augustus had built on the Palatine, and next to which Domitian had built his palace. The name is a very common one, occurring often in Martial, and it cannot be said with certainty that the same man is ever referred to elsewhere.

eloquent: the epithet implies that Sextus himself was a poet or orator.

Minerva: as patron of learning – see on V 1.1.

2   **the god:** see on V 3.6.

      domini: see on V 2.6.

      curas: often used by Martial of literary work.

4   **ducis:** commonly used as an imperial title. Horace had addressed Augustus as *dux bone* (*Carm.* IV 5.5).

6   In the Preface to Book I Martial listed, as his models for the frank language used in his epigrams, Catullus, Pedo, Marsus, and Gaetulicus. Albinovanus Pedo was probably the *praefectus equitum* of Germanicus, on whose German campaign he wrote an epic, of which 23 lines survive. None of his epigrams survive. Domitius Marsus, who enjoyed the patronage of Maecenas, wrote a well-known epigram on the deaths of Virgil and Tibullus, which alone survives of his works in various genres. The *Cicuta* mentioned by Philargyrius (on Virg. *Ecl.* 3.90) is thought to have been a collection of epigrams.

      Marsus and Pedo are mentioned together by Martial also at II 77.5 (and cf. Ov. *Pont.* IV 16.5–6), while Marsus occurs again along with Catullus at II 71 and VII 99. Catullus was for Martial the finest Latin epigrammatist, and the one to whom he would feel honoured to be placed second.

7   The implication is that Domitian had written a poem (presumably an epic) on the Capitoline conflict of December 69 (see on V 1.8). Quintilian (X 1.91) indulges in lavish flattery of the emperor's poetic genius, regretting that greater concerns have distracted him from the literary work which he undertook in his youth, and pointing out that no-one could write of wars better than the man who had waged them. It is implied by Valerius Flaccus (*Arg.* I 12f.) that Domitian had begun an epic on the Jewish War. While he was alive, his interest in poetry was fulsomely praised, but after his death it was dismissed as a pose (Jones, *Domitian*, 12).

      caelestia: the epithet, in court language, often means virtually 'imperial'.

8   **cothurnati:** the *cothurnus*, the high-heeled buskin worn by Roman actors appearing in Greek tragedies, is often used by metonymy for tragedy. The epithet is applied to Virgil (as at VII 63.5) because of the tragic colouring of his epic.

6

With due deference, Martial asks Domitian's chamberlain Parthenius to ensure that the emperor receives his book.

Parthenius, who was presumably a freedman, held the post of *a cubiculo* or *cubicularius*, which meant that he controlled access to the emperor, and therefore exercised great influence. Martial first mentions him at IV 45 and 78.8 (AD 88). At VIII 28 and IX 49 he celebrates Parthenius's gift of a toga. The first poem in Book

XI is addressed to him: this was written within a few months of the assassination of Domitian, in which Parthenius played a leading role. It was even claimed later that he had been one of the chief agents of Nerva's accession. At XII 11 Martial asks him to present a book to Nerva: this was presumably the abridged version of Books X and XI mentioned at XII 4, because, before Book XII was published, the Praetorian Guard had (in AD 97) savagely murdered Parthenius, against Nerva's wishes, in order to avenge the death of Domitian.

1   **si non est grave nec nimis molestum:** such polite phrases were common in colloquial speech. Compare Catullus 55.1 *oramus, si forte non molestum est* ('I ask you, if perhaps it is not troublesome'); Mart. I 96.1.

2   **Muses:** Parthenius was a poet himself. At XI 1 (an interesting parallel with this poem), Martial says (5–6): *libros non legit ille sed libellos* [i.e. petitions] / *nec Musis vacat, aut suis vacaret* ('he does not read books, but booklets, nor has he time for the Muses, or else he would have time for his own' – i.e. if he had the time he would write his own poetry). At XII 11.1–3 Martial again addresses the Muse:

> Parthenio dic, Musa, tuo nostróque salutem:
> nam quis ab Aonio largius ámne bibit?
> cuius Pimpleo lyra clarior exit ab antro?

('Muse, greet your and my friend Parthenius; for who drinks more copiously from the Aonian river? Whose lyre sounds more brightly from the Pimplean cave?').

3–8 **sic ... finiat ... et sis ... sic ... sentiat ... admittas:** the two verbs with *sic* express the wishes which Martial regards as conditional on the fulfilment of what is referred to by the verb *admittas*. In this type of expression the latter clause is usually constructed with *ut* + indicative, as at VII 12.1–4 *sic ... legat ... ut ... nec ... laesit.* See Nisbet and Hubbard's note on Hor. *Carm.* I 3.1.

     quondam: here of a time in the future, as at IV 13.9 *diligat illa senem quondam.*

4   **while Caesar is still in good health:** in view of what was to happen six or seven years later, the phrase has a cruel irony.

5   Anyone who was fortunate was naturally exposed to envy, which in the ancient world was regarded as positively malignant. Martial wishes that Parthenius may 'enjoy the favour of envy', a striking oxymoron.

6   **Burrus:** son of Parthenius. IV 45 celebrates his fifth birthday, when Parthenius makes an offering on his behalf to Apollo, to whom (as patron of song) he might well be devoted.

7   **chartam:** 'the manufacturer's and retailer's unit is the made-up roll, ... and the Greek word χάρτης, the Latin *charta*, does not mean a sheet but a roll' (E.G. Turner, *Greek Papyri: An Introduction* (Oxford, 1968), 4).

8   **the more sacred part of the palace:** presumably this refers to the emperor's private apartments (whereas the library referred to in the previous poem will have been a public institution).

9 **Iovis sereni:** this could mean 'calm weather', but Martial often compares Domitian with Jupiter (e.g. I 6.6), and identifies them again at VIII 15.2. Likewise Statius calls Domitian *Iuppiter Ausonius* (*Silv.* III 4.18).

10 **placido suoque vultu:** cf. V 78.24 *et vultu placidus tuo recumbes.*

12–15 A *libellus* might well contain a petition to the emperor (in fact *libellus* was the word used for a petition). Many such must have constantly turned up. But the elaborate appearance of this one shows that it is not a petition.

14 **cedar-oil:** papyrus was soaked in this to protect it from moths and worms. This gave it a yellowish tint. Persius uses the phrase *cedro digna* for poems worthy of immortality (I 42 – see Kissel's note).

purple: this refers to the *paenula* or wrapper which protected the wound-up roll. Purple was the favoured colour for it.

15 **knobs:** the ends of the rod, attached to the end of the papyrus, around which it was rolled, and appearing outside the papyrus. They were often coloured or gilded.

17 **nihil ... agasque: nihil agere** is the usual phrase for 'doing nothing'.

18 **dominum:** Domitian is gracefully described as master of the Muses.

19 Domitian will recognise the *libellus* as a work of literature, and will want to see it.

7

Martial uses a prayer to the god of fire as an opportunity for another (in this case well-deserved) compliment to the emperor.

Fires were extremely common at Rome, where buildings were crowded together and incorporated much timber in their construction (despite the attempt at regulation following the great fire of Nero's reign). Martial must be referring particularly to the conflagration of AD 80, which raged in the Campus Martius for three days and nights, destroying, among other buildings, the Serapeum, Iseum, Saepta, Poseidonium, Baths of Agrippa, Pantheon, Diribitorium, the theatre of Balbus, the stage of the theatre of Pompey, the Octavian buildings, and the Temple of Jupiter Capitolinus and the temples around it (Dio Cass. LXVI 24). Titus began the work of rebuilding, and Domitian carried it on, restoring the old monuments and adding magnificent new ones. The reign of Domitian was notable for its architectural achievement, in what B.W. Jones describes as 'a massive and spectacular programme of public building equalled by hardly any other emperor' (*Domitian* 79; see his account at 79–98).

1 The mythical phoenix (whose use in comparisons is jokingly described as corny at V 37.13) was supposed to regenerate itself by means of fire. Only one bird existed at any one time, and the length of its life was given differently by different authors, some (like Martial) saying 1,000 years, others 500, others other amounts. The phoenix appears on coins (e.g. of Trajan and Hadrian) as a symbol of a newly dawning golden age.

Assyrian: Martial seems to have taken the epithet from Ov. *Met.* XV 393, who says that the Assyrians call the bird the phoenix. Most authors locate it in Egypt or Arabia.

4 Rome has become as good-looking as its emperor. Domitian was handsome as a young man, and even in old age, though bald and fat, was proud of his *verecundia oris* (modest appearance'), boasting to the senate, 'So far at any rate you have approved of both my mind and my face' (Suet. *Dom.* 18.2).

5–8 Vulcan had a grudge against Mars because of his affair with Vulcan's wife Venus (described by Homer at *Od.* VIII 266f.). Three altars were set up by Domitian – one on the Quirinal, one in the Circus Maximus, and one near the Vatican – to ward off fires because of the great fire under Nero; every year at the Volcanalia the praetor in charge of the city *regio* was to make a sacrifice. (See Richardson, *Topographical Dictionary*, 21.)

7 **Lemnian:** the volcanic island of Lemnos in the northeast Aegean was the centre of the cult of Hephaestus (= Vulcan). According to Homer (*Il.* I 590f.), it was where he landed when thrown from heaven by Zeus for defending Hera against him.
chains: the chains of the net in which Vulcan caught his wife and Mars in the story told by Homer.

8 **patienter amet:** at first sight it might seem more natural to take Vulcan as object, but Shackleton Bailey, following Gronovius, translates 'love in moderation', and comments 'i.e. love Mars' (see his note at *AJP* 110 (1989), 136). In his Teubner edition he refers also to Nemes. *Ecl.* 4.56–7. The ambiguity is no doubt intentional, and adds a pleasant touch of humour.

8

Phasis was in the course of praising Domitian's edict restricting certain seats in the theatre to knights with the full equestrian property qualification, when he was ordered to leave these seats by an official.

Since this book contains no less than eight epigrams referring to this edict (8, 14, 23, 25, 27, 35, 38, 41), it must have been recent. Suetonius (*Dom.* 8.3) tells us that Domitian issued it as part of his part of his programme as censor. The custom of reserving the fourteen rows immediately behind the orchestra (where senators sat) for the *equites* may go back to the second century BC. It was confirmed by the Lex Roscia Theatralis of 67 BC, which was so unpopular that it took the influence of Cicero to ensure its acceptance. Augustus renewed and modified the law by his own Lex Iulia Theatralis (Suet. *Aug.* 44; see E. Rawson, 'Discrimina Ordinum: the Lex Iulia Theatralis', *PBSR* 55 (1987), 83–114 = *Roman Culture and Society* (Oxford, 1991), 508–545; also C. Schnurr, *LCM* 17 (1992), 147–160). The unpopularity of the law is shown by Appian's story that when Octavian ordered a soldier sitting among the knights to be removed, the troops were angry (*BCiv.* V 15). The law must have fallen into disuse; hence Domitian's edict. The Lex Roscia is indignantly referred to by Juvenal at 3.153–9.

Phasis is presumably ejected because he lacks the property qualification. Why then is he described as wearing a purple cloak? The answer is probably that it is a piece of ostentation intended to give a false impression of Phasis's status. Compare V 23.

However, Rawson (543–4) suggests that Phasis is being thrown out because he is improperly dressed, Augustus having laid down that spectators must wear the toga without cloaks. Suetonius (*Aug.* 44.2) tells us that he insisted that no–one in dark clothing (*pullatus*) should sit *in media cavea* (in the middle of the house), and *ib.* 40.5 shows that *pullatus* is contrasted with the wearing of the toga. Nevertheless, the wearing of cloaks (presumably over the toga) is implied by Suet. *Claud.* 6, which states that, as a mark of respect to Claudius, the equestrian order would stand up and take off their cloaks when he arrived at a show. Martial IV 2.1 tells of a *munus* (a show in the amphitheatre, rather than the theatre) at which everyone wore white except one man in a black cloak. Since it was winter-time, the rest were presumably wearing white cloaks.

1   **domini deique nostri:** this is the first occasion on which this combination occurs in Martial (see also VII 34.8). Suetonius (*Dom.* 13.2) records it as an example of Domitian's arrogance that in dictating a formal letter in the name of his procurators he began *dominus et deus noster hoc fieri iubet* ('our lord and god orders this to be done'), and that afterwards he insisted on being addressed in this way both in writing and in speaking. After Trajan's accession Martial insists *dicturus dominum deumque non sum* ('I shall not say lord and god' – X 72.3).

4   **Phasis:** the very rare Greek name suggests a freedman.

5   **lacernis:** the plural is hyperbolical. Phasis can only have been wearing one cloak.

10   **with his head thrown back:** Phasis is lounging in his seat. Throwing back the head was a stock sign of arrogance (Quint. *Inst.* XI 3.69; Pers. 1.129–30), whereas a lowered head showed humility.

12   **Leitus:** one of the ushers (*dissignatores*) charged with ensuring that the law was observed. They were under-officers of the *curatores ludorum* (magistrates in charge of shows), and were accompanied by lictors. They were probably imperial freedmen. Leitus may be a real person, though the etymology of the name (which occurs in Homer) would make it appropriate for a public official.

9

Attacks on doctors are very common in both Greek and Latin epigrams (e.g. Mart. I 30). The joke often centres on their leaving their patients worse off than they found them (usually dead). The profession was a profitable one, and anyone could enter it.

The epigram opens with a single word of three long syllables. After a pause, a swifter rhythm brings the doctor, and the crucial word *discipulis* is delayed by the vocative. The third line picks up *centum*, and again the crucial (and unexpected) word comes last. The last line is balanced between the matching phrases *non habui ... nunc habeo*, around the vocative set in the same position as previously.

2   **Symmachus:** the name is used for a doctor twice elsewhere in Martial (VI 70; VII 18). He is obviously not a real person. Doctors almost always have Greek names. The elder Cato had warned his son that the Greeks had sworn to kill off all the barbarians by means,of medicine, and that they charged fees so as to win people's confidence.

a hundred pupils: Philostratus tells of a sick man visited by two doctors accompanied by over thirty pupils (*VA* VIII 7).

10

A reflection on the fact that people tend always to neglect their contemporaries, and prefer buildings and authors from the past.

The tendency of Roman critics to prefer old literature to new is countered by Horace at *Ep.* II 1.18f. Martial has an amusing comment at VIII 69, where he asks a man who only praises dead poets to forgive him if he doesn't think it worth dying just to please him.

1-2 These words are imagined as being spoken by Regulus, the rest of the poem being Martial's answer. Pliny, in praising the literary work of Pompeius Saturninus, makes a similar ironic comment – 'it should not be held against his works that he is still alive' (*Ep.* I 16.8).

3 **Regulus:** the first of four references to him in this book (see also 21, 28, 63). He is often praised by Martial (I 12; 82; 111; II 74; 93; IV 16; VI 38; 64; VII 16; 31), whose works he greatly admired (VI 64.11). M. Aquilius Regulus was one of the most distinguished, or notorious, men of his time. Obviously a brilliant orator, he began his career by prosecuting three notable men at the end of Nero's reign, for which he was rewarded by the emperor. He was consul at some unknown date in the early or mid 80s. Under Domitian, he committed – according to his arch-enemy the younger Pliny – crimes as bad as those he had committed under Nero, but better concealed (*Ep.* I 5,1). He became extremely rich, largely (again, according to Pliny) from shameless legacy-hunting (*Ep.*II 20 13-4). He died about 105. Martial does not address him after Book VII, published c.92, which may be either because Regulus was too unpopular with Martial's other senatorial friends, or because Regulus failed to reward Martial adequately for his compliments. Martial's lavish praise of such a man may seem to do him little credit, but we should be wary of criticising him too seriously for knowing on which side his bread was buttered.

5 The Portico of Pompey was built by him in 55 BC next to the stage of his theatre in the Campus Martius, to provide shelter for the spectators in case of rain. It was rectangular, about 180 by 135m., with four parallel rows of columns. The central area was laid out as a garden, with four rows of plane trees, and it was ornamented with various works of art. References in literature show that it was one of the most popular places in the city – especially for picking up girls. Martial implies that there were newer porticoes which were less popular, but it is not certain which he was thinking of. Two other porticoes in the Campus Martius were the Porticus Argonautarum, built by Agrippa, and the Porticus Vipsania, begun by Agrippa's sister Polla, and completed by Augustus, but Martial must surely be referring to newer ones than these. One may have been the Porticus Europae, which he is the only author to mention (e.g. II 14). For a list of known porticoes, see Richardson, *Topographical Dictionary*.

6   After the first Temple of Jupiter Capitolinus was burnt to the ground in 83 BC, the rebuilding was begun by Sulla, but carried out for the most part by Q. Lutatius Catulus. He dedicated the new temple in 69 BC, and his name was inscribed over the entrance. It is likely that the columns were not of marble, but of stuccoed stone (Richardson, s.v. Iuppiter Optimus Maximus). In AD 69 it was burnt when the troops of Vitellius stormed the Capitoline (see on V 1.8). Vespasian rebuilt it, but it was burnt again in 80 (see on V 7). Domitian rebuilt it, dedicating it probably in 82, with much greater magnificence than ever before. For example, columns of white Pentelic marble were used, and the doors were plated with gold. It was still regarded as one of the wonders of the world in the 6th century.

7   Martial ignores the fact that the *Aeneid* was only published after Virgil's death. Ennius was included by Horace among the 'old poets' in the passage referred to above (*Ep.* II 1.50–52). Virgil himself clearly had the greatest respect for Ennius, but under the Early Empire his reputation declined. Ovid calls him *ingenio maximus, arte rudis* ('supreme in genius, but rough in artistry', *Tr.* II 424), and Seneca, according to Gellius (*NA* XII 2.10), claimed that Virgil only included rough and hypermetric lines so that the 'Ennian crowd' might recognise an archaic flavour in the new poem. O. Skutsch thinks that the story in Cassiodorus that Virgil called Ennius *stercus* ('dung') must have been invented in the Neronian period (*The Annals of Q. Ennius* (Oxford, 1985), 13–14). Statius speaks of the *Musa rudis ferocis Enni* ('the rough Muse of fierce Ennius', *Silv.* II 7.75), and at XI 90.5 Martial mocks a man who enjoys things like Ennius's *terrai frugiferai* (in fact, Virgil occasionally uses an archaic genitive of this type). Such tastes were becoming more common towards the end of the first century AD, and reached their peak in the time of Hadrian.

8   **Maeonides:** often used as a name for Homer, because of the tradition that he was born in Maeonia (in Asia Minor). Homer was reputed to have endured poverty and wanderings, and to have been fined at Athens as a raving madman (*RE* s.v. 2201–2).

9   Of Menander's 105 comedies, only eight won victories (Gell. *NA* XVII 4.6). He was less successful with his contemporaries than his rival Philemon, though posterity reversed the judgement.

10   In fact Ovid makes it clear that he was very well known in Rome, so that this is a humorous exaggeration. Shackleton Bailey suggests that, since Ovid says that Corinna's identity was known only to himself (*Am.* II 17.29; *Ars Am.* III 538), Martial's memory may have played him false, but this explanation seems unnecessary. Modern scholars doubt whether Corinna was real, but Martial takes it for granted that she was (compare VIII 73.10; XII 44.6). (Ov. *Am.* III 11.19, cited by Shackleton Bailey, would, if it referred to Corinna, suggest that she was well known, but there is no reason to suppose that it does.) As regards Martial's theme, one may compare Ovid's statement (*Pont.* IV 16.3) that 'greater fame comes after we are ashes'.

11   Martial addresses his book, a device which goes back to Catullus 35 (*Poetae tenero meo sodali,/ velim Caecilio, papyre, dicas* ('I should like you, papyrus, to say to my gentle friend, the poet Caecilius'), and probably to Hellenistic poetry, if not even earlier. The idea that books will be eager to go out into the world and win fame goes back to the last Epistle of Horace's first book (*Ep.* I 20), and is common in Martial (compare e.g. I 3).

12   It is interesting to contrast this joke with Martial's proud claim in I 1.4–6 that he is a poet 'to whom, enthusiastic reader, you have given, while he is alive and can appreciate it, such glory as few poets have after their deaths', and with that of V 13.4, 'What death has given to few, life has given to me'. Ovid had made a similar boast at *Tr.* IV 10.121–2, and compare Quint. *Inst.* XII 11.7. By contrast, at I 25 Martial had encouraged Faustinus to publish his books while he was still alive and could enjoy their success, making the point (8), *cineri gloria sera venit* ('glory comes too late when we are ashes').

11

Martial pays a compliment to his important friend Stella, in which he praises both his taste in precious stones and his poetical talent.

The four Greek nouns, with their exotic sounds, make a striking opening. By contrast, the second couplet uses simple but neatly pointed language.

1–2   Stella presumably wears all these jewels on the same ring. The ring is no doubt the same one referred to in the next epigram, from which it appears that there are ten gems, each bearing the representation of a girl. A ring set with several stones is included in a list of jewels worn by a girl described in an inscription (*CIL* II 3386): *in digito minimo duo gemmis adamantibus, digito sequenti anulus polypsephus zmaragdis et margarito* ('on her little finger two with diamond gems, on the next finger a many-stoned ring with emeralds and a pearl'). The wearing of large and elaborate rings as status symbols is borne out by literature (e.g. Mart. XI 37; Juv. 7.139–140), and testified by surviving rings (e.g. F.H. Marshall, *Catalogue of Finger Rings ... in the British Museum* (London, 1907), plate 21, etc.).

1   **sardonyxes:** this is a variety of agate, a variegated chalcedony which has layers. Sardonyx includes a layer of sard (a red chalcedony).
zmarǎgdos: the scansion suggests that the word may have been pronounced *zmarados.*
jaspers: a variety of chalcedony which could be smoky, milkwhite, yellowish, or bluish in colour. (On these gems, see R.A. Higgins, *Greek and Roman Jewellery* (London, 1961).

2   **twists:** he likes to feel his ring, and he may also want to shift its weight – see on V 61.5.
Stella: L. Arruntius Stella was a well-born and wealthy man, praetor in 93 and suffect consul in 101. He is often addressed or mentioned by Martial, from Book I to Book XI. Statius also praises his poetical gifts (*Silv.* I *Praef.*; I 2). At I 7, Martial says that Stella's poem about his pet pigeon is greater than Catullus's *passer.*
Severus: it is not certain who this is, but a likely candidate is Silius (or Catius) Severus, younger son of the poet Silius Italicus. He died in 94, before his father

(IX 86). He too was a poet. He is probably the same man addressed by Martial at V 80; VI 8; VII 34; 38; 49; 79; Vlll 61.

3 **gems:** for this metaphorical use, compare Tac. *Dial.* 22: *oratorem ... volo ... non ea solum instrui supellectile quae necessariis usibus sufficiat, sed sit in apparatu eius et aurum et gemmae, ut sumere in manus et aspicere saepius libeat* ('I wish the orator not just to be armed with such equipment as may suffice for essential purposes, but let there also be in his outfit gold and gems, so that people may take pleasure in picking them up and looking at them more frequently').

4 In Martial's opinion, the real ornament of Stella's hand is his poetical achievement, not his display of jewels. As Alan Ker (*CQ* 44 (1950), 18) points out, there is an 'elegant pun' on *manus*, which can mean 'handiwork' as well as 'hand' (e.g. Mart. VIII 50.2). Shackleton Bailey (Loeb) considers this metaphorical explanation of the 'gems' far-fetched, and suggests that the reference may be 'to some jewels described by Stella in his poetry'.

12

Stella's achievement in carrying ten girls on one finger surpasses the feats of famous gymnasts.

It is unusual for Martial to place two poems on the same theme side by side, but this epigram would be extremely obscure without the previous one. It will be noted that they are in different metres.

1–4 Gymnastic displays were put on in the new Stadium – the first permanent one in Rome – built by Domitian in the Campus Martius (the Piazza Navona follows its outline). He inaugurated the festival of the Capitolia in 86, and it attracted the best Greek athletes (see H.A. Harris, *Sport in Greece and Rome* (London, 1972), 62). See also VII 32; IX 38.

1 **pole-bearing forehead:** i.e. with his forehead provided with a pole (*pertica*) on whose tip he balances weights. Heraeus compared the Greek word κοντοπαίκτης, defined by *LSJ* as 'acrobat who balanced a pole on his head'.
Masclion: a very rare Greek name (e.g. *IG* XIV 977), derived, according to Heraeus, from *masculus*. Presumably a real person.

3 **Ninus:** also no doubt real. The name is found in a few Roman inscriptions.
omnibus: for *totis*, i.e. *tota vi lacertorum*, in contrast with *uno digito* in line 6 (Friedlaender).

7 It has been suggested that the ten girls whose portraits are engraved on the gem-stones might be Stella's future wife Violentilla (also called Ianthis) and the nine Muses; or Minerva and the nine Muses; or else ten of Stella's girl-friends (his affairs are hinted at in VI 21, and at Stat. *Silv.* I 2.29–30). See R.Durand, *Latomus* 5 (1946), 259–261.

13

Here we have a theme which is close to Martial's heart: his legitimate pride in the name which he, a poor provincial, has made for himself.

1   **Callistratus:** a name used several times by Martial for fictitious characters. The point here is that it is both Greek and grand-sounding. He must be a freedman (see line 6).

      pauper: 'poor' by contrast with 'rich', but that is not to say 'destitute' (= *egenus*). See XI 32, whose last line is *non est paupertas, Nestor, habere nihil* ('it is not poverty to own nothing, Nestor'): Kay points out that in the ancient world there was 'no easily definable middle ground between the very rich and the very poor'. At IV 77 Martial says, 'I have never asked the gods for wealth, content with a moderate amount and happy with what is my own', and terms this *paupertas*. Compare Seneca's definition (*Ep.* 87.40): *ego non video quid aliud sit paupertas quam parvi possessio* ('I do not see what poverty is other than the possession of a small amount').

2   **a knight:** Martial's equestrian rank was the result of his having held a titular military tribunate, which he may have been given by Titus. In order to qualify, he must have possessed at least 400,000 sesterces – enough to live on quite comfortably.

3–4   These lines are a reworking of I 1:

          Hic est quem legis ille, quem requiris,
          toto notus in orbe Martialis
          argutis epigrammaton libellis,
          cui, lector studiose, quod dedisti
          viventi decus atque sentienti,
          rari post cineres habent poetae.

      ('"It's him", I, the man you're looking for, Martial, famous throughout the whole world for his witty books of epigrams; to whom, enthusiastic reader, you have given, while he is alive and can appreciate it, such glory as few poets have after their deaths').

3   **throughout the whole world:** Martial had already made this claim in the first poem of his first book (just quoted), into which it may well have been inserted at a later date, as the works which we know he had previously published (the *Liber de Spectaculis,* the *Xenia,* the *Apophoreta*, and some youthful works, also perhaps some of his small collections or occasional *libelli*) would be unlikely to have brought him worldwide fame. The idea of this claim by a poet goes back to Alcman (Page, *Poet. Mel. Gr.* fr. 148). Compare also Hor. *Carm.* II 20.14; Ov. *Tr.* IV 10.128 in *toto plurimus orbe legor*. Martial repeats his boast at VI 64.25; VIII 61.3; X 9.3–4. He also speaks of being read at Vienne (in the South of France), in Vindelicia (on the Danube), among the Getic frosts (north of the Black Sea), and in Britain.

      'hic est': the expression used by a passer-by on recognising a famous man in the street. It is used by Cicero in retelling the story of Demosthenes's pleasure at being recognised by a woman carrying water (*Tusc.* V 36.103).

4   See on V 10.12.

5 The use of a large number of columns would imply a house of considerable size and architectural elaboration. The largest number would usually be in the porticoes surrounding the peristyle garden. By this period, it was likely that columns would be of marble, which was a conspicuous form of luxury: compare Hor. *Carm.* II 18.3–5 *non trabes Hymettiae / premunt columnas ultima recisas / Africa* ('[in my house] beams of Hymettian marble do not press down upon columns cut in furthest Africa').

6 **the wealth of a freedman:** such as Augustus's freedman Licinus (VIII 3.6). This had become proverbial. Compare Seneca's description of Calvisius Sabinus (sometimes claimed to be the model for Trimalchio) at *Ep.* 27.5 *et patrimonium habebat libertini et ingenium* ('he had both the property and the mind of a freedman'). At III 31 Martial tells a rich man with a Roman name that two men with Greek names (presumably freedmen) were or are even richer than he.

flagellat: a bold metaphor. The idea is that the money does not rest quietly in the cash-box, but is kept on the move, pushed to its fastest speed to get the greatest return. Compare II 30.4 *et cuius laxas arca flagellat opes* (' whose strong-box whips up extensive wealth'); Plin. *HN* XXXIII 164; Pers. 4.49. For the opposite, compare Stat. *Silv.* II 2.150–151 *non tibi sepositas infelix strangulat arca / divitias* ('your strong-box does not miserably suffocate hidden-away wealth'). Shackleton Bailey points out (*AJP* 110 (1989), 132) that the strong-box would contain not just coins and other valuables but records of money lent at interest: he cites VIII 37.1 and Juv. 13.136, also III 31.3 *servit dominae numerosus debitor arcae* (' many debtors are enslaved to their mistress, your strongbox').

7 **Egyptian Syene:** Syene (modern Aswan) was until the reign of Trajan the southernmost outpost of the Roman Empire (I 86.7). For the value of Egyptian property, compare X 15.6 *cum tua Niliacus rura colonus aret* ('although an Egyptian tenant ploughs your fields'). The younger Seneca owned property there (*Ep.* 77.3).

servit: land is often described as being the slave of someone; cf. I 116.6; VI 76.6.

8 **Gallic Parma:** Parma, in the broad Po valley in Cisalpine Gaul, was famous for its wool, which, according to XIV 155, was second only to the wool of Apulia (for which see V 37.2). Parmesan sheep are referred to as an investment at IV 37.5 (*ex pecore redeunt ter ducena Parmensi* ('my Parmesan flock brings in 600,000').

9–10 The extremely simple language and plain logic of the last couplet make a deliberate contrast with the elaborate poeticisms of the previous four lines.

14

Another epigram (compare V 8) about a man ejected from the knights' seats at the theatre. The reader is left to assume that Nanneius lacks the property qualification.

1 **Nanneius:** a rare name, used again in scazons at XI 61.
occupy: Shackleton Bailey translates as 'squat'.

2   **when it was permitted:** this must refer to the time before Domitian published
his edict, reaffirming the earlier laws.

4–5 The sense of these lines is not entirely clear. The *sellae* must be the seats of the
senators in the orchestra. Nanneius has been several times ejected from the
front row (*primus gradus* – line 1) of the knights' seats, immediately behind the
sellae, but still tries to sit there, crouching behind the seats of two senators in
such a way that he looks as if he is sitting between them. The common names
Gaius and Lucius were used conventionally by jurists when giving examples,
along with Titus and Seius (Juv. 4.13). English lawyers similarly use 'John Doe
and Richard Roe'.

   Rawson ('*Discrimina Ordinum*', cited on V 8, 535 n.129) argues against this
that other privileged groups must have divided the *equites* from the *plebs*, but,
as suggested above, the reference here is to the seats of the senators. She draws
attention to the different explanation suggested by S. Demougin (*L'Ordre
Équestre sous les Julio-Claudiens* (Paris, 1988), 808–9): Tacitus (*Ann.* II 83)
records among the honours paid to Germanicus after his death the naming after
him of a *cuneus iuniorum* ('wedge-shaped division of seating allocated to
younger men') by the equestrian order. As the honours to Germanicus were
modelled on those granted to Augustus's grandsons Gaius and Lucius after their
deaths, one might expect that two *cunei* were named after them, and Martial
may be referring to these. Nanneius is trying to sit in the space between the
two *cunei*. Rawson, however, points out that this is rendered unlikely by his
next move, to perch on the edge of the gangway, and suggests (not very
plausibly) that Gaius and Lucius may have continued to have seats placed for
them side by side in the theatre.

6   **hood:** a woollen cloak with a hood, used for disguise also at Juv. 6.117–8;
8.145.

7   **shamefully:** his appearance is disgraceful, like that of the genuinely one-eyed
woman at XII 22.1 (*quam sit lusca Philaenis indecenter* – 'how shamefully
Philaenis is one-eyed').

8   **gangway:** one of the gangways between the blocks of seats, where people who
could not find a seat might have to stand.

9   **bench:** one of the fourteen benches of the knights.

11   **Leitus:** the same name for an usher as at V 8. Martial's portrayal of Nanneius's
bizarre and uncomfortable position has a strikingly visual humour.

15

Strictly speaking, this is another 'introductory' poem, but Martial has presumably
postponed it because of the comparatively large number of such poems he has
already placed at the beginning of this book.

1   **Augustus:** the title was held by all Roman emperors except Vitellius.

jokes: Martial often refers to his epigrams as *ioci or lusus* ('playful pieces'),
e.g. I *Praef.* line 7; 35.13. He does not, of course, imply that all his poems are
humorous: he is being modest (like Catullus when he calls his poems *nugae* –
1.4).

2 Compare Martial's claim at the beginning of the Preface to Book I: *spero me secutum in libellis meis tale temperamentum ut de illis queri non possit quisquis de se bene senserit, cum salva·infimarum quoque personarum reverentia ludant* ('I hope that I have in my books pursued a course of such moderation that no-one who thinks well of himself may be able to complain about them, since they have their fun without infringing the respect due even to the lowest class of persons'). Roman emperors discouraged personal attacks on citizens, and Domitian as censor was likely to be particularly averse to them. But Martial's own character was in any case opposed to such an abuse of his power.

3-4 The most notable example of a proud recipient of Martial's praise was the younger Pliny, who at *Ep.* III 21 records his pleasure in Martial's epigram flattering him (X 20). He ends by admitting that Martial's poem may not survive for ever, but patronisingly states that at least Martial wrote as if it would (see pp. 12–13).

5 At I 5 Martial puts a two-line epigram into the mouth of Domitian, giving his supposed reply to I 4.

6 The emperor has asked what is the profit for Martial if the people he praises give him no reward, but he says that profit is not the main consideration since he enjoys writing like this. There is no reason why we should not take him at his word, despite poems where he complains that his praise does not always get the return which is its due. Pliny did, of course, provide a financial recompense.

16

Martial picks up the theme of the last epigram, telling his readers that his desire to please them by writing entertaining literature costs him dear, for, if he practised as a lawyer, he would become rich, whereas now all he gets in return is praise.

Since Martial had received the normal Roman rhetorical education (IX 73), he could have made a profession of the law, and this was in fact the one profession open to a man of social standing that was both respectable and profitable. Apparently friends, including even his fellow-Spaniard Quintilian (II 90), urged him to make a respectable living by so doing (see also I 17; II 30). The chief reason why he did not was doubtless disinclination, combined with his devotion to poetry.

1 **serious works:** the rest of the epigram shows that he means speeches to be delivered in the courts.

2 **friend reader:** Martial often addresses his reader, as Ovid had done in his poems of exile (cf. *Tr.* III 1.2 *lector amice*). Compare I 1.4 (quoted on V 10.12). Obviously Ovid was not in a position to give recitations. Martial's pride in his extensive renown makes it natural for him to look beyond a mere recital–audience. However, when he refers to his *auditor* at XII *Praef.* lines 9–10 he is indulging in nostalgia for what – now he was back in Spain – was no longer possible. His only other reference to an audience is at IX 81 (*lector et auditor*).

3 **legis et....cantas:** the two words are close in meaning, for *legere* can mean to read out loud to others (e.g. V 78.25), while *cantare* does not necessarily involve an audience (e.g. VII 88.5). Compare also VII 51 and VIII 61.3, and see W. Allen, *TAPA* 103 (1972), 1–14.

4   **amor:** picking up *amice* in line 2.

5   **the sickle-bearing Thunderer:** i.e. Saturn, who is called *falcifer senex* at XI 6.1. Cronos (usually identified with Saturn) used a sickle to castrate his father Uranos. *Tonans* is usually the title of Jupiter, but other gods are sometimes called 'Jupiter'; e.g. Virg. *Aen.* IV 638 *Iovi Stygio* (= Dis); Stat. *Achil.* I 48–9 *secundi ... Iovis* (= Neptune). See Housman, *CQ* 13 (1919), 70.

The temple of Saturn beneath the Capitol housed the *Aerarium Saturni*, so that 'to defend Saturn's temple' means 'to defend the interests of the Treasury'. A good example is a case referred to by Pliny at *Ep.* IV 12: a scribe had died in a province before his pay-day, and the quaestor was not sure what to do with his pay. The emperor referred the case to the senate, where one advocate put the case for the scribe's heirs, and another the case for 'the people' (i.e. the Treasury).

6   **sell words:** the *Lex Cincia* of 204 BC, which forbade orators to receive money or gifts in return for their services, had finally been abolished by Claudius, who legalised fees up to 10,000 sesterces. Nevertheless, Quintilian (*Inst.* XII 7.11–12) strongly disapproved of what he called the 'piratical custom' of orators striking a bargain with their clients before pleading their cause: the more honourable course was to leave it to the client to express his gratitude afterwards.

sollicitisque ...reis: the phrase comes from Hor. *Carm.* IV 1. 14 *pro sollicitis non tacitus reis.*

7   **Hispanas ... metretas:** large pottery vessels used for olive oil, which was one of the chief exports of Spain (especially Hispania Baetica). Lawyers were often paid in kind: see IV 46; Juv. 7.119–121.

merchant: as a Spaniard himself, Martial could presumably reckon on getting briefs from his merchant compatriots.

8   **sinus:** a fold in the toga or tunic was commonly used for keeping money.

9   Martial's book, instead of earning its living in the courts, is merely a dinner-guest and drinking-companion, and as such naturally earns nothing.

11–12 It is interesting to compare with these lines Pliny's justification (*Ep.* III 21) for having given Martial money for his journey back to Spain as a reward for the epigram in which he had praised him (see pp. 12–13). Pliny says that in the good old days it was normal to reward those who wrote eulogies of individuals or cities in this way, but that now, 'since we have ceased to do anything worthy of praise, we also think it bad form to be praised'.

12   **Alexis:** Martial several times refers to Alexis (*Eclogues* 2.1) as a real boy given to Virgil by Maecenas (VI 68.6; VII 29.7; VIII 55.12; 73.9–10). However, Donatus's life of Virgil (9) says that he was a present from Asinius Pollio. He also says that his real name was Alexander, that he was not lacking in erudition, and that he was one of two slave-boys particularly loved by Virgil. It is likely that all of this is mere fiction, derived from the figure of Alexis in the second *Eclogue*.

13   **belle:** *bellus* (diminutive of *bonus*) is usually used ironically by Martial, but
      the adverb is not ironic, and appears often in his poems, reflecting its common
      colloquial use (see Kay on XI 52.1).

14   **pretend not to understand:**   compare XI 108 (last poem in the book)
      'Although you could be satisfied by such a long book, reader, you still want a
      few distichs more from me. But Lupus wants his loan back and my slaves want
      their rations. Reader, pay up! You pretend you can't hear [*dissimulas*]?
      Goodbye then' (Kay). There too Martial jokingly pretends that all his readers
      owe him a financial reward for his epigrams, and not just those who are
      mentioned in them. Praise is not enough. Martial's revenge will be to turn
      lawyer after all, and deprive his public of their entertainment.

17

This satirical attack on an absurdly pretentious woman is neatly constructed: each of
the first three lines begins with *dum*, but the third *dum* clause spills over into the last
line with the word *nubere*, which is immediately picked up by *nupsisti*. The end of
the third line is picked up by the end of the fourth, with the repeated vocatives
followed by the crucial nouns in the dative, both beginning with *c*.

3   **Gellia:** a common name used several times by Martial.
      broad stripe: senators wore a broad purple stripe on their togas.

4   **a police sergeant:** a *cistiber* was a member of the *quinque viri cis Tiberim*
      ('board of five men on this side of the Tiber'), who had been first created as
      assistants to the *tres viri capitales*, responsible for policing Rome, when the
      senate in 186 BC took action against the Bacchanals. Coranus, the rich man
      who cheats the legacy-hunters in Hor. *Serm.* II 5, is described as *recoctus
      scriba ex quinqueviro* (55–6 – 'a scribe remoulded from a member of a board of
      five'). Cicero refers to them as the lowest rank of magistrate (*Acad. Pr.* II 136).
      In provincial towns similar offices were held by freedmen: it is not clear
      whether this was so at Rome, but such a humble magistracy would certainly not
      be held by a senator, nor – it would seem to be implied by this epigram – by a
      knight. See *TLL* s.v.

18

Martial explains to a rich friend why the only presents he sends him at the Saturnalia
are his own books: he does not want to seem to be fishing for gifts in return.
      The epigram was presumably written to accompany the actual gift of some *libelli*
('little books') to Quintianus. He is also addressed at I 52, which asks him to assert
the true authorship of Martial's *libelli* (described there too in the imagery of slavery)
if a plagiarist claims them as his. The name is a common one, but it is just possible
that he is the Pompeius Quintianus about whose death Pliny writes at *Ep.* IX 9. He is
there praised for his devotion to literature. The problem is that he would have to
have been very young at the time of Martial's first book.

1   **December:** the festival of Saturn began on December 17th, and by the reign of
      Domitian lasted from five to seven days. Friends sent each other *sigillaria*

(pottery or wax figurines) or presents. Martial's so-called Book XIII, the *Xenia*, and Book XIV, the *Apophoreta*, were both written for the Saturnalia (probably in 83 and 84 or 84 and 85): they consist of series of short poems (mostly single couplets), each designed to accompany a particular gift. The poems in the *Apophoreta* alternately describe gifts to be sent by rich and poor men.

napkins: at IV 46.17 a rich lawyer receives among his Saturnalia presents a *lato variata mappa clavo* ('a napkin adorned with a broad stripe' – like the one worn by Trimalchio, Petr. *Sat.* 32.2), whereas at VII 72.2 and X 87.6 they are poor gifts. It is surprising that napkins do not appear among the gifts listed in Book XIV.

2   **spoons:** these were the only eating implements in common use in the 1st century AD, and were often of silver even in poorer households (though they could also be of bronze, horn, or ivory). There were two types, the smaller round-bowled *cochleare* for eggs and shellfish, and the larger *ligula*, with pear-shaped bowl, used, for example, for eating cereal foods (D.E. Strong, *Greek and Roman Gold and Silver Plate* (London, 1966), 129, 155–6). They are mentioned as Saturnalia presents by Martial again at VIII 71.9; cf. also XIV 120; and VIII 33.23 (a New Year's gift).

wax candles: mentioned as Saturnalia presents at X 87.5 and XIV 42. They were not only useful, but had a symbolic significance, representing the increase in light after the winter solstice. According to Macrobius (*Sat.* I 7.33), the tribune Publicius had a law passed forbidding poor people to send anything more expensive than *cerei* to their richer friends (the implications of this provide a fascinating parallel to what Martial says in this poem), and that they were recognised gifts from poorer to richer is attested also by Varro (*Ling.* V 64) and Festus (54.16M).

sheets of papyrus: at XIV 10 Martial jokingly suggests that for a poet to send empty papyrus as a present is quite a substantial gift. Sheets of papyrus appear as Saturnalia gifts, along with napkins, also at Stat. *Silv.* IV 9.25–6.

3   **aged damsons:** plums from Damascus (*pruna Damascena*) appear as a Saturnalia gift at XIII 29 (*vas Damascenorum*):

> pruna pereginae carie rugosa senectae
>   sume: solent duri solvere ventris onus.

('Take plums wrinkled with the decay of foreign old age [Pliny says that the Italian sun was not strong enough to shrink them]: they are accustomed to relax the load of a packed stomach.')

senibus indicates that they were dried, like our prunes. For the use of the word, compare III 58.7 *senibus autumnis;* XI 36.6 *senem ... cadum* (both of wine); also Martial's fondness for *anus* similarly used (e.g. I 39.2).

4   **home-born:** a *verna* was a slave born in the owner's household. For the idea of the book as its author's young slave, compare I 3 and Hor. *Ep.* I 20. But the word also suggests that the books are witty, since home-born slaves were often encouraged to be cheeky and amusing: compare I 41.2, and the phrase *vernacula urbanitas* (the sort of wit characteristic of a *verna*) used at Petr. *Sat.* 24.2; Tac. *Hist.* II 88. Their wit makes the books suitable as Saturnalia presents. Sending his books as presents would involve Martial in the not inconsiderable expense of having copies made, but this is ignored for the sake of the point.

7   The comparison of gifts to hooks, and of the recipient to a fish, is more commonly applied to the situation – frequently mentioned under the Early Empire – where the gifts are sent by a legacy-hunter to his victim. Cf. IV 56.5 *sic avidis fallax indulget piscibus hamus* ('thus does the deceitful hook indulge the fishes'); VI 63.5–6:

> 'munera magna tamen misit', sed misit in hamo:
>   et piscatorem piscis amare potest?

('"But he sent great gifts", – yes, but he sent them on a hook; can the fish love the fisherman?').

Also, in a different context, Hor. *Ep.* I 7.74 *occultum visus decurrere piscis ad hamum* ('the fish seemed to hurry to the hidden hook').

8   **wrasse:** the *scarus* is the parrot-wrasse, which apparently does not rise to a fly (D'Arcy W. Thompson, *A Glossary of Greek Fishes* (London, 1947), 241). R.B. Veloso (*CPh* 75 (1980), 67–8) proposes the emendation *squalum*: 'a fly is a suitable bait to catch a member of the carp family, such as the *squalus* (either the chub or a related species), a fish commonly found in the Tiber (otherwise *quis nescit* line 7 becomes somewhat awkward)'. Shackleton Bailey does not mention this conjecture, which may presuppose too precise a knowledge of the behaviour of fish on the part of Martial.

9–10   The paradoxical conclusion is of a type which much appealed to Martial.

19

Martial again addresses Domitian, praising his reign, but complaining that poor men cannot find generous patrons. Their only hope is that the emperor will supply the deficiency. The epigram ends with a neatly deflating twist as Martial imagines Domitian's reaction.

Martial often complains about the meanness of patrons (compare Juvenal's seventh Satire), wishing that great patrons like Seneca and Piso could still be found. However, the fate of those two provides at least one good reason why distinguished senators might be wary of devoting too much attention to their *clientelae*.

The theme is closely related to that of V 18, with its reference to Saturnalian gifts.

1   **si qua fides:** a colloquial expression found also in Ovid and Petronius, and cf. Mart. I 13.3.

3   **triumphs:** Domitian's first triumph was after his war against the Chatti, and took place in 83; his second, over the Dacians, took place in 86 (Jones, *Domitian*, 129 and 139).

   more deserved: by comparison with the notoriously undeserved triumph of Caligula, and the supposedly undeserved one of Claudius. Jones admits that Domitian's first triumph was hardly deserved, but calls the second 'probably less undeserved than the first' (139).

4   **Palatine gods:** the gods worshipped on the Palatine, including Jupiter, Apollo, and Cybele, who deserve thanks for protecting the emperor and his people.

Shackleton Bailey thinks that the phrase may refer to the deified emperors (Augustus, Claudius, Vespasian, and Titus).

5   See on V 7. Domitian was a great builder, completing projects begun by his father and brother, as well as initiating his own.
       greater: not in the literal sense of physical expansion, since outward growth of the city was limited by the *pomerium*, or sacred boundary.

6   There is savage irony when one contrasts this line with Tacitus's words at *Agr.* 3.1: *primo statim beatissimi saeculi ortu Nerva Caesar res olim dissociabiles miscuit, principatum ac libertatem* ('right at the beginning of this most happy age Nerva Caesar combined things formerly incompatible, namely principate and liberty'). Similarly Pliny (*Ep.* IX 13.4) speaks of *primis diebus redditae libertatis* ('the first days of restored liberty'), and an inscription dated the day of Nerva's election was set up on the Capitol to *Libertas Restituta* ('restored Liberty'). But it has to be remembered that it was the senate that was chiefly at odds with Domitian, and these are the political slogans of the senatorial party.

8   The idea that a man may cultivate friendships in the expectation of a return seems to us an unworthy one, but one has to remember that in the sort of unequal friendships that existed at Rome between men who were at different social and economic levels the rich man expected the poorer man to provide him with services such as attendance and political support, so that the poorer man felt entitled to expect some recompense.

9   **sodali:** the word suggests 'boon-companion', rather than just 'friend'.

10   'Who is escorted by a knight, to whom he himself has given the status by providing him with the necessary financial qualification?' (Friedlaender). Compare XIV 122, written to accompany a present of rings (*anuli*):

         Ante frequens sed nunc rarus nos donat amicus.
               felix cui comes est non alienus eques.

       ('Previously friends frequently gave us, but now rarely. Happy the
         man whose companion is a knight who is not of another's making.')

       At IV 67 poor Gaurus asks an old friend, now praetor, for 100,000 sesterces to add to his 300,000 so as to become an *eques*. The younger Pliny gave a man 300,000 for the purpose (*Ep.* I 19). Of course, the financial qualification was not all that was needed, but, if a man was otherwise qualified (e.g., like Martial, by having held the military tribunate), but did not possess 400,000 sesterces, he was ruled out (see on V 8). The emperor, however, could provide both qualifications.

11   'A [single] spoon [out] of the half-pound [of silver] he [i.e. the patron] has received at the Saturnalia.' Patrons sometimes passed on gifts given to them by their clients (e.g. IV 88; VII 53). At VIII 71.8 a patron is given a *selibra in cotula* (in the form of a cup); so here the patron received the *selibra in ligulis,* but only passes on one of the spoons to the client. (This is Housman's explanation, approved by Heraeus.)

12   Shackleton Bailey, like some previous editors, regards *flammaris* (which occurs nowhere else) as corrupt. Housman (*JPh* 30 (1907), 236–8) conjectured *damnatis*, 'to men condemned to the toga', i.e. clients (because they had to wear the toga when calling on their patrons), but surely we need to be told of what

the *decem scripula* consist. Heraeus took *flammaris toga* to refer to a gold
plaque used to ornament wooden couches (citing Mart. IX 22.6; VIII 33.5;
Suet. *Cal.* 32.2), but this seems a peculiar present.

scripula: a *scripulum* was the twenty-fourth part of an *uncia.*

13   **regarded as extravagant:** by the patron – heavily sarcastic.

reges: the term *rex* is often used by Martial and Juvenal for a patron. Parasites
in Plautus and Terence use it as a form of address. However, Horace used it of
Maecenas (*Ep.* I 7.37 *rexque paterque audisti coram* ('you have heard yourself
openly called "king" and "father"'; and cf. *ib.* 17.43). Although its unpeasant
associations were more remote than those of *dominus*, they existed all the same,
and are emphasised here by *tumidi* (cf. Mart. II 18.5; also III 7.5 *regis superbi*).

14   **aureolos:** an *aureus* was worth twenty-five *denarii* (100 sesterces). The
diminutive is used for the sake of the metre.

crepet: *crepare* is more often intransitive, e.g. Mart. XII 36.3 *interdum
aureolos manu crepantis* ('sometimes some gold pieces jingling in the hand').

17   **for some time now:** Domitian had guessed in which direction the epigram is
moving, even before line 15 made it clear.

Germanicus: see on V 2.7.

nose: the nose was the organ of criticism (cf. I 3.6), and Ker translates 'with a
quiet sneer', but this sense is inappropriate here. That Domitian had a sense of
humour is shown by the fact that at I 5 Martial actually puts a humorous
epigram in his mouth.

20

Martial outlines to his old friend Iulius Martialis the sort of life he would like to
share with him, if they could free themselves from the business of life at Rome,
ending with the reflection that we should enjoy life while we can.

    The theme of this epigram is one that was very close to Martial's heart, and it is
no coincidence that it is addressed to one of his closest friends. Iulius Martialis was
probably about ten to fifteen years older than the poet. At XII 34 Martial says that
they have been friends for thirty four years, so he must have known Iulius virtually
from the time of his arrival in Rome. He addresses or refers to him in every book
except II and VIII. In three poems he is sent books, and once is asked to suggest
corrections. He had a house in the Via Tecta (on the Campus Martius) and a villa on
Monte Mario (north of the Janiculum). Closely comparable with this epigram is X
47, where Martial describes *vitam quae faciant beatiorem* ('what things make the
happier life'): the ingredients make up the same kind of quiet, sociable, and easy-
going life as here. However, the setting there seems to be the country, reflecting
perhaps his growing nostalgia for his Spanish homeland, as well as the atmosphere at
Rome at the end of Domitian's reign, whereas here it is definitely the city of Rome.

    This celebrated epigram provided a model for an epigram addressed by Clément
Marot to François Rabelais (Mayer, no. CLXXXIII), and for a longer poem by
Abraham Cowley (*Poems*, ed. A.R. Waller (Cambridge, 1905), 38–9).

3   **dispose of my leisure-time:** compare Plin. *Ep.* IV 23.1 *magnam cepi
voluptatem, cum ex communibus amicis cognovi te, ut sapientia tua dignum est,*

et disponere otium et ferre ('I was very pleased when I heard from mutual friends that you – as is appropriate for a man of your wisdom – are both disposing of your leisure-time and managing to bear it'). Pliny is addressing a friend who has retired after a distinguished career. His view is (§3): *et prima vitae tempora et media patriae, extrema nobis impertire debemus* ('we ought to apportion both the early and middle years of our lives to our fatherland, but the final ones to ourselves'). Since Martial at this time was aged about fifty, perhaps even Pliny would have conceded his right to 'retire' (though cf. Mart. II 90.3–4, quoted below on line 14).

4   **a truly full life:** compare I 15.4, where Martial tells Iulius Martialis that, although he is almost sixty years old, *numerat paucos vix tua vita dies* ('and yet you can scarcely reckon up a few days of real living'). *vita* is used in the sense that only the time one has enjoyed counts as one's real life. Not surprisingly, this sense of *vita and vivere* is common in Martial: cf. e.g. VI 70.15 *non est vivere sed valere vita est* ('true life is not just being alive but enjoying good health'); Catull. 5.1 *vivamus, mea Lesbia, atque amemus* ('let us live life to the full, my Lesbia, and let us love').

5–6 These lines show that, although Iulius must have been better off than Martial, he too had to pay court to his social superiors.

6   Compare Alfius's description of the joys of country life at Hor. *Epod.* 2.7: *forumque vitat et superba civium potentiorum limina* ('he avoids the forum and the proud thresholds of the more powerful citizens'); also Martial's rhapsody to Juvenal on the joys of Bilbilis (XII 18.4–5): *dum per limina te potentiorum sudatrix toga ventilat* ('while the sweating toga flaps you about across the thresholds of the more powerful citizens'). The reference in lines 5–6 is to the morning call which clients were expected to pay on their patrons (the *salutatio*).
     grim law-suits: a reference to the annoyance of becoming involved in a law-suit, or of having to turn up and support patrons in court: cf. II 90.10 *sit sine lite dies* ('may my days be free from lawsuits'); X 47.5 *lis numquam* ('never a law-suit') (on these poems see above). Iulius may have practised as a lawyer.
     the dismal forum: the forum was the place where all kinds of business were transacted. Again, patrons would expect their clients to accompany them there in order to boost their standing. Compare Hor. *Epod.* 2.7 (quoted above).

7   **ancestral images:** the wax images of ancestors with which the great man's *atrium* would be decorated (see Courtney's note on Juv. 8.1–9). So this picks up *atria* in line 5.

8   The taking of exercise by riding, or travelling in a vehicle. The word *gestatio* can also be applied to a building erected for the purpose, such as Regulus's portico at I 12 and 82 (and cf. Juv. 7.178–181). Insofar as Martial means a building, he must be referring to public ones like the Portico of Pompey (V 10.5).

9   **Campus:** the Campus Martius, where so many of the city's public amenities, including porticoes, baths, and temples, were situated. It was also traditionally the place for taking athletic exercise or swimming in the Tiber.
     the portico, the shade: see on V 10.5.

Aqua Virgo: an aqueduct brought into Rome in 19 BC by Agrippa to supply the baths he built in the Campus Martius. The water came from springs about eight miles along the Via Collatina, and was renowned for its purity and coldness. It was regarded as expecially suitable for bathing in (Mart. VI 42.16–21; VII 32.11; XI 47.6; XIV 163), and also supplied the famous private baths of Claudius Etruscus (Stat. *Silv.* I 5.25). The 'Acqua Vergine' that now supplies the Trevi Fountain comes from springs nearer Rome, but uses part of the ancient channel.

baths: the great *thermae* (hot baths open free of charge) of Agrippa and Nero were in the Campus Martius; those of Titus were near the Colosseum.

It will be noted that the five items mentioned in this line are closely inter-related: the *campus* gives the general setting; *porticus* suggests at once those in the Campus; *umbra* is what the *porticus* provide; *Virgo* is the aqueduct supplying the Baths of Agrippa in the Campus; *thermae* suggests these baths and those of Nero (singled out for special praise at VII 34.5).

10 **labours:** humorously paradoxical.

11 **lives his life for his own benefit:** cf. Plin. *Ep.* IV 23.3, 'apportion the final years to ourselves' (quoted above).

necuter: used here ln place of *neuter*, which would not fit the metre, in the sense *ne alteruter quidem.* It is not used elsewhere by Martial. (In fact, *necuter* is Schneidewin's conjecture: the MSS of the family read *neuter*, and this may be right, scanned *nĕŭter* – the original scansion of the word.)

12 An echo of Catull. 5.4 *soles occidere et redire possunt* ('suns can set but reappear'), in a similar context.

13 **pereunt et imputantur:** sometimes used as a motto on sundials; including the one designed by Wren at All Souls' College, Oxford.

14 It is a striking paradox to ask why one should hang about waiting to lead an easy life.

The theme of enjoying life while one can was an ancient and widespread one, given new vigour by its incorporation into the teaching of Epicurus. It was particularly significant for Horace: cf. e.g. *Carm.* I 11.7–8;

> dum loquimur, fugerit invida
> aetas: carpe diem, quam minimum credula postero

('while we are talking, grudging time will have fled: seize the day, trusting as little as possible in tomorrow').

It occurs also in Manilius and Persius, and often in Seneca. Compare Mart. II 90.3–4:

> vivere quod propero pauper nec inutilis annis,
> da veniam: properat vivere nemo satis

('if I hasten to live my life, though a poor man and not yet incapacitated by age, forgive me: noone hastens enough to live his life').

Martial's emphasis on enjoying the pleasures of life while one can is related to the popular idea that memories of those pleasures are all you can take with you when you die. This is the idea stated by St Paul (I *Cor.* 15.32) – 'If the dead rise not, let us eat and drink, for tomorrow we die'.

21

Greeting people by name was an important part of Roman social life: this is shown by the fact that rich men would emply a *nomenculator* to tell them people's names. Apollodotus's failing is all the more striking because a good memory was one of the chief requisites of the orator, so that he is a poor example to his pupils.

V 54 is a related epigram.

1   These common names are chosen because of their meanings ('tenth' and 'fifth'; 'thick' and 'thin'). It is easier to confuse names that have some sort of connection, even if – as in the case of the latter two – they are actually opposites.
     Regulus: see on V 10.3. As an orator himself, he will appreciate the joke.
2   **Apollodotus:** apparently coined by Martial. *Apollodorus* is the common form, but cannot be used in hexameter verse.
4   **learned them by heart:** in the same way as he would learn his speeches.

22

Martial tells a patron that the long and weary journey he has to undertake in order to greet him in the early morning would hardly be worth it even if he were actually there when he arrived.

Complaints about the arrogant and thoughtless behaviour of patrons are common in Martial. This epigram is given life by its colourful picture of the discomforts of the Roman pedestrian, which recalls the passage at Hor. *Epist.* II 2.65–76, where the poet speaks of the distractions that make it difficult to write at Rome, not least of which is the duty of paying morning calls. Martial's epigram has in turn influenced Juvenal's similar description at 3.239–267.

1   **in the morning:** see V 20.6N.
     wished and deserved: Martial wishes to see his patron out of friendship, and deserves to see him because of his dutiful attendance.
2   **Paulus:** Martial uses this common name several times for a mean patron, presumably because of its meaning 'small' (VIII 33; IX 85; X 10; XII 69), as well as in other contexts (e.g. V 4). It cannot possibly indicate a real person in this disparaging context.
     further away: even further away than it is in fact, so far that I don't go there.
     Esquiline: this hill (NW of the Colosseum) was one of the most fashionable places to live.
3   **the Tiburtine Pillar:** the name occurs only here. It was presumably some kind of monument, perhaps set up at a crossroads. *Tibur* is the Latin name of Tivoli, some 18 miles E of Rome.
4   The Temple of Flora and the Capitolium Vetus (a shrine of the Capitoline Triad, Jupiter, Juno and Minerva, older than that on the Capitoline Hill) stood on the northern slope of the Quirinal Hill. Not much is known about either, but the Temple of Flora probably stood near the modern Piazza Barberini (where Bernini's Triton Fountain stands), and the Capitolium Vetus just SE of the Palazzo Barberini.

At I 108.3 Martial says that his *cenacula* (a rented apartment in an *insula*) was up on the Quirinal. By the time he wrote Book IX (about AD 94), he owned a small house which was in the same area, probably W of the Palazzo Barberini, across the modern Via Quattro Fontane. It is not certain whether V 22 and VI 27 refer to the apartment or the house, though the fact that at VIII 61 Martial does not mention a house in the city as an enviable possession may imply that he did not yet possess one.

5 **the Suburan hill:** the continuation of the Subura (the street leading NW from the Forum), where it climbed between the Oppian and Cispian Hills to the Porta Esquilina (on whose site now stands the Arch of Gallienus, between S. Maria Maggiore and the Piazza Vittorio Emanuele). It is not clear why Martial should need to use the street: one might have expected him to follow the line of the modern Via Quattro Fontane. Perhaps he wanted to include a mention of a well-known steep and busy street, which would certainly be used by someone coming from the Forum.

The Suburan hill is similarly referred to by Juvenal at 5.76–9, where the client describes how he earned his dinner invitation:

> scilicet hoc fuerat propter quod saepe relicta
> coniuge per montem adversum gelidasque cucurri
> Esquilias, fremeret cum saeva grandine vernus
> Iuppiter et multo stillaret paenula nimbo;

('to be sure, this was the reason why I often left my wife behind and ran up the steep mountain and chilly Esquiline, when the springtime Jupiter was roaring with cruel hail, and my cloak dripped with much rain').

By contrast, at X 20 Martial tells his Muse to take his book to Pliny: *brevis est labor peractae / altum vincere tramitem Suburae* (4 – 5; 'it is a slight effort to surmount the lofty path at the end of the Subura').

6 **never ... dry:** either because of the rain, or the droppings of animals, or slops thrown out from shops and flats. The mud of the streets is mentioned at III 36.4.

7 **mandras:** 'herds', from the Greek μάνδρα, an animal-pen. The mules are presumably there to haul the loads of marble mentioned in the next line, which must be for public works, since private wheeled traffic was not allowed in the city during the day. Compare Hor. *Epist.* II 2.72–74 (see above):

> festinat calidus mulis gerulisque redemptor,
> torquet nunc lapidem, nunc ingens machina tignum,
> tristia robustis luctantur funera plaustris;

> ('the contractor hurries along with his mule and carriers, the huge machine whirls now a rock, now a beam, gloomy funerals struggle with stout waggons').

Juvenal (3.236–8) gives, as one of the reasons why poor men cannot sleep at Rome, *stantis convicia mandrae* – 'the abuse of the stationary herd', i.e. the abuse hurled by the herdsman when his herd cannot move).

8 Compare Juv. 3.254–9 for contractors' wagons carrying timber and marble as a peril of the streets.

10   This did not necessarily mean that Paulus was not in fact at home: at II 5.5
Martial tells a real friend, Decianus: *saepe domi non es, cum sis quoque, saepe
negaris* ('you are often not at home, and even when you are you are often said
not to be'). There Martial says that it is not worth making a round journey of
four miles not to see his friend, though it would certainly be worth going two
miles to see him.

11   **soaking:** presumably with sweat, as at XII 18.4–5 (to Juvenal – quoted on V
20.6). Clients were expected to wear the toga for the *salutatio*, which was
annoying, not only because it was hot, but because it was an expensive form of
clothing. Of course, the toga might also be wet from rain, as at Juv. 5.78–9
(quoted above on line 5).

12   **hardly ... worth all this:** he values Decianus more highly – see on line 10.
Compare also I 108.6, where he tells a friend who lives across the Tiber:

> migrandum est, ut mane domi te, Galle, salutem:
> > est tanti, vel si longius illa foret;
>
> ('I have to make a long journey to call on you at home in the morning,
> Gallus: it's worth it, and would be even if it were still further').

13   The point of this line is not clear: why should a man who fulfils his duties
(*officia*) as a client always have friends who refuse him the return of basic
courtesy? For the epithet *officiosus* in this context, cf. I 70.2; X 58.11–14. The
word always has a good sense: NB XII *Praef.* 4 *inter illas quoque urbicas
occupationes, quibus facilius consequimur ut molesti potius quam ut officiosi
esse videamur* ('even in the midst of those urban occupations, by means of
which we more easily bring it about that we should seem troublesome than that
we should seem dutiful').

    In his Loeb edition, Shackleton Bailey reads, instead of *habet, colet* ('shall
he cultivate?'), which he now prefers to his previous conjecture *cavet* (CPh 73
(1978), 279).

14   **rex:** see on V 19.13.
    unless you sleep: this suggests that Paulus has in fact gone out, presumably in
order to pay his own calls on greater men, rather than staying in bed till his own
clients arrive. Compare II 18. 3–4:

> mane salutatum venio, tu diceris isse
> > ante salutatum: iam sumus ergo pares
>
> ('I come to greet you in the morning, but you are said to have gone out
> earlier to greet someone else: so now we are equals').

There too he tells his patron (10): *qui rex est regem, Maxime, non habeat* ('a
man who is a patron, Maximus, ought not to have patron').

23

This epigram is a variation on V 8 (see on that poem for Domitian's theatre edict),
and has a similar point. Bassus now prefers purple because it implies the wealth and
status he does not really possess.

1   **the colour of grass:** the colour implied is probably *galbinus*, or greenish-
yellow. Men described as wearing clothes of this colour are all of a dubious

reputation, e.g. Mart. III 82.5; Juv. 2.97; *S.H.A. Aurel.* 34.2. Hence Martial's reference at I 96.9 to 'greenish-yellow morals' (*galbinos mores*), of an effeminate man. Compare W.S. Gilbert's 'greenery-yallery' young man (the aesthete Bunthorne in *Patience*).

The actual colour green (*viridis*) is used of the tunics of the chariot-racing team (e.g. Juv. 11.198), but not apparently otherwise of dress.

fueras: Martial likes to use the pluperfect when one might expect the perfect or imperfect (often for metrical reasons).

Bassus: a common name used quite often by Martial for fictitious persons.

3   **placid:** cf. V 6.10. One might expect a censor to be *tetricus* (severe).

censor: Domitian assumed the censorship in 85, and exercised its moral functions with great energy (hence Juvenal's attacks on him for hypocrisy). His theatre edict must have been issued in his capacity as censor, which traditionally involved the scrutiny of the lists of *equites* to ensure that they were properly qualified.

4   **Oceanus:** another usher (*dissignator*), like Leitus (V 8.12). He appears also at Mart. III 95.10; VI 9. The knights, who are now more clearly set apart from the rest, obey the orders of the usher, whereas an impostor like Bassus does not.

5   The wearing of purple clothes was a status symbol in imperial Rome (see e.g. Mart. I 49.32; M. Reinhold, *Purple as a Status Symbol in Antiquity* (Brussels, 1970)). Scarlet was second in value to purple. The *coccum* was the 'berry' (actually a kind of insect) of the scarlet oak; the *murex* was a shell-fish.

6   **dare verba:** 'cheat', 'deceive' – a common phrase.

7–8 'If elegant dress sufficed to give the right to a knight's place (for which the chief requirement was the possession of 400,000 sesterces, which Bassus does not own), then Cordus would have it before all others' (Friedlaender).

8   **Cordus:** Martial expects his readers to remember that at II 57.4 he had described Cordus as *alpha paenulatorum* ('A1 among coat-wearers'). Even if the reader did not know that epigram, he would be reminded of it three poems after this one (V 26). Cordus was probably a real person, for the Publius described as *meus* at II 57.3 was certainly real (cf. I 109), and Cordus is similarly called *meus* here. (However, the Cordus of III 15 must be fictitious. At III 83 he could be the real one.)

own a horse: Martial jokingly refers to the original function of the *equites* as cavalry, with horses supplied either by the state or by themselves. By this period many *equites* probably hardly knew one end of a horse from the other. Compare the prize-giving scene in the film *If*, where the knighted guests turn up in armour.

24

This very remarkable epigram in praise of a gladiator takes the form of a parody of a hymn. The idea was due to his having the name of a god. Each of the fifteen hendecasyllabic lines begins with the name, a type of repetition (anaphora), particularly associated with hymns. An even longer example is a late hymn to the Sun (*Anth. Lat.*, ed. D.R Shackleton Bailey, I (1982), no. 385), in which each of the last 23 lines begins with the word *Sol*. The commoner type of repetition involving *tu* or *te* is found at the opening of Lucretius's *De Rerum Natura*, and at Martial VIII 8, addressed to Janus, where *te* occurs four times in two lines. Compare, in the *Gloria in excelsis Deo* of the Latin Mass, *tu solus sanctus, tu solus dominus, tu solus altissimus, Jesu Christe.*

In each line the name is followed by a phrase, either in apposition, or participial, or a relative clause, expressing his qualities – in other words, a kind of litany. The closest pagan parallels are the so-called 'aretalogies' of the Egyptian goddess Isis, which stress her omnipotence, invincibility, and so on. .

The name Hermes was quite often used by gladiators, probably because of the god's association with speed, though there may also be an allusion to the role of Hermes as Psychagogos – the god who escorts souls to the underworld.

The most important contribution to the understanding of this epigram is H.S. Versnel's 'A Parody on Hymns in Martial V 24 and some Trinitarian Problems', in *Mnemosyne* 27 (1974), 365–405. See also G. Ville, *La Gladiature en Occident* (Rome, 1981).

1   **martial sweetheart of the age:** the phrase could be applied to both god and gladiator, though *Martia* more particularly applies to the gladiator's warlike occupation. The phrase *saeculi voluptas* resembles the words *lusus et voluptas* used by Martial at XI 13 of the famous actor Paris, but, as applied to the god, it recalls Lucretius's invocation of Venus as *hominum divumque voluptas* (I 1).

2   A general statement of Hermes's universal skill, which is picked up by *omnia* in line 15, and further explained in lines 11–13. It was extremely unusual for a gladiator to practise more than one type of fighting (Ville, 307).

3   This line parodies another typical feature of hymns, the use of 'polar expressions' – the linking of two opposites which are usually self-exclusive. The gladiator and the trainer normally had quite distinct jobs (Ville, 305–6). The use of *et ... et* emphasises this polarity.

4   **whirlwind:** Shackleton Bailey prefers Heinsius's conjecture *turbŏ* to the MS reading *turba*. Compare e.g. Cic. *Dom.* 137 *tu, procella patriae, turbo ac tempestas pacis* ('you, the gale of your fatherland , the whirlwind and storm of peace'). Shackleton Bailey translates *tremor* 'earthquake', which suits the sense of *turbo*, but when *tremor* has this sense it is usually made clear by the context (e.g. by reference to *terrae*, as at Virg. *G.* II 479). For the sense 'terror', compare V 65.5.

5–6 Even other famous gladiators are knocked down by Hermes. The name *Helios* occurs in a gladiatorial inscription from Asia Minor. According to Versnel (382), there is also a reference to the Sun as the highest of the visible sky gods. In hymns, gods are sometimes said to be so great that even the Sun must give way to them.
      sed unum ... sed uni: picked up by *ter unus* at the end. In hymns the words *unus* or *solus* or their equivalents often express the the fact that the deity praised is set apart from all others (compare *tu solus sanctus* etc, quoted above, or *tu sola potes* at Lucr. I 31).

6   **Advolans:** this occurs as the name of a race-horse, but not of a gladiator. However, a name suggesting speed is obviously appropriate.

7   **skilled at winning without wounding:** the rationalistic explanation is that Hermes wins by disarming his opponents, but the paradox (of the type known as an *ἀδύνατον*, or impossibility) suggests his superhuman qualities. Most gladiators would need to strike a blow, and inflict a wound, to win, but Hermes does not. The fact that his defeated adversary remains unscathed is to his credit: gladiators sometimes boast in their inscriptions of having 'saved many lives'.

8   **subpositicius:** the gladiator who replaced a fallen colleague (also known as *tertiarius*, Petr. *Sat.* 45.11). By an even more remarkable paradox than that in the previous line, Martial expresses the fact that Hermes never falls, and so never requires a substitute, by saying that he is 'his own substitute'. Ville (397) understands *subpositicius* in the sense of 'stand-in', for a gladiator unable to appear, since the other sense would imply that it was after all conceivable that Hermes might be defeated, but this is just what Martial is denying.

9   **locariorum:** although most of the seats at public shows were free, it seems that some (presumably the better ones) could be booked for a fee, and the *locarii* would then be speculators who bought the seats in order to sell them for a higher price (Ville, 431). When a famous fighter like Hermes was to appear, business would be brisker and higher prices could be charged.

10   **anxiety and torment of the female fans:** this recalls *saeculi voluptas* in line 1. For the *ludiae* (female fans) compare Juv. 6.104. At Pompeii graffiti refer to gladiators as the idols of the girls, and ivory tablets found there contain love-letters to gladiators. Their names and portraits appear on all manner of objects. Even Faustina, wife of the emperor Marcus Aurelius, was said (probably falsely) to have loved a gladiator. *cura* is often used of the pains of love, and for *labor* compare e.g. Hor. *Carm.* I 17.19–20 *laborantis in uno Penelopen vitreamque Circen* ('Penelope and glassy Circe, both tormented over the same man').

11–13   These three lines explain the *omnia arma* of line 2, each specifying a different type of fighting at which Hermes excelled. There is no certain evidence of any other gladiator practising more than one type.

11   **spear:** he fought as a *veles*, carrying a shield and *hastae amentatae*, javelins fitted with a strap so that they could be thrown from a distance with greater force. The spear is called 'war-like' because it was a weapon in actual military use. L. Robert (*Hellenica* III (Paris, 1946), 131–2) argues that this line is precisely illustrated by the helmeted figure on the famous Zliten mosaic (his plate XI) who is holding a long lance in his right hand and a small round shield on his left arm. (Despite what Ville says (307, n.191), he does not identify the man with a *hoplomachus*.)

12   The trident, called 'marine' because it was used for spearing fish, and was an attribute of Neptune, was the weapon used by the *retiarius*, a lightly armed fighter who tried to entangle his opponent in a net.

13   **casside languida:** it is not certain to what the 'drooping helmet' refers. The opponent of the *retiarius* was the Samnite, who wore a visored helmet with a tall crest, but some think that the reference is to the *andabata*, who wore a helmet without eyeholes, and full armour, while Ville (307, n.191) suggests a leather helmet. Perhaps the idea is that a man fighting blind will naturally tend to lower his head in self-defence. *casside* makes a contrast with the bare head of the *retiarius*. There may also be a humorous oxymoron in *languida timendus*, since *languida* often means 'weary'. Shackleton Bailey, however, suspects corruption in this word.

14 *Martis* picks up *Martia* in line 1, while *universi* relates to *omnibus ... armis* in line 2.

15 **omnia solus:** this 'polar' formula of praise is found in religious contexts. For example, Seneca says that God *solus est omnia* (*QNat*. I *Praef*. 13). Similarly, someone may describe his beloved as *omnia*, as at Ov. *Her*. 12.161 *deseror*, [*amisso*]... *coniuge, qui nobis omnia solus erat.*

et ter unus: *unus est omnia* is naturally also found as a formula of praise in both religious and erotic contexts (for the latter, compare for example, Livy XL 11.3 *Demetrius iis unus omnia est*). *ter* is often used as a superlative, in phrases like *ter felix or ter magnus*, with no reference to actual number. Here, however, there is an allusion to the three gladiatorial spheres in which Hermes excels (11–13), and there is also a connection between the god Hermes and the number three – a connection which, possibly as early as the 2nd century BC, gave rise to his Greek title Trismegistos (thrice greatest). It is possible that Martial is alluding to this title.

unus (which picks up *unum* and *uni* in lines 5–6) is frequently used in invocation to the gods, e.g. *CIL* X 3800 *te tibi una quae es omnia dea Isis*. Here *ter* is applied to *unus* for comic exaggeration, precisely because of the illogicality of doing so. It is probable that Martial is mildly satirising the exaggerated eulogies that must often have been written about gladiators.

25

For the fourth epigram in the book on the subject of Domitian's theatre edict (compare 8, 14 and 23), Martial takes quite a different line from the previous ones: here he is sympathetic towards the man who is being ejected for lack of the property qualification, and uses the incident as pretext for an attack on patrons who waste their money on foolish extravagance instead of using it to help their poorer friends. Similarly at IV 67 an old friend asks a praetor for 100,000 sesterces to add to the 300,000 he has already, but the praetor says he is giving it to the charioteers Scorpus (see on line 10) and Thallus. For the miserliness of patrons, see on V 19.

The structure of the poem is exceptionally lively. It opens with the long numeral, followed by the long name, but the first pentameter, with its interjected *ecce* and quadruple imperatives, has staccato urgency. The two questions in the second couplet give the impression of a man actually shouting to the audience. Four more questions follow (a veritable inquisition), the third emphasised by *rogo*. The final couplet addresses the hypothetical culprit with a rhetorical double *o*, and (as often in Martial) adds to the attack on his meanness a revelation of his hypocrisy and short-sightedness.

1 **quadringenta** (sc. *milia sestertium*): 400,000 sesterces were the equestrian property qualification.

Chaerestratus: the name occurs only here in Martial. The fact that it is Greek suggests a freedman. It is broad-minded of Martial to suggest that a freedman deserves equestrian status.

2   **Leitus:** as at V 8.12; 14.11.

3   **io:** the word more often expresses delight, like 'hurrah'; e.g. XI 2.5 *io Saturnalia*; Catull. 61.117f. *io Hymen Hymenaee io.*

4   The person in a position to call him back is the friend rich enough to provide him with the necessary money.

5–6 Generous patrons are rewarded with a degree of immortality (*non ... totus*) by being praised by Martial. To be remembered after death was extremely important to the Roman way of thinking, since this was almost the only consolation which the dead man's spirit could enjoy. Hence the importance attached to tombs and epitaphs, as well as to the family cult.

7   **rogo** ('I ask you') emphasises Martial's turning from flattery to reproach. The questions in lines 7–10 both refer to extravagance in connection with public shows.

7–8 The rich man, when putting on a show in the theatre, pays for liquid (sometimes sweet wine – Plin. *HN* XXI 33), scented with saffron, to be sprayed over the stage. This was done by means of hidden pipes, which sent up the spray to a great height (Sen. *Ep.* 90.15). See also *Spect.* 3.8. The custom went back at least to the time of Lucretius (II 416).

rubro.. nimbo: cf. VIII 33.3–4 *hac ... nebula ... rubri ... croci.* Saffron is regularly described as red in Latin: hence the description of dawn as *croceus* in Virgil etc. *nimbi* is used of clouds of perfume (in a bedroom) at X 38.8. (At XIV 112 *nimbus* is used of a glass sprinkling vessel, but here – as at X 38.8 – the word is used in its basic sense, *pace* W. Hilgers, *Lateinische Gefässnamen* (Düsseldorf, 1969), 231).)

9–10 An amount equivalent to the entire equestrian qualification is 'given to a horse' (rather than to a would-be knight), in the sense that it pays for the horse's rider, the famous charioteer Scorpus, to be commemorated by gilded equestrian statues. A similar phrase occurs in IV 67 (on which see above), line 8 – *quod non vis equiti, vis dare, praetor, equo*? ('what you do not want to give to a knight, praetor, do you want to give to a horse?'). The word 'horse' here must refer to an equestrian statue, as at VIII 44.6.

The idea that a bronze horse (plus horseman) cannot appreciate the rich man's generosity is pleasantly humorous.

caballo: the 'vulgar' word for horse, used contemptuously. (As so often, the vulgar form is the one from which the romance languages derive their words – cheval, cavallo, caballo.)

10   Martial's picture of Scorpus's golden nose glittering wherever you look is nicely comic. Flavius Scorpus was the best-known charioteer of the time. At IV 67 (see above) a praetor is going to give him well over 100,000 sesterces. At X 74 his wealth is contrasted with that of a poor client: it is claimed that in one hour he, as victor, carries off fifteen heavy sacks of gold. (The wealth of jockeys is mentioned by Juvenal at 7.114.) Two epigrams also in Book X (50 and 53) commemorate his death, at the age of only twenty-seven (X 53.3). So he must

have died sometime between December 96 and summer 98, and at the date of Book V must have been somewhere between eighteen and twenty years old. Martial says at X 53.3–4 that Lachesis, counting his victories, thought he must be an old man. An inscription to another charioteer says that Flavius Scorpus won 2,048 victories.

Monuments to charioteers, in the form of statues and busts, were common at Rome, and impressed foreign visitors such as Lucian and Galen. Naturally they were particularly numerous at race-courses such as the Gaianum, across the Tiber. A number of examples survive. Several inscriptions mention a Scorpus: these include a marble *cippus* (cylinder) with a damaged relief, recording a victory and the names of the four horses, and the tombstone of T. Flavius Abascantus (doubtless a keen fan), which includes a relief showing Scorpus driving a chariot (illustrated in Balsdon, *Life and Leisure*, plate 16b), while a third was set up by Scorpus and Incitatus to their deceased patron. The last of these three Scorpi was a Claudius Scorpus, so the name was obviously a traditional one for charioteers.

aureus: bronze statues were often gilded.

12   Martial points out that the rich man himself reads his epigrams and admires them: if he were generous, he could be praised in them and read about by others.

26

An epigram of four scazons which refers back to II 57, in which Martial attacked an unnamed man who put on a great display of wealth, though in fact he had had to pawn his ring to buy a meal. Lines 3–4 read:

> Quem non lacernis Publius meus vincit,
> non ipse Cordus alpha paenulatorum

('a man whom not even my friend Publius beats when it comes to cloaks,
nor Cordus himself, A1 among coat-wearers').

It is most unusual for Martial to refer back to an epigram in an earlier book. This one closely follows another (23.8) which also refers to Cordus.It appears that Cordus (assuming that he was a real person) took offence at what (granted Martial's fixed principle of not attacking real people by name) must have been intended as no more than a mild joke, and Martial here makes it clear that no offence was intended by turning the joke against himself.

The simplicity of the poem, with its single sentence leading neatly to the final punch-line, is effective.

1   **alpha ... paenulatorum:** a *paenula* was a coat of thick rough wool or leather worn as a protection against cold or rain by people of all classes. Cordus must have worn a particularly splendid specimen. *alpha* occurs nowhere else in Greek or Latin in this sense, except at *Apocalypse* 1.8 – 'I am alpha and omega, says the lord God'; also 21.6; 22.13. (That the names Alfius (or Alphius) and Olfius (or Olphius) at IX 95 might be chosen with reference to A and Ω is suggested by P.T. Eden, *Mnemosyne* 47 (1994), 685–7.)
Cordus: see on V 23.8.

2 recently: Book II was published about three or four years before Book V.

4 beta ... togatorum: *beta* is chosen simply because it is subordinate to *alpha*. The *togati* are clients who have to wear the *toga* while accompanying their patrons (see on V 22.11). Martial disparages himself by identifying himself with the class of dependants. He may intend to recall that the ostentatious victim of II 57, with whom Cordus had been compared, was described as being followed by a *grex togatus* (line 5).

27

Yet another epigram on the theatre edict, the new twist here being that the man concerned, who has every right to equestrian status except the formal qualifications, should have more sense than to risk being thrown out of the knights' seats.

The interpretation and text of the poem have been much disputed. It would mean little if it were not set within the series of related epigrams. Shackleton Bailey first (*CPh* 73 (1978), 278) suggested that *habe* should be read in line 2 – 'For the rest, have what commoners have', i.e. don't take privileges to which you are not entitled. He now prefers to follow Schneidewin in supposing that a missing couplet would have made clearer what is meant by *cetera*.

It is comparatively unusual for Martial not to address a named person: the only other example in Book V (apart from 33 and 60, where the omission forms the point) is 62.

2 As the poem stands, *cetera* must refer to material possessions, and in particular the amount of property. It is true that *cetera plebis habes* is an unexpected way of describing what the man has *not* got, but the sense seems to be guaranteed by the other epigrams in the series. The man's lack of wealth puts him a on a level with the *plebs*.

4 pale with fear: like Chaerestratus in V 25, when the approach of Leitus is pointed out to him.
Oceanus: see on V 23.4.

28

Martial tells Aulus about a man so grudging with his praise that no-one, however, virtuous, can avoid his censure: he is to be pitied. The epigram neatly combines a moral point that was important to Martial, for whom virtue deserved to be praised, with appropriate compliments paid to eight leading contemporaries. This is in itself a reproach to Mamercus.

In the letter which he wrote after Martial's death (*Ep.* III 21.2–3), Pliny admits that he rewarded Martial for writing in his praise, and claims that this was an ancient custom which had died out in modern times, when *postquam desiimus facere laudanda, laudari quoque ineptum putamus* ('since we have ceased to do things worthy of praise, we also consider it bad form to be praised').

The construction of the nine scazons is logical: the first two explain the problem about Mamercus, the next four lines pay the eight men their compliments, while the seventh sums up Mamercus's reaction to them. The antithesis expressed in the last two lines gives Martial's verdict.

1   *bene* goes with *sentiat* as well as *loquatur*, in the sense 'have a good opinion of someone' (compare Book I *Praef.* 2).

Mamercus: a fictitious name used elsewhere by Martial only once (II 88).

2   **Aulus:** this is presumably Aulus Pudens, mentioned in sixteen epigrams spread throughout almost all the books of Martial. He was a centurion from Sarsina in Umbria, and was interested in literature (see M. Citroni, 'La carriera del centurione A. Pudens', *Maia* 34 (1982), 247–257). Address by the *praenomen* is a sign of familiarity.

3   The Curvii are specified as *fratres* (' brothers') to make it clear that this is a real plural, and not simply generic like those in the next three lines. Their full names were Cn. Domitius Afer Titius Marcellus Curvius Lucanus, and Cn. Domitius Afer Titius Marcellus Curvius Tullus. They had almost identical careers, both reaching the consulate in about 79, and it even seems that Tullus succeeded his brother as proconsul of Africa. They also shared their business interests and estates, and when Lucanus died (by about 94), he left everything to Tullus. They are mentioned at least four times by Martial, who praises their *pietas* (brotherly love) also at I 36.3. A less attractive picture of the brothers emerges from Pliny, who describes them in his *Letters* as mean and greedy, especially in the way they tricked Lucanus's daughter Lucilla out of her inheritance. However, when Tullus died he left his property to Lucilla after all, to the surprised pleasure of Pliny, who describes Tullus's will as 'full of *pietas*' (*Ep.* VIII 18.2).

4   **Nerva:** this is Martial's first reference to the future emperor Nerva, whom he praises in similar terms at VIII 70.1, before he became emperor (*quanta quies placidi tantast facundia Nervae* – 'quiet Nerva's eloquence equals his gentleness'), and at XII 5.3–4 (*contigit Ausoniae procerum mitissimus aulae | Nerva* – 'Nerva, mildest of all the nobles of Italy, has reached the palace').

Ruso: P. Calvisius Ruso Iulius Frontinus was consul in 79, and proconsul of Africa. His distinguished career continued into the reign of Trajan.

5   **Macer:** presumably the same Macer to whom X 18 and 78 are addressed. In the former, he is referred to as curator of the Via Appia; in the latter he is about to go off to govern Dalmatia. Martial praises him for his *rara fides amorque recti* ('exceptional trustworthiness and love of virtue'), and emphasises that his *pudor* (self-restraint) will ensure that he will return poorer rather than richer. Both epigrams imply that he was an admirer of Martial's verse.

Mauricus: Iunius Mauricus, a distinguished senator, was noted for his firmness and righteousness. In AD 70 he asked Domitian (who was standing in for Vespasian) to publish the names of informers. In 93 he was banished by Domitian (his brother, Q. Iunius Arulenus Rusticus, was less fortunate: he was put to death in about the same year for writing a panegyric on his fellow-Stoics Thrasea Paetus and Helvidius Priscus). He returned after Domitian's death, and his friend Pliny tells two striking stories about him (*Ep.* IV 22) – how he denounced the informer Veiento at a dinner-party given by Nerva, and how in Trajan's cabinet he expressed the opinion that gymnastic contests should be banned at Rome. Pliny praises him for his firmness and devotion to truth, for his wisdom and experience. He was consul at some unknown date.

6   **Regulus:** see on V 10, whose theme is related to that of this poem.
       Paulus: unidentified. The name is very common.

7   **robiginosis:** here metaphorically for 'envious' or 'malicious'. In the Preface to Book XII the word *robigo* is used of the teeth of malicious townspeople. The assonance with *rodit* is striking.

8–9 Instead of condemning the man, Martial pities him.

<h2 style="text-align:center">29</h2>

The joke depends on the Roman superstition that anyone who ate hare would be beautiful for a week. The elder Pliny describes this as a frivolous joke, but thinks there must be some reason for so widespread a belief (*HN* XXVIII 260). A possible explanation is the similarity of the words *lepos* (hare) and *lepos* (charm), which decline identically, apart from the scansion (*lepos* – charm, *lepŏris*).

Martial claims that a lady-friend sent him a hare, repeating the superstition, to which he ironically replies that she has obviously never eaten hare herself. The Roman fondness for hare is shown by the fact that Apicius gives fourteen recipes for it. Martial describes it as the best to eat of all quadrupeds (XIII 92).

The epigram is constructed as a pair of conditional sentences, giving a neat logic. Gellia is addressed in the first and fourth lines by her name, and in the third by the lover's slang expression *lux mea*, which the reader at first takes seriously, but recognises, on reading the last line, as ironical. The crucial positioning of the words *tu leporem* at the end is notable. Gellia's impolite suggestion that Martial's looks require improvement is turned against her.

The epigram is quoted by the author of *S.H.A. Alex. Sev.* 38, when telling how the emperor Severus Alexander ate hare daily (see R. Syme, *AJAH* 2 (1977), 92).

1   **Gellia:** see on V 17.3.

2   **Marce:** the address by the *praenomen* is a sign of familiarity.
       septem ... diebus: the use of the ablative for 'time during which' is common in post-Augustan writers. Pliny (see above) says nine days. This period was probably suggested by the *nundinae*, the market-day on every ninth day. Martial's use of a seven-day period is due to the fact that by the first century AD use of the sevenday week had become extremely widespread (Balsdon, *Life and Leisure*, 61–5).

3   **lux:** this term for the beloved goes back to Plautus.

<h2 style="text-align:center">30</h2>

Martial tells his fellow-poet Varro that, as it is the Saturnalia, he should drop his own composition for a while and read the poems Martial sends him instead.

Varro is not otherwise known. He would appear to have had old-fashioned tastes (by no means uncommon at this time), for tragedy was no longer written for the stage, and neither lyric nor elegiac poetry had any real life after the Augustan period. Mimes were performed, but this was not a serious genre.

The epigram is constructed in the form of a single sentence, with Varro addressed both at the beginning and in the penultimate word (a common device in Martial). The first two couplets define Varro's own spheres of literary activity, each one described by an elegant periphrasis, with a pair of stylish gerundives and double negatives, followed by two different forms of command – one an imperative and positive, the other a negative subjunctive – each in effect urging Varro to stop. Then Martial uses another imperative to tell Varro what he should do instead (and another gerundive), and the Saturnalia are referred to obliquely. The final couplet is a characteristically unexpected joke, designed partly to avoid any accusation of conceit in actually asking someone to read his poems.

1   **Sophocleo ... cothurno:** a reminiscence of Virgil's praise of Asinius Pollio in his 8th *Eclogue* (line 10, *sola Sophocleo tua carmina digna coturno* – 'your poems alone worthy of the Sophoclean buskin'), which was also imitated by Ovid, *Am.* I 15.15. The *cothurnus*, the high boot, was regularly used as the symbol of tragedy.

2   **Calabrian lyre:** the reference is to Horace's lyric poetry. Martial calls him Calabrian again at VIII 18.5 and XII 94.5, although his birthplace, Venusia, was actually in Apulia. However, vagueness about South Italian geography was not uncommon, and Horace himself says that he is doubtful whether he is Lucanian or Apulian (*Serm.* II 1.34).

3   This Catullus was a writer of mimes in the time of Caligula, and is probably the Valerius Catullus described by Suetonius (*Cal.* 36.1) as a young man of consular family who claimed to have had sexual relations with the emperor. His mimes were still popular in the time of Juvenal, who calls him *urbanus* (13.111; see also 8.186–7). At a revival of his *Laureolus* in AD 80, a real criminal was crucified (Mart. *Spect.* 7.4). (P. Wiseman, *Catullus and his World* (Cambridge, 1985), 192–3) implausibly identifies the mime-writer with the Republican poet.)

4   Elegy was personified as a lady with an elegant hair-style. So Ovid, in his elegy for Tibullus (whom he calls *cultus, Am.* I 15.28), asks her to loosen her hair as a sign of mourning (*Am.* III 9.3).

5   December is naturally 'smoky' because it is cold and fires are lit for warmth. For the Saturnalia, see on V 18.1. The general licence and jollity associated with the festival made it an obviously suitable occasion for light-hearted poetry, a point already made by Statius (*Silv.* I 6.1–8; 93). So Martial asks Silius Italicus, the epic poet, to read his poems at this season (IV 14), and he uses the fact that Book XI is published in December to make it more than usually improper (XI 2; 6; 15). Compare also XIV 1 (see below) and 185, where Martial says that Virgil's *Culex* is more suitable Saturnalia reading than the Aeneid.

7   **appropriate:** better suited to the season.

8   Gambling was legal only at the Saturnalia. Gambling for nuts was particularly associated with small boys (see on V 84.1), which provides here a touch of irony.

perdere nuces recalls XIV 1.12, where Martial says, in justification for his having written the short poems in that book, that the Saturnalia are not the time for writing on grandiose mythological subjects, and, to the suggestion that he should 'play with nuts', he replies *perdere nolo nuces*. At XIII 1 he says that his book is his substitute for gambling (line 7 – *haec mihi charta nuces*).

31

This epigram describes a remarkable spectacle seen in the amphitheatre, when bulls allowed boys to leap around on their backs waving weapons, and to hang from their horns. Martial often describes similar events in the arena, a fact which indicates that the shows were not always as bloody as is usually thought, and were often more like a modern circus. Seven poems in Book I deal with a show at which lions allowed hares to jump in and out of their mouths, and I 104 also refers to tamed leopards, tigresses, stags, bears, boars, and bisons, and to dancing elephants. Roman animal trainers must have been extraordinarily skilful.

The elder Pliny, in a rather obscure passage (*HN* VIII 182), says that he saw bulls which fought when commanded, allowing themselves to be swung round by the horns or lifted up off the ground, and even acted as charioteers. See J.M.C. Toynbee, *Animals in Roman Life and Art* (London, 1973), 149f.. However, the most striking parallel is with the famous bull-leaping frescoes found in the Palace at Knossos (N. Marinatos, *Minoan Religion* (Columbia, 1993), 67, with figs. 57–8). These seem to show young acrobats seizing charging bulls by the horns, leaping over their backs, and landing behind them on their feet. According to Marinatos (218–20) it is doubtful whether such a trick would be possible, and more likely that the youths leapt sideways over the animals' backs. The so-called Boxers' Rhyton (214) shows the feat in the context of athletic contests, and also reveals the danger involved, as one man is being gored. She suggests that the practice may have formed part of an initiation ceremony, and this idea is supported by a modern parallel from the Hamar tribe of Southern Ethiopia (W.G. Arnott, *LCM* 18 (1993), 114–6), where youths aged 19 or 20 leap sideways over the backs of between fifteen and thirty bulls, as a test of manhood.

The epigram begins strikingly with the imperative *aspice* (used to open an epigram also at XIII 58; IV 3), as if the reader were in the amphitheatre with Martial, and ends with a characteristic paradox.

1   **insultet:** *in* + *saltare*, 'dance upon', but also with a play on the sense 'insult'.
4   **ventilat:** 'shakes about', in the word's basic sense. It is often used of weapons.
5   I.e.the fierce animal is unmoved and remains still.
    non esset: the subject is the *ille* of line 3.
7   Shackleton Bailey holds (*CPh* 73 (1978), 278) that '*gestus* is impossible': hence his conjecture *trepidat* (though he points out in his Teubner edition that *trepidant gesti* would also be possible).
8   The bull is concerned in case the boy's trick fails to come off as a result of his failing to keep still.

32

A neatly constructed couplet making a surreal joke about a miser's will. By the *Lex Falcidia* of 40 BC a man was obliged to leave his next of kin at least a quarter of his estate. But Crispus is so mean that he does not even fulfil the minimum requirement of the law: he leaves everything to himself. This absurd joke also appears in the first couplet of an eight-line epigram by the Neronian Greek epigrammatist Lucillius (*Anth. Pal.* XI 171 – 'The money-loving Hermocrates, when dying, made himself in his will heir to his property'), the remainder of which adds two further jokes; and in the collection of funny stories, dating from about the fourth century AD, known as *Philogelos* ('A mean man writing his will put himself down as the heir'). The Lucillian epigram was later imitated by Palladas (*Anth. Pal.* VII 607).

Note that Martial does not – as do Lucillius and the *Philogelos* version – characterise the man as mean at the outset, so that this fact emerges only from the last word, which is given added emphasis by being made the reply to an enquiring question from the friend to whom Martial purports to be describing the incident.

Some editors, including Shackleton Bailey, interpret the epigram as meaning that Crispus was a spendthrift and had used up all his wealth, so that he 'gave it to himself' in a metaphorical sense. But this seems impossible in view of the clear antithesis *non dedit uxori ... [sed] sibi*, where *dedit* must have the same sense in both instances, and in view of the explicit words *tabulis ... supremis*. See W. Burnikel, *Untersuchungen zur Struktur des Witzepigramms bei Lukillios und Martial* (Wiesbaden, 1980), 101–5: he sees this as an example of direct imitation of Lucillius by Martial.

1   **quadrantem:** the fourth part of his estate (not the coin called *quadrans*).
    Crispus: a common *cognomen*.
    Faustinus: a wealthy friend of Martial, and clearly a sympathetic one, who is addressed or referred to nineteen times. Several times he is told a joke.
2   **cui dedit:** understand *bona* as object. Shackleton Bailey compares Quint. *Decl. Min.* 264 *thema: ne liceat mulieri nisi dimidiam partem bonorum dare* ('no-one should be allowed to leave more than half of his property to a woman').

33

The fate in store for the lawyer must presumably be a reciprocal attack on the part of Martial, although, as his fixed principle is never to attack real people by name, the threat is not intended seriously, and the man probably did not exist.

There is no proper name in the epigram (see on V 27), for the obvious reason that it is addressed to the unknown man.

The concise structure of the couplet is similar to that of V 32.

1   The profession of *causidicus* is apparently chosen chiefly with a view to the alliterative effect, although it is also relevant that lawyers are in the business of seeking redress for their clients. The word *causidicus* tends to indicate a lawyer who plies his trade for profit, and is somewhat disparaging.

qui sit: the use of *qui* as a substantive (instead of *quis*) is not uncommon, especially in literature with an archaic flavour. See Fordyce's note on Catullus 61.46.

34

This is the first of two poems in this book (the other is 37) on the death of a little slave-girl, born in his own household (V 37.20), of whom Martial had been particularly fond. Several years later he published an epitaph for her (X 61), which may well have been inscribed on her actual tomb. It was common for Roman slave-owners, and especially those who (like Martial) had no children of their own, to take great pleasure in the children of their slaves. Martial laments the untimely deaths of his slaves also at I 88; 101; XI 91. Such poems were not uncommon under the early Empire: see Kay's note on Mart. XI 91.

One of the most ancient purposes of the epigram was the provision of epitaphs, and this usage extended itself to the writing of either literary and non-functional epitaphs, or epigrams otherwise commemorating a dead person. This one incorporates in its last couplet a variation on a common epitaphic formula, but the previous eight lines more unusually recommend the girl to the protection of Fronto and Flaccilla, generally taken to be Martial's own dead parents. Some have argued that they are Erotion's own parents, but their names are unlikely ones for slaves, and it would be a little odd to call her own parents her *patroni* (line 7). The argument that her own parents would be more of a consolation to her is self-defeating: the whole point is that Martial asks his own parents, who presumably had never seen Erotion, to look after her.

1   The line is elegantly constructed, with *hanc ... puellam* framing the personal pronoun and the chiastic addresses to the parents. The name *Fronto* is very common, *Flaccilla* less so.

2   'Kisses' might suggest a girl-friend of mature years, but the word *deliciae* is regularly used of a pet, whether human or animal, such as, for example, Publius's puppy Issa (I 109), or Bassa's baby (IV 87).

3   **parvula** makes it clear that the subject is a young child.
    Erotion: a Greek diminutive form of Eros. Slave-names formed from Eros are extremely common. In Plautus's *Menaechmi* Erotium is the name of a prostitute. There is only one Erotion in the Index to Volume VI of *CIL*, and that is a man (presumably a freedman – 17801). Martial nowhere else uses the Greek diminutive form in *–ion*, but his fondness for other Greek forms makes this less surprising.

4   **the Tartarean dog:** Cerberus is usually said to have had three heads, though Hesiod gave him fifty, and Pindar (followed by Horace at *Carm.* II 13.34) a hundred.

5–6 The fact that it was her 'sixth winter' that carried her off is stated in both the other epigrams dealing with her. What exactly is meant by saying that she was six days short of completing her sixth winter is not easy to say: perhaps she died six days before the (calendar) beginning of spring.

7   **old patrons:** if Martial had freed Erotion (and perhaps he had), he would have been her official *patronus*. By extension, his parents could well act as her patrons in the underworld. *veteres* means primarily 'old' in age (Martial himself was probably getting on for fifty when Book V was published), but there is also a play on the sense 'longstanding' – even though the child is so young.

inter tam veteres: Shackleton Bailey objects (*AJPh* 110 (1989), 136) that '*tam* is foolish as well as unnecessary, since Erotion was five years old when she died', but there is surely no need to take it so literally – it is a pleasant joke. He prefers Heinsius's *inter iam veteres*, but one would tend to take *iam* with *veteres*, which is not what is wanted.

lasciva: the word by no means always has a bad sense. It is often combined alliteratively with *ludere*.

8   Erotion would naturally speak of Martial to his parents.

9–10 It was extremely common to use in epitaphs the formula *sit tibi terra levis* ('may the earth be light upon you') – so common that it is often abbreviated to *STTL*. Since the dead person's spirit was envisaged as still having some kind of existence, the wish was a quite literal one. The formula often serves as the basis for variation. Martial may well have recalled an epigram by the Hellenistic poet Meleager (*Anth. Pal.* VII 461), which goes: 'Hail, earth, mother of all: upon Aesigenes, who was previously not heavy upon you, may you now in turn rest lightly'. Meleager's epigram certainly seems to have been the source of an epigram found on a child's tombstone at Corfinium (in central Italy) which may predate Martial's (*CLE* 1313). Note how Martial reverses the order of Meleager's poem so as to save up the point that the girl was not heavy on the earth for the final climax, expressed by means of asyndeton and the chiastic arrangement *nec illi ... fueris ... non fuit ... tibi*.

The formula could also be parodied, as in the epigram about Sir John Vanbrugh, architect of Blenheim Palace:

> Ly heavy on him, Earth, for he
> Laid many a heavy stone on thee.

9   **bones:** although cremation was the usual method of dealing with corpses at this period, references to 'bones' and so on are quite regular.

35

Another epigram on Domitian's theatre edict (see on V 8). The victim in this case is a rich and boastful Greek who turns out to be a slave. The metre (scazons) hints that the poem is satirical.

1   **dum:** Martial often begins an epigram with a dum-clause, which arouses the reader's anticipation. Here the *dum*-clause goes on for no less than five lines, while the verb of the main clause is postponed to the beginning of line 6, and the climactic subject to its end.

redire: in the financial sense of the English noun 'return'.

Patras: on the north coast of the Peloponnese.

2   Note the alliteration of *c* in this line.

ducena: understand *milia sestertium.* The use of the distributive form of the numeral is normal in this sense. This was half the equestrian property qualification.

scarlet-clad: see on V 23.

Euclides: a rare Greek name, which sounds grandiose, but is presumably chosen for the meaning it suggests – 'well locked-up'.

4   Leda was wife of Tyndareos, king of Sparta, and Euclides's property is in the Peloponnese. Greek inscriptions recording supposed descent from mythical figures such as Ajax, Hercules, or the Dioscuri are not uncommon, and Claudius's freedman Pallas claimed descent from the kings of Arcadia (Tac. *Ann.* XII 53). But descent from Leda sounds especially comic in view of the fact that after her encounter with the swan she laid an egg.

5   **suscitanti**: the single word neatly exposes Euclides's situation.

      Leito: see on V 8.12.

6   The emphatic noun followed by three adjectives (tricolon) in asyndeton memorably sums up Euclides's pretensions.

7   No man of standing would carry around the key to his house (or – more probably – store-room): that would be in the custody of a trusted slave.

8   **Fabullus:** Martial several times addresses someone of this name (quite a common one) in epigrams of this type. Note the emphatic repetition of *clavis* at the end of the line. Its personification is amusing.

36

Martial makes it clear to his friend Faustinus (see on V 32) that those whom he praises owe him some return. This is generally taken to be financial, but it could have taken other forms as well. It should be noted that the suggestion that the man he has praised has cheated him would seem to imply that the man had actually commissioned the epigram in which he was praised. This would be a different matter from spontaneous praise on Martial's part of someone he admired.

It can hardly be coincidental that Martial places this epigram after several others which do not in fact praise anyone still living – otherwise the hint would be too palpable. No doubt Faustinus himself was open to no criticism on this score.

The structure of the epigram is simple, with the vocative placed in Martial's favourite position as penultimate word in the hexameter, and the final comment saved up for the last word of all.

2   **imposuit:** IV 40 ends with the same word: the subject there is a patron who, despite the fact that he is now wealthy, has failed to reward Martial's long service as a client. There it is Fortune who says he has cheated – in other words, she was mistaken in thinking that he deserved her favour. Professor Willcock thinks that the sense is the same here, but the context makes it less obvious.

37

In this variation on the theme of V 34, Martial again praises the dead Erotion, with a dazzling list of comparisons, and uses his own grief at her loss to make a pointed

contrast with a man who has just lost a rich , but unloved, wife, and rebukes Martial
for making such a fuss about a mere slave-girl.

Martial shows his usual skill in varying the construction of his sixteen
comparisons – first three comparatives (*dulcior ... mollior ... delicatior*); then *cui nec
praeferas* followed by *nec ... -que ... -que*; then *quae vicit* followed by three different
objects; then *fragravit* followed by three *quod* clauses; and finally *cui comparatus*
followed by three subjects. The name of the girl, identified at the beginning only as
puella, is deferred until line 14. So the reader might take the poem to be an account
of (or perhaps addressed to, since *puella* could be vocative) the poet's mistress. This
impression might be strengthened by the analogous use of a playful triplet of
comparisons in an erotic context at Virg. *Ecl.* 7.37–8 (based on Theoc. 11. 20–21).
Lines 15–17 form a succinct epitaph. But in line 18 Paetus appears, with his public
but very conventional display of grief, and Martial gets in his sting in the tail by
pointing out that Paetus has a consolation in his wife's fortune.

. This epigram has often been criticised: the great German writer Lessing, for
example, found the ending disconcerting. However, E.J. Kenney has pointed out
that an ancient reader would expect the second poem to be different from the first,
and that the metre – the scazon – would give him a clue that the content would be
satirical (*Greece and Rome*, 11 (1964), 77–81). As mentioned above on V 34,
poems mourning the deaths of young slaves are not uncommon in the early Empire.
One may compare the grief expressed by Cicero and Pliny in similar circumstances,
but it is noteworthy that each takes a defensive attitude against the possible criticism
that such grief was inappropriate (Cic. *Att.* I 12.4; Plin. *Ep.* VIII 16.3). Martial's
epigram provides a striking rebuff to any such critics, in emphasising the hypocrisy
of so much conventional mourning, and – by contrast – the genuineness of his
feelings for Erotion.

The poem has been further discussed by P. Watson (*CQ* 42 (1992), 253–268).
She argues that the erotic language is an indication that Erotion was for Martial a
puella delicata (cf. 34.2 *deliciae*), and that there is a sexual element. However, as
she does not suggest that Martial had done anything more with Erotion than perhaps
'engage in some sort of sexual play' (26), and does not deny that Martial's grief is
genuine, it is difficult to find much that is helpful in her line of approach.

Whether the poem succeeds as a whole, or not, must ultimately be a matter of
taste, but it is worth emphasising that there is no reason to doubt the seriousness or
sincerity either of Martial's affection for Erotion or of his moral criticism of the
hypocrisy of Paetus.

Ben Jonson made a famous adaptation of the opening lines in the last stanza of
Her Triumph, from *A Celebration of Charis*:

> Have you seene but a bright Lillie grow,
>> Before rude hands have touched it?
> Ha' you mark'd but the fall o' the Snow
>> Before the soyle hath smutch'd it?
> Ha' you felt the wooll o' the Bever?
>> Or Swans Downe ever?
> Or have smelt o' the bud o' the Brier?
>> Or the Nard in the fire?

Or have tasted the bag of the Bee?
O so white! O so soft! O so sweet is she!

1   **senibus voce dulcior cycnis:** the MSS read *dulcior mihi*, but Shackleton
Bailey argues (i) that old swans are not generally 'sweet'; (ii) that the
comparisons in lines 1–13 do not apply to Martial alone. He suggests that the
corruption may have arisen from the erroneous transposition to *dulcior voce*,
which would not scan, and so was corrected by a scribe. (See the apparatus to
his Teubner edition, and also his Loeb edition, III, 317–8.) It is possible also
that reminiscence of Virgil *Ecl.* 7.37–8 *thymo mihi dulcior Hyblae, candidior
cycnis,* played a part. On the other hand, this reading has the disadvantage of
making the first comparison more specific than the second and third. For the
comparison with the 'swansong', Shackleton Bailey compares Sen. *Phaedr.* 302
dulcior vocem moriente cycno ('sweeter in voice than a dying swan'); Stat.
Theb. V 341 *mitior et senibus cycnis ... vox* ('a voice milder even than aged
swans'). (The relationship between this passage, published in 90–91, and that
of Martial, is impossible to determine.) Martial uses the phrase *senibus cycnis*
again, with reference to singing, at IX 42.2.

The 'song' of the dying swan is identified as the wailing sound made by the
collapsing lungs of the whooper swan by W.G. Arnott, *Greece and Rome* 24
(1977), 149–153.

2   The wool of Tarentum (modern Taranto) in South Italy was particularly fine,
which was reckoned to be largely due to the pure water of the river Galaesus in
which it was washed. Martial several times refers to this (IV 28.3; VIII 28.4;
XII 63.3; XIII 125), as does Horace at *Carm.* II 6.10. Phalanthus was the
legendary founder of the Spartan colony of Tarentum.

3   The volcanic Lucrine lake, between Pozzuoli and Baiae, and separated from the
Bay of Naples only by a narrow dyke, was famous for its oysters. 'Martial is
saying playfully that Erotion was delicious enough to eat ... one says such
things to children and pet animals' (Kenney). This 'gives the game away' that
he is not talking about a mature woman. Martial had used the phrase *stagnum
Lucrinum* at III 60.3: see K.M. Coleman, 'The Lucrine Lake at Juvenal 4.141',
CQ 44 (1994), 554–6.

4   Pearls from the Red Sea (*Mare Erythraeum*). At I 109.4 Publius's puppy is
called *carior Indicis lapillis* ('more precious than Indian jewels'), and *Margarita*
(pearl) is the name of a dog both in Petronius (*Sat.* 64.9) and on a dog's
tombstone in the British Museum. At VIII 28 pearls appear (along with lilies,
ivory, swans, snow etc.) in comparison with a white *toga*.

5–6 These three comparisons all combine whiteness with freshness. Ivory was a
luxury material much prized by the Romans.
dentem: elephants' tusks are commonly called teeth.

6   **snow:** perhaps the commonest of all comparisons for whiteness. It goes back
to Homer, where the horses of Rhesus are said to be whiter than snow (Il. X
437).
lily: also a common comparison. 'Untouched' suggests the girl's virginity.
(The use of the lily as a symbol of chastity is confined to Christian writers.)

7–8 Three comparisons describing Erotion's hair, and in particular its reddish-golden colouring.

7 **Baetic:** Baetica was the part of Spain through which ran the river Baetis (the Guadalquivir) – modern Andalusia. It was famous for its wool, whose quality (like that of Tarentum – line 2) was ascribed to the purity of the river's water. It had a natural colouring that did not need to be dyed. The wool is described at IX 61.3 as yellow (*flava*); at XII 98.2 as golden (*aurea*); and by Pliny (*HN* VIII 191) as reddish (*rutilus*).

8 **the knots of the Rhine:** Tacitus (*Germ.* 38) says that it was the distinguishing mark of the Suebi (of North Germany) to twist their hair and tie it up in a knot. This is referred to by Martial at *Spect.* 3.9 (of the Sygambri, another German tribe), by Juvenal (13.164), and by several other authors, and can be seen represented on bronze figures and on Trajan's Column. A terracotta mask of the 2nd century AD, on display in the British Museum, shows a German with a knot of hair over his right ear (GR 1867.5 – 8.644). Furthermore, an actual head found in 1948 and now in the Schleswig-Holsteinisches Landesmuseum at Schloss Gottorp, Schleswig, has perfectly preserved hair tied into a knot over the right temple. The hair is now red, but was originally blond. Juvenal calls the hair of the Germans blond (*flava* – 13.164); Tacitus and Seneca call it reddish (*rutilae* – Tac. *Germ.* 4; *rufus* – Sen. *Dial.* V 26.3).
nitelam: a shortened form of *nitedulam*. This type of dormouse is distinguished from *glis* at Plin. *HN* VIII 224. The *OLD* identifies it as the garden dormouse or lerot. Its colour is described by Servius as reddish (*rubeus* – on Virg. *G.* I 181). On dormice see J.M.C. Toynbee, *Animals in Roman Life and Art* (London, 1973), 204.

9 **the rose-garden of Paestum:** the famous roses of Paestum (south of Naples) are praised by Virgil, Propertius, Ovid and others. They were said to bloom twice a year.

10 The honey from Mount Hymettus near Athens was the most celebrated in the ancient world, and is still famous.

11 If a lump of amber (a substance deriving from the exudations of a now extinct species of pine-tree) is held in the hands and rubbed, it gives off a scent of pine and camphor. This practice is referred to by Martial at III 65.5; IX 12.6; XI 8.6 (describing fragrant kisses); and by Juvenal (6.573). See P. Watson, *LCM* 17 (1992), 23–27.

12 Peacocks were well-known in Italy in Martial's time. They were bred in large quantities, and sold for high prices. Chiefly admired for their appearance, they became a favourite dish for wealthy gourmands in the late Republic (Mart. XIII 70; Juv. 1.143). The peacock was also familiar in literature and art as the sacred bird of Juno, and so of ladies of the imperial house. (Toynbee, 250–3.)
indecens: not in the same sense as at V 14.7.
erat: since *comparatus* stands for *si compararetur*, one might expect *esset*, but compare Virg. *G.* II 132–3 *et, si non alium late iactaret odorem,* | *laurus erat*: and Ov. *Am.* I 6.34 *solus eram, si non saevus adesset Amor*. In each case the indicative adds emphasis to the statement in the apodosis.

13   **squirrel:** the implication is that the Romans found squirrels particularly lovable. They occasionally appear in art (Toynbee, 293). The Greek name σκίουρος means 'shadow-tail'.

      phoenix: see on V 7.1. 'The phoenix is always turning up.'

      Lines 12–13 were translated by Robert Burton in *The Anatomy of Melancholy* (Part 3, Section 2, Member 3), when discussing 'Symptoms or Signs of Love-Melancholy'; ''tis not Venus' picture that ... no, no, but his divine mistress forsooth, ... to whose service he is wholly consecrate, whom he alone adores,

> To whom conferr'd a peacock's undecent,
>
> A squirrel's harsh, a phoenix too frequent.'

      (The last four words were used as the title of a verse-play by Christopher Fry.)

14   **busto:** strictly the place where the body was burned, but used for the tomb also. Erotion had no doubt been cremated (see on V 34.9)

15–16   Compare X 61.2 *crimine quam fati sexta peremit hiems.* It is especially common for fate to be reproached in epitaphs of those who die young (R. Lattimore, *Themes in Greek and Roman Epitaphs* (Urbana, 1962),183f.).

16   **as yet incomplete:** compare V 34.6.

18   **et:** 'and yet', a common usage in Martial.

      my friend: somewhat sarcastic.

      Paetus: a common *cognomen* ('cross-eyed').

19   Note the alliteration of *p*. Beating the breast and tearing the hair were the stock signs of grief (e.g. II 11.5) – and so all the more likely to be employed when genuine grief was absent.

20   **vernulae** is emphatic. For the word, see on V 18.4.

21   **and yet I remain alive:** there has been no suggestion that Martial's grief for Erotion might kill him, or drive him to suicide, but the exaggerated reaction characterises Paetus's affected performance. For a comparison between Paetus's words and the stock 'consolation' of philosophy, see Watson, 264. She emphasises the commonplaces of the injunction not to indulge in excessive grief, and, in particular, not to give up the will to live, and the use of examples (in this case, that of Paetus himself).

22   The four adjectives (the last three of which occur also at V 35.6) balance the list in line 17, and emphasise the lady's superiority to little Erotion – but it is the last that Martial seizes upon. Kenney draws attention to the absence of any reference to Paetus's affection for his dead wife.

      The list of adjectives in asyndeton is common in tomb inscriptions. Watson (263) cites e.g. *CLE* 237 and 1136. She also points out that it is usually moral qualities which are mentioned, rather than social standing and wealth, as here.

23   The rhetorical question praising Paetus's Stoic fortitude prepares for the final stab.

24   **ducentiens:** understand *centena milia sesterium.*

      et tamen vivit: picking up *et tamen vivo*, a device Martial learned from Catullus (e.g. 24.8 and 10).

      For similar sarcasm at the expense of a man who had married his wife for her money, compare II 65.

38

Martial produces another variation on the theme of the theatre edict by making fun of a man who does possess the equestrian property-qualification, but has a brother, whom he wishes to have regarded as a knight, even though he does not himself possess the qualification.

The epigram has a lively and staccato construction, including rhetorical questions, abrupt parentheses, and imperatives. The name of the victim appears no fewer than five times (three in the vocative), though his brother is never named.

The text (the reading of the last words of lines 3 and 7), and the punctuation (of lines 2–3 and line 7) have been much disputed, but this interpretation follows Shackleton Bailey's text (which is the same as Lindsay's Oxford text).

1   **Calliodorus:** a rare name used several times by Martial in satirical contexts, no doubt because of its convenient scansion. The fact that it is Greek suits the use of actual Greek words.
     census: the Latin word relates to the inspection of the knights traditionally held by the censors every *lustrum* (five years).
2   **Sextus:** there is no particular reason for identifying this man with the Sextus of V 5.
     The last two words of the couplet repeat its first two words, providing further emphasis.
3   The Greek proverb σῦκα μερίζει means 'divides up figs', the point being that a fig is too small to be worth dividing (compare the English expression 'to make two bites of a cherry'). Similarly the equestrian qualification of 400,000 sesterces represents a unit which, when divided, loses its character as the minimum qualification.
4   As at V 23.8, Martial jokes about the original function of knights. Two knights on one horse would look ridiculous. *uno* and *duos* frame the line.
5–6 The twin sons of Leda, Castor and Pollux, were characterised as a horse-rider and a boxer (Homer, *Iliad* III 237). Since Calliodorus wants to be counted as a knight (= horseman), his brother is jokingly called Pollux.
6   **eras:** for the indicative, see on V 37.12.
7   'Since you (plural), are one, will two of you (singular) sit down?' The effect is impossible to achieve in English, which does not distinguish between singular and plural 'you'. The faulty grammar symbolises the faulty logic.
     sedebis here must refer to sitting in the theatre: hence *surge* in the next line, which is what the official would order those not properly qualified to do (compare V 8.12; 25.1).
8   **surge:** following *sedebis*, the alliteration of s in these lines adds to the effect.
     σολοικισμόν: English 'solecism'. The word was said to derive from the corrupt version of the Attic dialect spoken by the Athenian colonists of Soloi in Cilicia.The grammatical fault actually occurred in the question which Martial addressed to him, but the grammatical impossibility symbolises the false logic and downright impossibility of Calliodorus's position.

9 The story was that Castor and Pollux loved each other so dearly that, when Castor was killed in battle, Pollux prayed that he might·die too: Zeus gave him the choice between living in heaven or sharing with Castor the fate of living alternately on earth and in heaven. Pollux at once chose the second course. Compare Martial I 36. The parenthesis puts bluntly the absurdity of the notion that both brothers might sit in the equestrian seats.

10 **alternis:** understand *vicibus* – 'in alternate turns'.
   sede: picking up *sedere* at the end of the previous line and *sedebis* in line 7.

39

Martial complains that he is impoverishing himself in sending gifts to a rich man who keeps on changing his will.

   Under the early Empire, childlessness was extremely common (the causes of the remarkable decline in the birth-rate which led to this are still not clear). Naturally rich people's friends, real or assumed, hoped to become their heirs, and went to great pains to win their favour. Many rich people would encourage such attentions. The signing of a will was at Rome a public occasion, to which the rich man would invite his important friends as witnesses. Naturally this would serve as the signal to his 'friends' for an urgent effort to attract his attention, in the hope of being included in the will. Charinus is rich (this can be taken for granted, though Martial never states it), and – encouragingly – he coughs persistently, which suggests that he is consumptive and has not long to live. He exploits his 'friends' by constantly making new wills.

   Martial is not, of course, writing autobiographically: he has more sense than to behave like this. He is satirising both the greedy rich man and the greedy legacy-hunter. Compare, for example, I 10, where a man's desire to marry an ugly (and, one presumes, rich) woman is explained by her cough.

   The first three hendecasyllables set out the situation; the next three tell Charinus what he should do; the final four give an absurdly exaggerated account of Martial's financial situation. In each section Charinus is addressed by name.

1–2 **supremas ... tabulas:** as in V 32.1.
1 **thirty times:** three and its. multiples regularly stand for an indefinitely large number.
2 **Charinus:** this Greek name, used for a stock figure in Doric comedy, and also by Plautus for a character in his *Mercator*, is used by Martial in various satirical contexts.
3 **Hyblaean honey:** Hybla is a mountain in Sicily, often linked with Hymettus in Attica (V 37.10) as sources of the best honey. Thyme was reckoned to be the best food for bees (XI 42.3–4).
   placentas: the elder Cato gives a recipe for these cakes, made of flour, semolina, water, oil, sheep's cheese, and honey, and cooked on bay leaves (*De Agri Cultura* 76). They were thick and flat, and were cut into slices (Martial III 77.3; VI 75.1; IX 90.18; André 215).
5 The chiastic arrangement *signa rarius, aut semel fac* amusingly emphasises the absurd contrast between the making of wills and dying.

6 The cough as a hopeful symptom is often mentioned (e.g. I 10, referred to above; Horace *Serm.* II 5.106–7), but *mentitur* suggests that Charinus is faking, like the woman in II 26. Similarly in Petronius (117.9) a man who is pretending to be rich in order to attract legacy-hunters is told to cough frequently. Note the alliteration of *t*, which is onomatopoeic.

6 *sacculus* is regularly used for a purse or money-bag (e.g. Catullus 13.8). *loculus* means a money-box, but it could be carried (e.g. Hor. *Serm.* I 6.74).

8 Croesus, king of Lydia in the sixth century BC, was proverbially rich.

9 Irus was the proverbial beggar (from *Odyssey* XVII): compare Martial VI 77.1; XII 32.9.

10 Martial would be impoverished if he had been sending Charinus the poor bean-dish on which he himself usually lives, let alone the rich honey-cakes he has actually been sending.

conchis was a dish of cooked beans or peas, probably made into a purée. Like boiled chickpeas (*cicer* – I 41.6), it was a food eaten by poor people (who could rarely afford meat). Hence the question which the mugger asks his poor late-night victim at Juv. 3.293, *cuius conche tumes*? (See André 36; also Apicius V 4, with André's notes.)

40

Martial uses a theme found several times in the *Greek Anthology*: poets describing statues of Aphrodite or Athena, or comparing statues of each, often refer to the Judgment of Paris. He had already used it at I 102:

Qui pinxit Venerem tuam, Lycori,
blanditus, puto, pictor est Minervae.

('The painter who painted your Venus, Lycoris, has flattered – I'd say – Minerva.')

The idea here is much the same. Naturally Minerva is jealous when Venus is portrayed, but it is Minerva who is patron of artists: compare e.g. Ov. *Fast.* III 831–2 'worship Minerva, you who use the graving-tool and set the panel on fire with colours, and you who make rock soft with skilled hand'. Minerva's disfavour ensures that Artemidorus's picture is a dud.

The epigram is a masterpiece of neatness: the asyndeton in the first line, with variation of tenses, and the Greek name (appropriate for an artist) placed in Martial's favourite penultimate position, are followed by the sarcastic question.

1 **Artemidorus:** an athlete of this name is mentioned at VI 77, and is perhaps the man addressed at VIII 58, but at IX 21 it is clearly a fictitious name (combined with Calliodorus, for which compare V 38). It was a common name at Rome.

2 **are you then surprised?:** for a similar question, cf. *Anth. Pal.* XI 149 (Anon.), where the couplet hinges on the words τί τὸ θαῦμα; ('what's so surprising about that?').

41

The effeminate Didymus makes a great fuss about his being qualified to sit in the seats reserved for the knights. Martial has his doubts, but of one thing he is certain –

that Didymus has no right to sit in the seats reserved for married men of the *plebs*. These had been set aside by Augustus, in his theatre edict (Suet. *Aug.* 44.2). J. Carter (in his commentary) suggests that regular marriage may have been infrequent among the poor, as in early Victorian London: hence Augustus's desire to encourage it. Presumably this regulation too had been revived by Domitian.

The concessive clause which occupies the first three lines characterises Didymus by means of exotic vocabulary and bizarre comparisons, after which the verb governs no less than seven objects, emphasising Didymus's obsession with equestrian privilege. After this Martial intervenes, addressing Didymus by name, to lead up to the final punch-line, restricted to the last three words.

1   **eunuch:** Domitian had banned castration, probably in 82 or 83 (Jones, *Domitian*, 31,107), but he himself had a favourite eunuch called Earinus (praised by Martial at IX 11–13), and the ban itself indicates that the practice had not been uncommon at Rome. Eunuchs were inevitably targets for crude jokes, as for example Mart. II 45 and III 81, each of which poems characterises its victim as a *Gallus*. This word denoted a worshipper of the Phrygian goddess Cybele, who – like Attis in Catullus 63 – had castrated himself as a sign of his devotion.

2   **the Celaenaean concubine:** i.e. Attis. Celaenae is a town in Phrygia. Cybele was supposed to have loved him (hence 'concubine'), and to have caused him to castrate himself so as to avoid his marrying another woman.

3   **wails:** cf. XIV 204 (of a Gallus) *aera Celaenaeos lugentia matris amores* ('the bronze cymbals which grieve for the Celaenaean love of the Mother'). The Galli held processions at Rome and elsewhere, playing trumpets, horns, drums, and cymbals, and singing Greek hymns, while collecting money. See Apuleius *Met.* VIII 24.

   entheae: here (and only here in Greek or Latin) in an active sense, but in its more usual passive sense e.g. at XI 84.4 *cum furit ad Phrygios enthea turba modos* (' when the divinely inspired band raves to Phrygian measures').

4   **rows:** the fourteen rows assigned to the knights (see on V 8).

   edicts: see on V 8.

5   **knights' uniforms and the Ides:** on the Ides of July each year the knights held a solemn procession (*transvectio*) across the Forum, wearing their special parade uniform (a shortened form of toga, purple, with a crimson border, according to Dion. Hal. VI 13). The date was supposed to be that of the battle of Lake Regillus, where Castor and Pollux were said to have appeared at the head of the *equites*. On the knights' uniform, see Demougin, 782–4, and on the *transvectio ib.* 150–6.

   buckles: although not technically military decorations (there is no reference to them in V. Maxfield, *The Military Decorations of the Roman Army*, London, 1981), these were sometimes given to soldiers as rewards; for example, by the praetor Quinctius to his *equites* in Spain in 185 BC (Livy XXXIX 31.18). Here they presumably indicate knights who had (or wanted to pretend that they had) served in the army (and not – like Martial – merely held honorary posts). *TLL*, s.v. 644.54, compares Plin. *HN* XXXIII 39, who refers to a letter in which

Brutus complained that at Philippi tribunes wore gold *fibulae*. A connection between gold *fibulae* and cavalry ornaments is suggested also by Livy XXVII 19.12 (with Val. Max. V 1.7); XXX 17.13. The incongruity of Didymus's emphasis on the military aspect of the equestrian order is comic.

6   **pumice-smoothed:** pumice-stone could be used to remove bodily hair: see e.g. XIV 205 *sit nobis aetate puer, non pumice levis* ('let my slave-boy be smooth by reason of his age, not pumice-stone'); Juv. 8.16; 9.95. Depilation was taken to be a sign of effeminacy: cf. e.g. II 36; and see V 61.6. Didymus's contempt for the 'horny-handed' poor is evident.

7   **scamnis:** the use of this rather uncommon, mostly poetical, word adds solemnity.

8   **Didymus:** this Greek name means 'twin'. Its plural can mean 'testicles' – perhaps a hint at what Didymus lacks. The name is used again at III 31.6 and XII 43.3.

42

An elaboration of the paradox so neatly set out in the final line, whose argument is similar to that of an epitaph which appears several times on English church monuments. Dr Johnson produced a Latin version of a celebrated example at Doncaster, dated 1579:

> That I spent, that I had;
> That I gave, that I have;
> That I left, that I loste.

(D.N.Smith and E.L.McAdam, *The Poems of Samuel Johnson* (Oxford, 1974), 227–8).

In view of Martial's frequently expressed interest in receiving gifts, it is easy to suggest – as do, for example, Bridge and Lake – that this poem is intended as a hint, but that is hardly fair. We have no way of knowing how generous he was himself. But perhaps this is why there is no addressee.

2   Note the striking alliteration in this line. The flame is 'impious' because piety required that one should respect the household gods (cf. IV 64.29 *pios Penates*).

3   According to Plutarch (*Crass.* 3.1), Crassus used to lend money to friends without interest; on the other hand, Antoninus Pius, before becoming emperor, lent widely at what was described (S.H.A. *Anton. Pius* 2.8) as the very low rate of 4%.

5   **steward:** see on V 35.7. The line was pleasantly translated by Melmoth (quoted by A. Amos, *Martial and the Moderns* (London, 1858), 108):

> The am'rous steward to adorn his dear,
> With spoils may deck her from thy plunder'd year.

6   This line recalls Prop. I 8.10 *provectas auferet unda rates*.

43

Martial was fond of the theme of bought teeth – bought by an old woman who wishes to appear younger than she is, and so one aspect of the common satirical attack on old women. This goes back to Old Comedy, and is frequent in the *Garland of Philip* and later epigram. Horace says how amusing it is to see Canidia's teeth fall out (*Serm.* I 8.48–50).

The theme seems unattractive to us, but Martial's poems on the subject were much imitated in the sixteenth and seventeenth centuries, and it is remarkable that V 43 was the only one of his epigrams translated by Ezra Pound:

> Thais has black teeth, Laecania's are white because
> she bought 'em last night.
> (First printed in *Imagi*, 1950.)

1   **Thais**: the name of a celebrated courtesan. It occurs often in inscriptions from Rome, and Martial uses it seven other times, always for a prostitute, or at least (as is implied here) a woman no better than she should be.
snow-white: presumably made of ivory (I 72.4).
Laecania: also used at VII 35 of a dubious female.
Note the chiastic arrangement of the line, with alliteration of *nigros ... niveos*.

2   **What's the reason?**: a rhetorical question of a type common in epigram. The best-known example is Catullus 85 *odi et amo. quare id faciam fortasse requiris* ('I hate and I love. Perhaps you ask why I do this.').
emptos ... suos: again chiastic, but separated rather than side by side.

<h2 align="center">44</h2>

Martial writes here (as he does from time to time) in the person of the patron, rather than the client, and tells a revealing little story. It must have been far from uncommon for the client to abandon his former benefactor when he had found a grander one. Like the anonymous poem *Laus Pisonis*, which flatters Piso for his patience with his trying clients, such evidence reminds us that there were two sides to this relationship.

The hendecasyllables have a lively and humorous tone, strongly reminiscent of Catullus: the repeated question in the first sentence (compare e.g. Catullus 29.1 *quis hoc potest videre, quis potest pati...?*) contains another question in parenthesis. Then comes the paradox of the man running away from the person he used to look for, with *conclavibus* providing comic bathos. As the penny drops (*sic est*), Martial compares Dento to a dog, which always goes off after whatever food is most tempting. Even less flatteringly, he suggests that, as soon as the new host finds out what Dento is really like – which won't take long – he'll have to come back to gnaw bones with Martial.

1   This line is used again at VII 86.3, where it is Martial who has not been sent his usual invitation to a birthday party.

2   **Dento**: a real *cognomen*, one of the many which derive from bodily defects ('Toothy'). Here it is chosen on purpose, for a man who loves to chew (at VIII 31 Martial uses it neutrally).

5   The baths were an obvious place to look for dinner invitations, since dinner followed the bath: compare Selius at II 14.11–13.

theatres: not necessarily at a performance, since the porticoes attached to
theatres were much used for strolling: compare again II.14.10.

conclavibus: this word, which strictly means any room that can be locked up,
was presumably a polite euphemism for a public lavatory. (It occurs in this
sense only in Martial and the glossaries.) It seems to us an odd place to go for
dinner invitations, but then Roman public lavatories, with their multiple seats,
were much more sociable than ours. For the same ploy, compare XI 77:

> In omnibus Vacerra quod conclavibus
> consumit horas et die toto sedet,
> cenaturit Vacerra, non cacaturit.

('The reason why Vacerra spends hours in every public lavatory and sits there
all day is that he wants a meal, not a shit.')

7–8 The combination of *unctiore* and *canem* recalls Hor. *Serm.* II 5.83 *ut canis a
corio numquam absterrebitur uncto* ('just as a dog will never be scared away
from a greasy hide').

8 **greater**: both literally and as belonging to a greater man.

9 **sed**: 'and at that', a common use in Martial. Compare I 117.7 *et scalis habito
tribus, sed altis* ('and I live up three flights of stairs – long ones at that').

10 **popina dives**: an oxymoron, since *popina* usually refers to a low-class eating-
house (see on V 70.3).

45

A neatly constructed little attack on a woman who wants to be thought younger than
she is. For the theme, see on V 43. Naturally a pretty girl has no need to go around
telling everyone that she is a pretty girl.

1 **dicis...dicis**: the repetition, picked up by *dicere* in line 2, is tellingly emphatic.
Bassa: Martial uses this common name for a woman six times (and *Bassus* six
times).

46

This is one of three epigrams on the subject of kissing a boy called Diadumenos. III
65 gives an exotic list of comparisons for the fragrance of his kisses, but he is
addressed as *saeve puer* ('cruel boy'), and we gather that he begrudges them. At VI
34 he is asked to give non-stop kisses, and asks how many, but is told (with explicit
reference to Catullus) that counting is inappropriate.

Sullivan (164–6; 200) takes it for granted that Diadumenos is an actual slave-boy
of Martial, but this is not a necessary inference, and the name, despite the fact that it
was used for real people (there are about twenty in the index to Volume VI of *CIL*),
tends to suggest otherwise. The Diadumenos was one of the most famous statues of
Polyclitus: it showed a youthful athlete putting on the garland of victory. Pliny (*HN*
XXXIV 55) contrasted it with the same sculptor's Doryphoros: the latter represented
viriliter puerum ('a boy with the qualities of a man'), while the Diadumenos
represented *molliter iuvenem* ('a young man with feminine qualities'). The
Diadumenos, which was obviously very popular, exists in numerous copies: the one
from Vaison in the British Museum is inferior to the one from Delos in the National

Museum at Athens. (G.M.A. Richter, *The Sculpture and Sculptors of the Greeks* (New Haven , 1970) 191–2, figs. 695–7).

It is furthermore clear that Martial is influenced by Catullus's poems about the kisses of Iuventius: while VI 34 relates to Catullus 48, III 65 and V 46 recall Catullus 99, which apologises to the angry boy (again the word is *saevitia* – line 6) for having stolen a kiss.

It is interesting to consider that this poem was reckoned by Martial to be harmless to the *matronae puerique virginesque* (V 2. 1) .

The first couplet explains the poet's state of mind, while the third line, with telling repetition of *saepe*, and the vocative in the favourite penultimate position, explains what he does; the fourth line sets out the consequence, expressed in paradoxical antithesis.

1 **basia ... luctantia carpsi:** from Ovid, *Met.* IV 358 *luctantiaque oscula carpit*; already imitated by Martial at IV 22.7–8 *luctantia carpsi / basia.*

3–4 The idea that anger is a stimulus to passion is too common to need illustration, but Martial gives it a bizarre twist by saying that he actually beats the boy so as to make him angry, and cause him to refuse to let Martial kiss him, so that he will have to beg for permission.

3 **caedo:** used here in its normal sense, although it is often used metaphorically for *futuo* or *pedico* (J.N.Adams, *The Latin Sexual Vocabulary* (London, 1982) 145–6).

47

Like V 44, this epigram deals with a traditional butt of humorous attack, the parasite. This one boasts of his astonishing success rate, but the truth is that, unlike the poor client in Juvenal (1.133–4), if no-one else feeds him, he cannot afford to feed himself, and goes hungry.

The first line gives Philo's hyperbolical boast, and then arouses our interest by confirming its truth, so that the second line can deliver the explanatory blow.

1 **cenasse domi:** for the phrase cf. II 11.10 *maeroris igitur causa quae? domi cenat* ('what then is the cause of his grief? He dines at home'); Kay on XI 24.15, 'to eat at home was the ultimate indignity for the client and was to be avoided at all costs (see II 11; 14; 18; 27; V 47; VII 20; IX 14 etc): avoiding it is the trademark of the genus *kolax–parasitos*'. For the noun *domicenium*, see V 78.1.
   Philo: used only here by Martial, this common Greek name is often found at Rome.

48

At I 31 Martial had prayed to Apollo to ensure that his centurion friend Pudens should win promotion to the primipilate, in return for which he would dedicate to the god the long hair of his beloved slave-boy Encolpos. Nothing in this epigram suggests that Pudens had won his promotion, and presumably, after waiting some five years, Encolpos had finally persuaded his master to let him cut his hair without further delay.

For Aulus Pudens, see on V 28. At IV 13 Martial had congratulated him on his idyllic marriage, but it is clear that this had made no difference to his interest in boys (cf. VIII 63).

The *primuspilus* was the senior centurion of a legion. Promotion to the post usually came at the age of about fifty. On discharge from it, after his year of office, the man received a special bonus. The question of whether it automatically brought equestrian status has been much discussed. B. Dobson ('The Centurionate and Social Mobility during the Principate', in *Recherches sur les Structures Sociales dans l'Antiquité Classique*, ed. C. Nicolet (Paris, 1970), 106) claims that it did, Demougin (364) that it did not.

M. Citroni, in the article cited on V 28, argues that Pudens did win his promotion, primarily on the evidence of VI 58, which Martial sends to Pudens when he is on campaign in the North, probably in the Dacian war. Martial tells how a recent illness of his own had almost proved fatal, and hopes that his own recovery will be accompanied by the safe return of Pudens to Rome, and ends (line 10): *et referes pili praemia clarus eques* ('and you will bring back the rewards of the primipilate, a distinguished knight'). Citroni points out that VI 58 will naturally date from one year later than V 48, and that a year is the normal length of service in the primipilate. It is important for his argument to suppose that the rank did automatically bring equestrian status, but see above. He explains Martial's failure to mention Pudens's promotion at V 48 on the ground that it had actually come rather late, and so it was more tactful not to, but this is scarcely convincing.

The likelihood is that Pudens never achieved his ambition. Encolpos (a name whose sexual connotations explain its use, in the form Encolpius, for Petronius's narrator) may have been a nickname given by Pudens to his favourite, but it does occur as a real name. Good-looking slave-boys were ordered to grow their hair long (*pueri capillati*), but would wish to have it cut off because this was a sign of reaching adulthood and turning to heterosexuality. Compare e.g. XII 18.24–5, where Martial tells Juvenal about the pleasures of his life in Spain:

> dispensat pueris rogatque longos
> levis ponere vilicus capillos

('my smooth-skinned bailiff gives the slaves their rations and asks permission to cut off his hair'); also IX 36; XII 84.

Supposing that Encolpos was twelve or thirteen at the time of I 31, he would have been about seventeen at this time. It would not in fact be the cutting off of the hair that would alter his relationship with Pudens, but the onset of manhood, because of the general assumption in the ancient world that, whereas a sexual relationship with an immature male was perfectly natural and blameless (quite apart from obviously being more attractive to a boy-lover like Pudens), a relationship with a mature male would suggest a passive role, which was reprehensible. Thus Strato (*Anth. Pal.* XII 4) says that boys are most lovable between the ages of twelve and seventeen, but beyond that age they will want to 'answer back'. The physical sign of maturity is bodily hair, and most obviously the beard: hence lines 7–8. It is a common theme of Greek epigram that this will destroy a boy's attractions, and cf. Mart. IV 7; Hor. *Carm.* IV 10.

1 The arresting opening, with its reminiscence of Virgil's *omnia vincit amor* (*Ecl.* 10.69), provokes the reader's curiosity to know what aspect of love's tyranny will be illustrated. The answer turns out to be rather unexpected: it is only his love for Encolpos that has forced Pudens to give his permission.

3 **and wept:** a pleasantly sentimental touch.

3–6 Three flattering mythological examples of boys, the first of whom prevailed upon his father against his better judgment, while the other two both cut off their hair in unusual circumstances.

3 **cessit habenis:** *cedere* is regularly used with the ablative in this sense; compare e.g. Virg. *Aen.* IX 620 *cedite ferro*; *OLD* s.v. 12a.

4 Having persuaded his father Apollo (the Sun) to let him drive his chariot, Phaethon was unable to control it, so that there was danger that the earth might be set on fire. Zeus had to bring him down with a thunderbolt. See also V 53.4. The reference to Apollo is significant, as the vow of I 31 had been made to him, presumably because, as the type of male beauty, he was regarded as the protector of pederasts.

5 The example of Achilles is easily explained. To prevent his being drafted to fight against Troy, he was hidden by his father Peleus, or his mother Thetis, among the girls of Scyros, until Odysseus found him out by means of a characteristic trick (hence *deprensus*), when he offered them gifts of jewellery, among which he put weapons, which Achilles chose. Presumably he would at once have cut short his hair. The reference to Hylas is less obvious. After the death of his father Theiodamas in battle, he was taken by Hercules to be his 'page', and accompanied him on the voyage of the Argonauts. When sent to fetch water, he was dragged down into the spring by its nymphs. *raptus* must surely refer to this, and he is imagined as having cut off his long hair (specifically mentioned by Theocritus at 13.7) to symbolise his turning to heterosexuality (according to Theocritus, 13.72, he became immortal). The example of Hylas is particularly appropriate here since he was the beloved of a great warrior (whereas Achilles was a great warrior himself).

7–8 The reader is kept in suspense about the person addressed (*tu*), until the penultimate word. The personification of the beard is comic.

8 **so great a reward:** there is an amusing illogicality in asking the beard to show the gratitude of its owner by not appearing.

49

The theme of hair (with the reference to a *puer capillatus* at line 5) links this epigram with the previous one, but it is in a different metre, is longer, and instead of real people it deals with a fictitious man.

Attacks on physical defects were very common in ancient satirical writing, and baldness is mocked by Martial again at VI 12 and 57 and X 83 (the last close to V 49). It hardly seems a decent subject to us, but our sensitivities are not those of our forebears (see Sullivan, 168). However, it might seem surprising that Martial should attack this particular defect, since, according to Suetonius (*Dom.* 18.2), Domitian, who had begun to lose his hair when a young man, was so sensitive on the subject that he took personally any jokes or slanders aimed at other people. However, his supposed sensitivity may well have been exaggerated: he did after all publish a book about baldness (see Jones, *Domitian*, 13, 31, 185). In any case, he might have made an exception for a clever witticism such as this one, in which he himself plays a role: the victim's absurdity lies in growing what hair he still has so long.

1   **sitting:** obviously this would make the effect more striking – especially from behind.

2   **Labienus:** Martial uses the name in four other epigrams, always in a satirical context. It is not a common *cognomen*.

3   **calvae:** used as a substantive to denote the hairless scalp. Cf. VI 57.2 etc.

5   **even a boy:** in other words, long enough for a *puer capillatus*.
     possint: for the subjunctive, compare Ov. *Fast.* II 105–6 *capit ille coronam | quae possit crines, Phoebe, decere tuos.*

7   Compare Eumolpus's lament for the heroes' lost hair at Petr. *Sat.* 109.9, line 4: *areaque attritis ridet adusta pilis* ('after the hairs have been worn away, the burnt-up area laughs' – the language is intentionally ridiculous).

8   **December:** the reference is to the great Saturnalian feast for the whole people of Rome put on by Domitian on December 1st 88, and described by Statius at *Silv.* I 6 (see also Suet. *Dom.* 4.5; Jones, *Domitian*, 105).

9   **meals:** according to Statius (28–34), a good-looking crowd of slaves served the sitting people with *panaria* (literally 'bread-baskets'), white napkins, and 'elegant banquets'. The fact that Statius says of these slaves 'you would think that they were so many Idaean servants', i.e. Ganymedes, adds extra point to the comparison in line 5.

10   **you came back:** this is a little surprising, since Statius describes the whole people, *parvi, femina, plebs, eques, senatus* (line 44), as dining there and then 'at one table' (surely hyperbole). But then Labienus could hardly have eaten three meals at once.

11   **Geryon:** the triple-bodied monster whose oxen Hercules had to steal as one of his labours. Cf. V 65.12. Hercules killed him.
     Geryonen: Housman argued that Martial must have had in mind the nominative *Geryones* (as at V 65.12) – *JPh* 31 (1910), 253–4.

12   **vites censeo:** the paratactic construction is common with words of command or advice.
     the portico of Philippus: this portico, which surrounded the Temple of Hercules Musarum ('of the Muses') in the Campus Martius, was where wigs were sold. Cf. Ov. *Ars Am.* III 165–8:
     >   femina procedit densissima crinibus emptis
     >   proque suis alios efficit aere suos.
     >   nec pudor est emisse: palam venire videmus
     >   Herculis ante oculos virgineumque chorum.
     ('A woman comes forward really thick with bought hair, and she makes someone else's hair stand in for her own by means of cash; nor

is she ashamed of having bought it. We see hair openly on sale before
the eyes of Hercules and the virgin choir' [i.e. the Muses].)
Labienus might well go there to find a solution to his problem.

The Temple of Hercules Musarum was built by M. Fulvius Nobilior after he
took Ambracia in 189 BC: it contained statues of Hercules and the nine Muses.
The portico was built in 29 BC by L. Marcius Philippus, son of the stepfather of
Augustus by his first wife (cos. 38), who also rebuilt the temple. Its east wall
was common with the Portico of Octavia. See Richardson and Nash.

50

Another attack on a parasite, but here, as at V 44, Martial takes on the role of the
host who suffers the injustice of his guest. The humour of the epigram arises chiefly
from the absurdly hyperbolical language, and especially the pretended assumption by
the author that Charopinus's attitude is in fact justifiable.

The first half of the poem explains Charopinus's complaints. In the second we
have a rhetorical question, followed by a moralistic comment, whose sting is
counterbalanced by the less serious mock-polite requests of the final couplet.

1   **ceno domi:** the fact that these words are usually applied (as at V 47) to the
     disappointed parasite provides an amusing element of the unexpected to the last
     word *vocavi*, which shows that Martial is actually speaking in the character of
     host.
     Charopinus: only here in Martial. Its metrical form is handy. Not an
     uncommon Greek name, it was rare at Rome.
2   **inimicitiae:** usually used in the plural.
3   **potes:** 'you have it in you to'. Compare I 14.5 *unde potest avidus captae leo
     parcere praedae*? ('how can the greedy lion spare its captured prey?').
5   The idea that in not sharing his meal with Charopinus Martial is stealing from
     him entertainingly emphasises the absurdity of his anger. The idea that a man
     should be allowed to commit at least one theft is equally daft.
6   Plain speaking from Martial at last: expecting others to feed you is just greed.
7–8 It is pleasant to imagine Charopinus watching Martial's kitchen for signs of
     activity, which the cook tries to conceal.
8   **det tibi verba:** *dare alicui verba* regularly means 'to cheat'.

51

An attack on a man who is concerned to put on the appearance of a busy and
successful lawyer, but is so surly that he will not even utter one word to return a
greeting. Martial criticises a man for this social defect again at IV 83.3, interpreting
it as a general insult.

The victim is not given a name, which is comparatively rare in Martial.

2   **shorthand-writers:** one of these appears as a gift at XIV 208, where Martial
     says that however fast someone speaks his hand is faster, and has completed its
     job before the tongue has finished. They are referred to several times by
     Seneca, Quintilian, and the younger Pliny, and some are commemorated in
     funeral inscriptions.

smooth-cheeked chorus: a striking phrase suggesting their youth and elegantly concerted movements. Perhaps their youth suggests that the man has just gone out and bought them.

3 **notebooks:** *codicillus* is the diminutive of *codex*, the parchment 'book' which was just beginning to replace the papyrus roll (see C.H. Roberts and T.C. Skeat, *The Birth of the Codex* (London, 1983); L.D. Reynolds and N.G. Wilson, *Scribes and Scholars* [3] (Oxford, 1991), 27–8). The *codicillus* was used for petitions, legal documents (hence 'codicil'), etc.

5 These three are chosen primarily for their fame as orators, though also as outstanding examples of Roman virtue (which would include civility). The elder M. Porcius Cato was the first orator to leave a substantial body of published speeches. 'Tullius' is Cicero. M. Junius Brutus was much admired for his oratory by Cicero, who named one of his dialogues on oratory after him, and also dedicated to him the *Orator*.

6 **Rufus:** a very common name. It might conceivably refer to Martial's friend Canius Rufus, who had a keen sense of humour (see I 61.9).
   fidiculae: the diminutive of *fides*, a lyre, also refers to an instrument of torture at Sen. *Dial.* V 3.6; Suet. *Tib.* 62.2; *Cal.* 33. The rack seems a likely identification, from the analogy of tightening the strings.

7 There were very many Greeks and Greek-speakers from the East in Rome at this time, and a knowledge of Greek was obviously widespread (hence Martial's occasional use of Greek words). So a Greek-speaker might well greet people in his own language, and even a Latin-speaker might think it fashionable to use a Greek greeting (like the use of the Italian 'ciao' today).

8 **let's greet him:** the verb *saluto* is related to the verb *salvere*, and the greeting consisted of the word *salve* (or its alternative *ave*) to which the person greeted responded likewise.

52

Since the giving of presents was such an important part of Roman social relations (Sullivan, 13), it is not surprising that Martial often writes on the theme. It was an important one for Seneca, who wrote in his *De Beneficiis* (II 10.4): *alter statim oblivisci debet dati, alter accepti numquam* ('one man should forget at once that he has given, whereas the other should never forget that he has received'). He also states (II 11.2) *qui dedit beneficium taceat, narret qui accepit* ('let him who gave the benefit keep quiet, but let him who received it tell the story'). He returns to the point at VII 22, criticising those who go around telling everyone about their own generosity.

The first line emphasises Martial's gratitude, but the question in line 2 proposes a paradox, which is answered in just two words. The next couplet reveals that Martial has found out about Postumus's behaviour precisely when he was showing his own gratitude. The third couplet is a masterpiece of compression, its three sentences (in asyndeton) leading up to the moral expounded in the last two lines, which begin (as often) with an emphatic *crede mihi*, and where the name of the man addressed is repeated from line 2.

This epigram appears to have suggested an adaptation to Jean Ogier de Gombauld, whose epigrams were published in Paris in 1657. His epigram was imitated in turn by Matthew Prior:

> To JOHN I ow'd great Obligation;
> But JOHN, unhappily, thought fit
> To publish it to all the Nation:
> Sure JOHN and I are more than Quit.

(*The Literary Works of Matthew Prior*, ed. H.B. Wright and M.K. Spears (Oxford, 1971) 454, 951–2.)

2   **Postumus:** this common *cognomen* is quite often used by Martial for a victim. He is a patron also at IV 26 and 40.

4   **dixerat:** the use of the pluperfect, where one might expect the perfect, is common in Martial (see Friedlaender's note on I 107.3), as well as in other poets. Clearly metrical convenience played a part in this: see Citroni on I 30.1.

5   **belle:** the colloquial epithet *bellus* (diminutive of *bonus*) was fashionable under the early Empire. It was explained by Fordyce, on Catullus 22.9, as referring to 'one who knows and observes the usages of polite society'. It is usually ironical in Martial.

7   **crede mihi:** often used by Martial (as by Ovid) to emphasise a point, e.g. I 3.4; I 5.11; 41.2.

8   **are wasted:** a striking exaggeration. What Martial means is that the gifts lose their capacity to inspire gratitude, and so cease to 'be' gifts.

53

Martial suggests to an author who writes on hackneyed mythological topics that his works deserve to be either thrown in the water or burnt. In several epigrams Martial rejects mythology as trite and irrelevant to real life (see VIII 3; IX 50; X 4). The enthusiasm for epic poetry inspired by the example of Virgil partly explains the widespread preference at this period for such themes, but another important aspect was their comparative safety (Juv. 1.162–4).

The joke about bad poems deserving to be soaked in water goes back to Cicero (*Q Fr*. II 13.1), and occurs again at Tib. I 9.50. Martial liked it (I 5; III 100; IX 58; XIV 196). The more obvious punishment of burning goes back much further: see Nisbet and Hubbard on Hor. *Carm*. I 16.3. Martial's source here seems to be an epigram by Lucillius (*Anth. Pal*. XI 214):

> Γράψας Δευκαλίωνα, Μενέστρατε, καὶ Φαέθοντα,
> ζητεῖς τίς τούτων ἄξιός ἐστι τίνος.
> τοῖς ἰδίοις αὐτοὺς τιμήσομεν· ἄξιος ὄντως
> ἐστὶ πυρὸς Φαέθων, Δευκαλίων δ' ὕδατος.

('Having written about Deucalion and Phaethon, Menestratus, you ask what either of them is worth. We shall value them according to their own characteristic. Phaethon is really worthy of fire, and Deucalion of water.')

The two epigrams are interestingly compared by W. Burnikel (*Untersuchungen zur Struktur des Witzepigramms bei Lukillios und Martial* (Wiesbaden, 1980), 16–18). He points out that Martial has refined the sarcastic point of Lucillius's poem, and heightened the irony. Unlike Lucillius, Martial does not actually specify the 'water' and 'fire', relying on his readers to understand the metonymy (he points out that Martial's poem is barely comprehensible without a knowledge of Lucillius's). Lucillius has the victim ask the question, whereas in Martial it is the author himself. Martial expands the number of subjects from two to four, which carries the further implication that Bassus writes too much.

The chiastic arrangement of the first line, with repeated *quid scribis*, is contrasted with the next line where the two objects each end half of the line. The fourth line has its subjects in corresponding positions.

1-2 The implication seems to be that Bassus writes tragedies, for the four individuals named provided titles for (among others) Aeschylus (Niobe), Sophocles (Niobe, Thyestes), Euripides (Medea, Andromache, Thyestes), Ennius (Medea, Andromache, Thyestes), and Seneca (Medea, Thyestes).

1 **Colchis:** probably 'the Colchian woman', i.e. Medea, rather than Colchis itself. For the subject, cf. Juv. 1.10–11.

my friend: Martial pretends to be giving friendly advice.

Thyestes: brother of Atreus, who served up his children for him to eat.

2 **quo tibi:** for thus use, compare Hor. *Epist.* I 5.12 *quo mihi fortunam. si non conceditur uti?*.

Bassus: see on V 45.1.

3 **materia:** it is the play on this word which provides the epigram with its point. In the context, the reader takes it to mean 'subject-matter', but the final line shows that Martial is intending it in the sense of 'physical material'.

mihi crede: see on V 52.7.

4 **Deucalion:** he and his wife Pyrrha were the only survivors when Zeus flooded the earth.

Phaethon: see on V 48.4.

54

Another epigram on the same theme as V 21. There is a delightful absurdity in the idea of making a note of the names of those one might happen to meet in the street. The fact that the *nomen* Calpurnius was so common intensifies the absurdity.

1 **extemporalis:** a post–Augustan technical term of rhetoric (e.g. Petr. 6.1).

meus rhetor: this use of *meus* is colloquial; e.g. Petr. 62.4 *homo meus*; M. VII 72.16; IX 85.1; Hofmann, *Lateinische Umgangssprache* [3], 200.

2 **Calpurnius:** used only here by Martial.

et: 'and yet'.

55

Dialogue epigrams of this type are not uncommon in the *Greek Anthology*, though this is the only 'pure' example in Martial. It is not necessary to assume (as Friedlaender does) that the poem was inspired by an actual representation, though the description is certainly very precise.

The eagle was described by Homer (*Iliad* XXIV 292–3) as the favourite bird of Zeus, and in art it is regularly associated with him. The idea of showing him riding one, as here, was of oriental origin. He is often shown holding thunderbolts.

The eagle replies in single words until her final reply, which brings in Ganymede, who more usually rides the eagle. The story of Ganymede first appears in Homer (*Iliad* XX 231f.), where Aeneas tells how the third son of Tros was snatched up by the gods to be Zeus's wine-pourer, because of his beauty. Later it was supposed that he had been carried up to heaven by an eagle: this was the subject of an anonymous epigram in the *Garland of Meleager* (*Anth. Pal.* XII 67), and of later epigrams, and also of a famous bronze statue-group by the mid-4th century BC sculptor Leochares (Plin. *HN* XXXIV 79). It is likely that the group showed the eagle looking at Ganymede (see my note on Mart. I 6.1, with plate 1b – unfortunately reproduced sideways).

1   **dic mihi:** a rhetorical device used by Martial to begin an epigram also at I 20; XIV 179; 215. Compare the frequent use of the imperative εἰπέ to open epigrams (and especially dialogue poems) in the *Greek Anthology*.
     queen of birds: because *aquila* is feminine.

56

The most celebrated treatment of the poor rewards for literature in Imperial Rome is the seventh *Satire* of Juvenal. Martial had claimed in Book III, which he sent back to Rome from Forum Cornelii, that he would return when he had metamorphosed into a *citharoedus* ('lyre-singer', 4.7) – in other words, when he could ply a profitable trade. Compare also IX 73.

An amusing contrast is provided by Petronius (*Sat.* 46), where the blanket-maker (*centonarius*) Echion says that his little son is learning literature and also some law, so that he will possess a profitable skill: he intends him to be 'a barber, or an auctioneer, or at any rate a barrister'.

The common *cognomen* Lupus is used nine times by Martial. The fact that at X 48.6 a 'Lupus' is invited to dinner along with known friends of Martial shows that at least that one must be real. On the other hand, in some epigrams the name must be fictional: e.g. at XI 55 it is used for a legacy-hunter (no doubt with reference to the meaning 'wolf'). The other uses of the name are more ambiguous (VI 79; VII 10; X 40; XI 18; 88; 108: see Kay on XI 18, 55 and 108).

The epigram opens with the question: Martial's negative reply is given in five lines, its four sentences each expressed differently. Another question introduces Martial's positive advice, whose two sentences use constructions which echo earlier ones.

3   **teachers of grammar and rhetoric:** for the combination, compare (in a similar context) IX 73.8 (also X 70.12). These represented the two principal stages of the Roman educational system: the first taught literature, and the second rhetoric, so that the two pieces of advice in the following lines correspond separately to these.

5   **Cicero and Virgil:** already the canonical masters of Latin prose and verse.

6   **Tutilius:** this may be the rhetorical writer referred to by Quintilian at III 1.21. He may also be the Tutilius referred to politely by Pliny at *Ep.* VI 32.1. He was the father-in-law of the man addressed in this letter, who, although called Quintilianus, cannot be the famous bearer of that name.

7   **abdices:** a legal technical term.

9   **discat citharoedus:** for the construction, compare Petr. *Sat.* 46.7 (paraphrased above): *destinavi illum artificium docere aut tonstrinum aut praeconem aut certe causidicum.* See *TLL* V.1.1731. 45f.

    citharoedus aut choraules: the same words occur in a hendecasyllable at XI 75.3. A *citharoedus* sang lyric poetry (Greek or Latin) while accompanying himself on the *cithara* (lyre), while the *choraules* led the choir on the αὐλός or *tibia* (see Kay, l.c.). Suetonius records the large sums paid to two *citharoedi* by the supposedly stingy Vespasian (19.1): they received 200,000 sesterces each for their performances at the rededication of the Theatre of Marcellus. Juvenal claims that the fees paid to the singer Chrysogonus and the famous *citharoedus* Pollio for teaching rich men's sons are beyond any comparison with those of a rhetorician (7.175–7).

11   The profession of auctioneer was profitable (see above), but despised, not just because it involved money, but because it required shouting and joking (compare Mart. I 85). At Mart. VI 8 a man marries his daughter to an auctioneer, rejecting two praetors, four tribunes, seven barristers, and ten poets. At Juv. 7.5–6 desperate poets turn auctioneers.

    It is odd that the profession of architect is combined with that of auctioneer, as it was considered respectable, and obviously required much more intelligence. It was certainly profitable, and the prolific building works carried out under the Flavians provided plenty of occupation, whether in public or private practice (Friedlaender, *SG* I[10] 173–4).

57

Strictly speaking, only a slave would address someone as *domine*. However, under the Empire the use of the word as a polite form of address, whether within the family or in a wider social circle, became common. Seneca refers to his brother as *dominus meus Gallio* (*Ep.* 104.1). The freedmen at Trimalchio's dinner-party use similar civilities (e.g. Petr. *Sat.* 57.2; and cf. 41.3). Their use has been attributed to oriental influence.

However, it would obviously be remarkable for a free man to use such an address to a slave (though one instance occurs in an inscription of the third century AD – *CIL* VI 33840). J. Svennung (*Anredeformen* (Uppsala, 1958), 342) comments that nothing could show more clearly how the sense 'lord' was forgotten, and how the word had become a mere title. One explanation might be suggested by Seneca, who says that *domine* is sometimes used when people cannot remember names (*Ep.* I.3.1). See also M. Bang in Friedlaender *SG* [10] IV 85–6; *TLL* V.1.1925.3f.

Shackleton Bailey thinks that the answer lies in the erotic use of *dominus*, which is applied to slaves, with deliberate irony, at Mart. XI 70.2 (see Kay); XII 66.8; and XIII 69.2. This leads him to suggest that the doubtfully attested reading *meum.* may be preferable to *tuum*. However, the formal situation implied by *resaluto* makes this explanation less plausible.

Clément Marot wrote two versions of this poem (*Épigrammes*, ed. C.A. Mayer, CLXVIII and CLXIX): in each he uses 'Monsieur' for *dominus*, and 'valet' for *servus*.

1   Cinna: a not uncommon name, often used by Martial.

58

Martial returns to the theme of *vera vita*, as in V 20. (For this sense of *vivere* and *vita*, see on V 20.4). The name Postumus (for which see on V 52) must surely be chosen (as Friedlaender suggested) to recall Horace, *Carm*. II 14 (*Eheu fugaces Postume Postume*). Horace also expressed this Epicurean idea that one should enjoy life while one can at *Carm*. I 11.7–8:

> dum loquimur, fugerit invida
> aetas: carpe diem, quam minimum credula postero.

('While we are speaking, niggardly time has fled: seize the day, trusting as little as possible to the next one.')

It was a theme close to Martial's heart: see my note on I 15, and compare II 90.3–4 (addressed to Quintilian):

> vivere quod propero pauper nec inutilis annis,
> da veniam: properat vivere nemo satis.

('For the fact that I make haste to enjoy life, although poor and not incapacitated by age, forgive me: no-one makes enough haste to enjoy life'.)

Abraham Cowley wrote a charming version of this poem (*Essays, Plays and Sundry Verses*, ed. A.R. Waller (Cambridge, 1906), 454–5):

> To morrow you will Live, you always cry;
> In what far Country does this morrow lye,
> That 'tis so mighty long 'ere it arrive?
> Beyond the Indies does this Morrow live?
> 'Tis so far fetcht this Morrow, that I fear
> 'Twill be both very Old and very Dear,
> To morrow I will live, the Fool does say;
> To Day it self's too Late, the wise liv'd Yesterday.

The basic form of Martial's epigram is common in his work: P.'s statement is followed by questions intended to show up how misguided it is, with Martial's own words of wisdom at the end. It is ingeniously held together, not just by the repetition of the name in the same positions in lines 1 and 7 and 2 and 8, but by the repetition of the vital word *cras*, used no fewer than three times in the first couplet. Its appearance at the beginning of the final couplet, followed shortly by *hodie*, leads to the final punch-word, its polar opposite *heri*.

Martial's joke is to treat P.'s 'tomorrow' as if it were a commodity whose supply is doubtful, with regard to its time of arrival, its location, and its purchasability.

2   cras istud: the use of *cras* as a substantive recalls Persius 5.67–9 (e.g. 68 *iam cras hesternum consumpsimus* ('we have already used up yesterday's tomorrow').

4   Parthians and Armenians: these troublesome Oriental peoples were only too well-known in Rome, and so Martial uses them to suggest a distant locality.

5   Priam and Nestor were proverbial for longevity (e.g. Mart. II 64.3). Martial means that P. has been saying 'tomorrow' for an incredibly long time.

7   cras vives: the opening of the final couplet picks up the opening of the poem. With this couplet compare the ending of I 15 (11–12):

> non est, crede mihi, sapientis dicere 'Vivam':
>> sera nimis vita est crastina: vive hodie.

> ('The wise man does not – believe me – say 'I shall live later'.
> Tomorrow's life is too late: live today.')

For the future tense *vives*, cf. Sen. *Ep.* 45.12–13 *nullius non vita spectat in crastinum. quid in hoc sit mali quaeris? infinitum. non enim vivunt sed victuri sunt* ('Everyone's life looks to tomorrow. You ask what is the wrong in this? It is beyond measure. For they are not living, but about to live.')

59

For the theme, compare V 18. L. Arruntius Stella, suffect consul in 101, was a distinguished and rich friend of Martial, who addresses him often from Book I to Book XI. He was a poet.

4   pots: the earliest types of Saturnalia gifts were *sigillaria*, figurines generally of pottery, but sometimes of other materials (along with *cerei* or wax candles). *Sigillaria* could be used as children's toys, or else, if they represented deities, put in household shrines. At Rome they were sold in a special market. For examples of pottery figurines, see e.g. Mart. XIV 171; 178; 182. For other pottery objects, see e.g. Mart. XIV 114; 119. The sending of a gift obliged the recipient to reciprocate: see Mart. IV 88.

exoneratus: 'released from your obligation'. For this sense, see *TLL* V.2.1548.3f.

60

Martial addresses someone who thinks he can ensure that his name will live for ever by making vicious attacks which will provoke Martial into replying in kind. Since Martial makes a rule of never mentioning real people by name in a disparaging way (see the Preface to Book I), the hope would have been a vain one anyway.

Although dogs were much appreciated as companions and helpers of men in the ancient world (cf. e.g. Mart. I 109), they were also proverbial for viciousness; hence the abusive nickname of the Cynic philosophers. When Trimalchio's wife Fortunata is insulting him, the final word that provokes him into rage is *canis* (Petr. *Sat.* 74.9).

The epigram was adapted by Clément Marot (*Épigrammes*, ed. C.A. Mayer, CLXXXI) for an attack on his quarrelsome friend Étienne Dolet: it is amusing that Dolet is named in the title.

2   **gannitibus:** *gannio* (like *latro*) is an onomatopoeic word particular to dogs.

5   **qualiscumque:** for its use in a derogatory sense, cf. e.g. I 70.17; Catullus 1.9; *OLD* s.v. 2b.

       throughout the world: for Martial's pride in his worldwide fame, cf. I 1.2 *toto notus in orbe Martialis.*

8–10   Martial alludes here to the proverb (familiar in both Greek and Latin) 'dog doesn't bite dog'.

9   Compare Hor. *Ars P.* 358 *bis terve*, with Brink's note.

10   **to bite the dog's skin:** i.e. to respond to his attacks in kind, since dogs like chewing leather.

11   **scabie:** with a play on two senses, the metaphorical one of an itch-like desire to do something, and the literal one of the 'mange' of a dog's hide. Martial will not even scratch someone, let alone bite him.

61

Martial warns a man that his wife's effeminate-looking legal agent is cuckolding him. The theme of XII 38 is related, but there Martial tells the husband that the man who hangs around his wife (who is described as *crine nitens*, 'with shiny hair', and *crure glaber*, 'with smooth legs') provides no cause for fear, as he is not interested in sexual activity with women.

     Women who retained control of their own property would often employ a *procurator* to act as their legal agent, and generally this would be a trusted freedman (Friedlaender, *SG* [10] I 278f.). At XII 49 Martial addresses one,

> rerum quem dominum vocat suarum
> et credit cui Postumilla dives
> gemmas, aurea, vina, concubinos (2–4)

     ('whom the rich Postumilla calls master of her affairs, and to whom she entrusts her jewels, her golden objects, her wine, her male concubines'):

she is described as his *patrona* (6), so he was presumably her freedman. Procurators could become close friends of their employers, and there are examples of gravestones set up by such men for their employers (e.g. *ILS* 1200; *CIL* XI 6022). Interesting evidence of their activities is provided by Cicero's attack on Aebutius in his *Pro Caecina.*

     It might seem surprising that a married woman (as opposed to a spinster or widow) should employ a *procurator*, but a curious parallel is provided by the epitaph of Pudens, who was employed by Aemilia Lepida, wife of Drusus son of Germanicus: he was a freedman of her father. Tacitus (*Ann.* VI 40) tells how, despite making many attacks on her husband, she got away with it until her father died, when she was accused (with reason) of committing adultery with a slave, and killed herself (AD 36). In his epitaph Pudens is made to boast that he guided Lepida's morals, and that, had he lived, she would have remained the granddaughter-in-law of the emperor.

     Presumably Marianus is imagined as having married his wife by the less formal (and more usual) method, by which she retained control of her property.

     The likelihood that a *speciosus procurator* might commit adultery with his master's wife is confirmed by the bizarre murder story which forms the subject of

Seneca's *Controversiae* VII 5. Jerome refers three times (*Ep.* 54.13; 79.9; *Adv. Iov.* I 47) to the danger to a wife's reputation posed by her having a *procurator calamistratus* (see below): the words he uses in the first two passages suggest that he has this epigram of Martial in mind.

The structure of the poem is most effective, with the first half of the first hexameter repeated as the second half of the first pentameter, and the questions of lines 1–6 leading up to Marianus's unwilling reply. Sarcastic comment on this prepares for the final couplet, in which the fourfold repetition of *res* emphasises the scornful picking-up of Marianus's words, and *crispulus iste* recalls the first couplet, the punch being reserved for the final word.

This is the first of nine successive epigrams in elegiac couplets – a surprisingly long unbroken run.

1   **crispulus:** the diminutive is used sarcastically of a conventionally handsome man at Sen. *Ep.* 66.25 (*comatum et crispulum*). Curls were associated with effeminacy: at Petr. *Sat.* 97.2 Giton is described as *crispus, mollis, formosus*. They might have been artificially produced by the use of *calamistra* (curling-irons), hence e.g. Plaut. *Asin.* 627 *cinaede calamistrate*.

2   **Marianus:** a not uncommon *cognomen* used twice elsewhere by Martial.

3   **dominae:** if the *procurator* was a freedman of the wife (see above), then the word would allude to their former relationship, but there is also a hint of the use of the word by lovers. Furthermore, a husband might address his wife as *domina* (M. Bang in Friedlaender, *SG* [10] IV 87).

   garrit in aurem: the phrase is used by Persius at 5.96, and by Martial at I 89. Compare the English 'a word in your ear'.

4   **sellam:** presumably a sedan chair, mentioned together with a litter (*lectica*) at XI 98.12 (Blümner, *Privataltertümer*, 445f.). As the woman is carried along, the man walks beside.

   dexteriore: the comparative is used only here by Martial.

5   This line is generally interpreted by reference to Juvenal 1.28 *ventilet aestivum digitis sudantibus aurum*, where Crispinus is represented as wearing a 'summer ring' because he cannot endure the weight of a larger jewel, and moving the ring up and down his finger as it gets sweaty. Presumably the *procurator*, in similar circumstances, moves his ring from finger to finger. It has to be admitted, however, that without the Juvenal parallel the line would be very hard to understand. It might be easier to take it (with Shackleton Bailey) to mean that he wears many rings (like Charinus at Mart. XI 59, who wears six on each finger: see Kay's note), a practice dismissed as effeminate foppery at Sen. *QNat.* VII 31. But the epithet *levis* then has little point, and the verb *currit* seems odd too.

6   Satirical attacks on men who depilate their bodies are common in Martial and elsewhere: the practice was reckoned to be a sign of passive homosexuality (see Kay on XI 43.10). It is curious that in the modern world it is habitual with macho bodybuilders. Hair might be removed by plucking (e.g. Suet. *Jul.* 45.2), with pumice stone (e.g. Mart. V 41.6; XIV 205; I 117.16), or with pitch (Plin. *HN* XIV 123; XXIX 26). Contrast the out-of-work gigolo Naevolus in Juvenal's

9th *Satire*, whose woeful state is indicated by his *fruticante pilo neglecta et squalida crura* (1. 15 – 'legs neglected and squalid with sprouting hair').

violata: for the sense 'disfigured', compare I 53.6; Virg. *Aen.* XII 67–8.

7   **res agit:** here in the sense 'looks after her legal business'.

8–9 The *procurator*, as a legal expert and man of business, might be expected to look stern and therefore reliable – certainly not like a pansy.

10 **Aufidius Chius:** a *iuris consultus* (legal expert) of this name is referred to in a fragmentary legal text (*Fragm. Vat.* 77). At Juv. 9.25 Naevolus (see above) is described as having been *notior Aufidio moechus* ('a more notorious adulterer than Aufidius'). It would add point to the comparison if the lawyer Aufidius had a reputation for adultery, but there is no evidence for their identity.

11 **the slaps of Latinus:** the actor Latinus (a favoured companion of Domitian) was well-known for his role as the lover of Thymele, who makes a fool of her jealous husband Panniculus, subjecting him to such indignities as being slapped on the face. Compare II 72 (where *testes* in line 8 has a double meaning); and see I 4.5, and Courtney's notes on Juv. 6.44 and 8.191 and 197. The situation in which a pretty young woman married to an impotent and foolish old man takes a dashing young lover, who then runs rings round the husband, has been a stock comic plot for centuries.

13–14 For the legal sense of *res ... agere* (line 7), Martial substitutes the more general sense 'minds your business': compare e.g. Plaut. *Curc.* 671 *volo meam rem agere.*

13 For the colloquial effect of these brief questions, see Hofmann, *Lateinische Umgangssprache*[3], 102–3; 197. He compares e.g. Cic. *Verr.* II 5.70 *quo igitur? quo putatis?*

62

Martial complains that, although he has a suburban villa, he cannot afford to furnish it properly. He had in fact owned a small estate at Nomentum (now Mentana), fifteen miles NE of Rome, since at least c.83 (see my note on I 105), but this poem need not be taken as factually autobiographical. It is hard to say whether the absence of a named addressee makes this more or less likely. However, it must be noted that Martial claims to have bought the estate, whereas it was suggested by Friedlaender that, since Seneca had vineyards at Nomentum, it might have been given to Martial by Seneca or his heirs.

The paradoxical situation described in the first two couplets is resolved in the third by means of Martial's ingenious suggestion that a benefactor who furnished the house would be welcome to stay there. The compression of the last line is masterly.

1 Shackleton Bailey rightly argues (*AJP* 110 (1989), 136) that *hospes* is not vocative, but goes with *maneas*. The vocative would imply that the person addressed either was already a guest or had been in the past.

iure tuo: without exceeding the bounds of what is yours by right.

hortis: the plural generally refers to pleasure-gardens (whereas the singular refers to a vegetable garden), and so often stands for a suburban estate.

4 **asked for mercy:** a wounded gladiator asking for his life would raise a finger
– the literal meaning here. Martial's furniture has fought a good fight, but
finally packed it in. For the phrase, cf. e.g. Cic. *Cons.* ap. Lact. *Div. Inst.* III
28.9 *cedo, inquit, et manum tollo* ('I give in, he says, and raise my hand'); Mart.
Spect. 31.5. T. Wiedemann, *Emperors and Gladiators* (London, 1992),
reproduces several representations of the practice (figures 3, 5b, 9c, 10, 11, 12,
15, and see pp.95–6).

5 **nec = ne ... quidem.**
cushion: couches usually had mattresses: see G.M.A. Richter, *The Furniture
of the Greeks, Etruscans, and Romans* (London, 1966), plates 530f.. Mart. XIV
162 describes a pillow stuffed with hay, but wool or feathers were the superior
materials (see Kay on XI 56.9).

6 **webbing:** the webbing of beds could be made of flax or leather (C.L. Ransom
Williams, *Couches and Beds of the Greeks, Etruscans and Romans* (Chicago,
1905), 62f.; Richter, *Furniture*, 106.

63

Ponticus claims to want Martial's real opinion of his literary efforts, but Martial
naturally tells him what he wants to hear. In return, Ponticus wishes him well, on
condition that he is telling the truth. Since Martial is not fulfilling this condition, he
suggests that the wish should fall on Ponticus instead – because it is worthless.

VIII 76 is similar: a man wants Martial to give him his true opinion, so he tells
him that the truth is that he doesn't want to hear the truth.

1 **Marcus:** address by the *praenomen* was a sign of familiarity. This form of
address is rare in other authors, but common in Martial (compare V 29.2).
libellis: in Martial the diminutive usually refers to books of poetry (cf. Catullus
1.1), but it could refer to other works of literature (see *TLL* s.v.).

3 **Ponticus:** the name is used seven times by Martial in various contexts.

4 **Regulus:** see on V 10. He published a biography of his young son after his
death (Plin. *Ep.* IV 7), and also a *libellus* attacking Arulenus Rusticus and
Herennius Senecio (*ib.* I 5), but Martial is hardly likely to refer to that. He
must have published other works.

5 **sic:** the use of this word to express a wish or prayer which is conditional is not
uncommon. The condition can be expressed by an *ut* clause, as at Catullus
45.13, or by an imperative, as at Catullus 17.5 (see Fordyce on these passages).
Here it is understood to be the veracity of Martial's opinion.

6 **Capitoline Jupiter:** with whom Domitian was often compared, or even
identified (see on V 6.9).
immo: several times used by Martial to introduce his final point (e.g. IV
84.4).

64

The theme is related to that of V 20 and 58. The idea that drinking wine is the way
to enjoy life while you can is best known from Horace (*Carm.* I 11; and cf. I 9; II
14). Martial's poem is a variation on his own II 59, in which a small diningroom

called the *Mica* points out that from it can be seen the *Caesareus tholus*, which must refer to the Mausoleum of Augustus, and urges the diners to enjoy a drinking-session, complete with perfumes and roses, since (line 4) *ipse iubet mortis te meminisse deus* ('the god himself bids you remember death').

1   **four ladles-full:** a *sextans* was one sixth of a *sextarius*, which was one sixth of a *congius*, which was one eighth of an *amphora*. There were two *cyathi* (ladles) to a *sextans*. Two *sextantes* were equivalent to one *triens*, which was a common size of wine-cup (e.g. I 106.8). At XII 27 Martial contrasts himself, drinking *sextantes*, with a man who is drinking *deunces* (a *deunx* is eleven twelfths of a *sextarius*), so the *sextans* presumably indicates moderation.
     Callistus: Martial uses common Greek names for the slaves. This one (meaning 'most beautiful') occurs again at VIII 67.5, for a slave of his own (not necessarily real).
     Falernian: this wine, from Campania, was generally reckoned at this time to be the best Italian variety.

2   The Romans usually drank their wine mixed with water, and it was regarded as a sign of intemperance to drink it neat (see I 11.4; VI 89; Virg. *Catal.* ll.1f.). The water was usually warm (cf. I 11.3). However, by the first century AD, the practice of cooling wine was known in Italy. The wine was usually poured through the snow in a strainer, so as to filter out any impurities. Mart. XIV 103 describes a *colum nivarium* (a strainer or colander for snow), through which the wine would be poured, but XIV 104 describes a *saccus nivarius* (snow bag), used apparently to melt the snow down into cold water, which was then added to the wine. The latter process seems to be referred to here, but, according to Seneca (*QNat.* IV 13.9), some people put lumps of snow into their cups to keep their wine cold while they were drinking. Snow was available at Rome, at a price, all year round. See R.J. Forbes, *Studies in Ancient Technology*, VI[2] (Leiden, 1966), 104f.; Mart. XII 17.6.
     aestivas ... nives: a striking oxymoron.
     Alcimus: quite a common slave-name, at I 88 this is the name of a dead slave of Martial himself.

3   The application of perfumed oil to the hair was normal practice at Roman drinking parties.
     amomo: the oriental shrub Cardamom was used to make an exotic perfume. See also VIII 77.3; XII 17.7.

4   The host would supply the guests with garlands of roses for their hair.
     wearied: the idea that the weight of the roses wearies the head is a piquant hyperbole.
     sutilibus: literally 'sewn together', like the boat at Virg. *Aen.* VI 414.

5   **Mausolea:** spondaic hexameters are comparatively rare in Martial (fourteen examples), and are used to accommodate unusual names or words. The fourth foot is always dactylic. See T. Birt in Friedlaender's edition, pp.40–41; Sullivan 228.
     The reference is most obviously (as at II 59 – see above) to the vast mausoleum built in the northern part of the Campus Martius by Augustus. It could

probably be seen from Martial's apartment on the Quirinal (for which, see on V
22.4). The plural may be taken to include the tomb of Julia, also on the
Campus Martius, where Julius Caesar was buried. (See Richardson, s.v.
Mausoleum Augusti.) One is tempted to think that it includes the Templum
Gentis Flaviae, which was built by Domitian, on the site of the house in which
he was born, as his family mausoleum, and to which Vespasian's and Titus's
ashes were probably transferred (Richardson, s.v.), as that must have been very
close to Martial's apartment, but this is unlikely as the temple is first referred to
only in Book IX.

65

Martial uses the magnificence of the shows put on by the emperor as an occasion for
flattery. His point of comparison is provided by Hercules, which enables him to pass
neatly from the destruction of ferocious creatures to the deification which was
Hercules's reward, and is foreseen as Domitian's. Hercules was generally seen as the
model of a mortal who achieved divine status (hence his role in Seneca's
Apocolocyntosis). The labours of Hercules were, of course, one of the corniest of
poetical topics, which helps to explain why Martial refers to them in such
extraordinarily recherché language.

Domitian presumably enjoyed being compared with Hercules (as Commodus did
later); hence his dedication of a temple to Hercules outside Rome with a statue
bearing his own features. This is commemorated by Martial at IX 64, 65 and 101:
the latter poem compares the deeds of Hercules unfavourably with those of
Domitian. This epigram also recalls *Spect.* 32, where Martial tells the emperor that
the feats of Carpophorus, who killed twenty wild beasts at once, excel those of
Hercules.

The entertainment of the people of Rome by means of shows was a vital element
of imperial propaganda: hence the construction by Vespasian and Titus of the
Amphitheatrum Flavium (the Colosseum), and the shows with which it was
launched, and hence Martial's *Liber Spectaculorum*, a book of poems about those
shows, whose own success as propaganda probably led to his receiving the *ius trium
liberorum* (privileges of a father of three), his titular tribunate, and so his equestrian
rank (see Introduction p. 1). See also Mart. I 6.

The *venationes* (hunting displays) referred to here may possibly have formed part
of the games put on in November 89 to celebrate Domitian's double triumph over the
Chatti and Dacians (Jones, *Domitian*, 151; G. Ville, *La Gladiature en Occident*
(Rome, 1981), 154).

1   **astra polumque:** this hendiadys is used again at VII 56.1. For *astra ... dedit*,
     cf. XIV 124.2; and for *astra* IX 65.10; 101.22.
     his stepmother's opposition: the enmity of Juno, angry because Jupiter had
     fathered Hercules on Alcmene, dogged him throughout his life. Hercules is
     called Alcides because his grandfather was Alceus.
2   **Nemees terror:** the same phrase is used of a lion at IX 71.7. *Nemees* is a
     Greek genitive (compare the accusative *Geryonen* in line 12). The Nemean
     lion is included in the list of exploits of Hercules surpassed by Domitian at IX

101.6, along with the Erymanthian boar. Erymanthus is a range of mountains in Arcadia.

3 The defeat and killing of the giant Antaeus was not one of the canonical Twelve Labours. He lived in Libya. The point of *castigatum* ('punished') is that he had the unsociable habit of forcing all comers to wrestle with him: after defeating them he killed them.

ceroma means the layer of mud which formed the wrestling ring. O. Reinmuth (*Phoenix* 21 (1967), 191f.) suggests that the word acquired this sense, from its former significance of a medicinal salve, because the wrestlers' bodies became smeared with the mud of the floor, and the word was then applied to the floor itself. The use of *ceroma* to stand for the wrestler himself is a bold metonymy.

4 Eryx was another wrestler overcome by Hercules: he was the son by Butes of Aphrodite, who had a famous shrine in west Sicily, where the mountain and town were named after him. See Virg. *Aen.* V 412–4.

5–6 The story of the monster Cacus, who lived on the Palatine Hill, and terrorised the district, until he made the mistake of stealing eight of Geryon's cattle from Hercules, who killed him, was told to Aeneas by Evander at *Aen.* VIII 184–275.

5 **was accustomed:** Martial humorously pretends that the trick which Cacus played on Hercules, when he dragged the cattle backwards into his cave so that their footprints would lead the wrong way (*Aen.* VIII 209–212), was habitual to him.

6 **non rectas:** despite the gender used here, Evander specifies that there were four bulls and four cows. The line recalls (but in this respect differs from) both Ov. *Fast.* I 550 (*traxerat aversos Cacus in antra ferox*) and Prop. IV 9.12 (*aversos cauda traxit in antra boves*).

7 **quota pars:** the phrase is used in similar eulogistic contexts at *Spect.* 34.3 and VIII 36.3; cf. *quanta ... portio* at *Spect.* 17.2.

8 **in the morning:** the fighting of wild beasts took place in the morning of show days: see Mart. XIII 95; Ov. *Met.* XI 26; Balsdon, *Life and Leisure*, 298; G. Ville, *La Gladiature en Occident* (Rome, 1981), 393.

9 For the Nemean lion, see on line 2.

10 **tua ... hasta:** the spear of the beast-fighter belonging to you .
Maenalian: Maenalus was a mountain-range in Arcadia, so the reference is the same as in line 2.
collocat: 'lays out', as a dead body.

11–12 Hercules had to go to the Far West, to the island of Erytheia, to steal cattle from the triple-bodied monster Geryon (cf. V 49.11). The latter is called *pastor* because of them, as at Ov. *Met.* IX 184–5 *pastoris Hiberi | forma triplex*. *pugna triplex* is an ingenious variation on Ovid's phrase.

12 **you have someone:** some editors take this to be a reference to the *bestiarius* Carpophorus, who is compared with Hercules at *Spect.* 17 and 32 (see also 26).

13–14 The Hydra was a monster which lived at Lerna, near Argos: it had seven heads, but as Hercules cut off each two more grew in its place. Hence the need for 'frequent counting'. The Hydra is mentioned at IX 101.9.

14 Crocodiles, presumably from Egypt, had first been shown at Rome in the games put on by M. Aemilius Scaurus in 58 BC, and thirty-six were killed at the games of 2 BC. See G. Jennison, *Animals for Show and Pleasure in Ancient Rome* (Manchester, 1937), 50, 64; Balsdon, *Life and Leisure*, 303, 305, 312f..

16   quickly: Hercules died a premature death through the poison of Nessus.
late: Horace had expressed the same wish to Augustus at *Carm.* I 2.45 *serus in caelum redeas* ('may you return late to heaven').

66

A social inferior would be expected to greet his social superior first: the distinguished lawyer Philippus was paying a compliment to the auctioneer Mena when he greeted him first at Hor. *Epist.* I 7.66 (*salvere iubet prior*), and Mena apologises for not having seen him in time to anticipate him. So the fact that Pontilianus never does so is a sign that he refuses to regard Martial as his social equal.

The importance of greeting, which would take the form *salve, Martialis*, is shown by the fact that rich men kept slaves called *nomenculatores* to remember the names of those with whom they were acquainted (cf. Mart. X 30.23; and see on V 21).

2   sic eris?: the punctuation is due to Housman, *CQ* 13 (1919), 71. *sic = talis*: Housman compares e.g. Ter. *Phorm.* 527 *sic sum: si placeo, utere*.
aeternum ... vale: Martial uses the words with which Aeneas made his last farewell to the dead Pallas (Virg. *Aen.* XI 98). Housman explains, 'You are to me as dead', comparing IX 6.4 *non vis, Afer, havere: vale* ('you don't want "good-day", Afer, so goodbye'.
Pontilianus: used twice elsewhere by Martial in satirical contexts. It is a very rare name (even the *nomen* Pontilius is rare).

67

The reference here is to the myth concerning the two daughters of Pandion, king of Athens (hence 'Attic birds'). Procne was married to Tereus, king of Thrace, who raped her sister Philomela and then cut out her tongue. Philomela wove the story into a tapestry, and Procne took revenge on Tereus by serving up their son Itys to him as a meal. When Tereus found out and chased them he was turned into a hoopoe, Philomela into a nightingale, and Procne into a swallow. (The earlier Greek version reverses these two.)

It is not unusual for a poet like Martial to base a poem on a novel idea about an old myth: what is remarkable here is that the 'lead-in' to this takes the form of what appears to be a direct observation of natural history. There was a belief in the ancient world that some swallows (or house-martins, which were not distinguished from swallows) did not migrate, but hibernated (Arist. *HA* 600 a 16; Plin. *HN* X 70), and this belief also existed in eighteenth-century England (see Gilbert White's letter to the Hon. Daines Barrington of February 12 1771, in his *Natural History of Selborne*).

However, it is inconceivable that a swallow could have overwintered even in Rome, according to Dr C.M. Perrins of the Edward Grey Institute of Field Ornithology at Oxford. He suggests two possible explanations:

1. The returning swallows found in the nest the remains of a fledgling from the previous year, pulled it out, and dropped it on the ground. They would certainly clean out the nest before reusing it. The problem about this is that the fledgling's remains would be so decayed that they would be unlikely to be mistaken for a freshly-dead bird.

2. If more than two birds fancy a particular nest, there is sometimes a fight in which one of them dies. However, as swallows have comparatively weak bills and legs, they are unlikely actually to kill each other.

F. Capponi (*Ornithologia Latina* (Genova, 1979), 297 n.10) argues that there is some evidence that swallows might, in exceptional and rare cases, hibernate: he does not refer to this passage.

4 deserter: a deliberately paradoxical word, since this bird 'deserted' its companions by staying behind.

5–6 Martial means that the murderous disposition of swallows goes back to Procne, who deserved to suffer the fate she inflicted on her son.

68

The Romans greatly admired blond hair, which explains why even Dido is described by Virgil as having *flaventis comas* (*Aen.* IV 590). So, if a woman was to wear a wig (cf. Martial VI 12.1; XII 23.1), she would be likely to buy a blond one, as Ovid's girl did after her attempts at dyeing her own mousy hair led to disaster (*Am.* I 14). Hers was made with hair from Germany (line 45). Blond hair was regarded as characteristic of Germans (Juv. 13.164–5; cf. Mart. V 37.7–8). Martial's epigram plays on the reader's initial assumption that Lesbia has been sent a blond wig because her hair is *not* blond.

1 Arctoa: this epithet first occurs in Seneca's tragedies, and is often used in epic. The pompous effect adds to the humour here.

Lesbia: Martial uses the name seven times, always in erotic contexts. He obviously borrows it from Catullus. The use of this name suggests to Shackleton Bailey (Loeb) that Martial must have a satirical motive: 'perhaps ... she dyes her hair to excess'.

69

Martial compares the crimes of Antony and of Pompey's murderer Pothinus also at III 66: his point there is that Antony is more guilty because Pothinus did the deed for the benefit of 'his master', whereas Antony did it for himself. The similarity between the two deaths lay partly in the fact that each man was beheaded, and partly in the widespread horror aroused by their brutality.

Epigrams dealing with historical subjects are not uncommon in the *Greek Anthology* from the Hellenistic period onwards, but Martial wrote them comparatively rarely: there are three examples in Book I (13, 21, 42), and cf. II 80; III 66; V 74; VI 32. He probably felt that the stock *exempla virtutis* had become hackneyed – above all through their frequent use in rhetoric.

The rhetorical origin of this poem is indicated by the dramatic device of the direct address to Antony, and the two indignant questions he is asked, leading up to the final paradoxical hyperbole.

The theme of Seneca's *Suasoria* 6 is whether Cicero should beg Antony for mercy: his murder is compared with that of Pompey (see also Sen. *Tranq.* 16.1). In his *Controversia* 7, C. Popillius Laenas is accused of immorality because, despite having been acquitted on a charge of parricide when defended by Cicero, he nevertheless murdered him. Popillius is named as the military tribune who did the deed by Appian (*BCiv.* IV 19–20). He mentions that Cicero had defended him, but Seneca (*Contr.* 7.2.8) admits that the story that the charge was parricide was an invention of the declaimers, who (as in this *Controversia*) liked to contrast this with his later murder of the 'father of his country'. Plutarch names the murderer as the centurion Herennius (*Cic.* 48).

1   **Phario:** this epithet is used, as a metrically convenient equivalent to 'Egyptian', several times by Latin poets (see *OLD* s.v.). Pharos was the name of the island off Alexandria on which stood the famous light-house.

      Pothinus: the eunuch tutor of the boy Ptolemy XII, who, after the death of the latter's father Ptolemy Auletes in 51, was *de facto* regent, and as such was responsible in September 48 for giving the order for the murder of Pompey. The deed was carried out by Achillas and Septimius.

2   **tabula:** for the sense 'proscription list', cf. e.g. Sen. *Suas.* 6.3; Juv. 2.28. The notion that the murder of Cicero was a worse crime than the deaths of all the others proscribed by the Triumvirs in 43 BC is a characteristic rhetorical hyperbole.

3   **against the mouth of Rome:** in the sense that when Cicero spoke Rome spoke: cf. III 66.4 *hoc tibi, Roma, caput, cum loquereris, erat* ('this was your head, Rome, when you spoke'). **ora** is plural for singular.

      Romanā stringis: in his note on Catullus 64.357, Fordyce points out that the treatment of a final open vowel before a combination of s and another consonant presented a problem to Latin poets. It is more common for such vowels to be left short than for them to be lengthened (see M. Platnauer, *Latin Elegiac Verse* (Cambridge, 1951), 62–3).

      Professor M. Willcock suggests that *Romanā ... in ora* might mean 'on the Roman shore', which avoids the metrical oddity. The fact that Pompey was murdered on the shore is well-known. Cicero was murdered at Caieta, on the coast of Latium, while being carried from his villa towards the sea (Plut. *Cic.* 47–8; App. *BCiv* IV 19).

4   In fact, Cicero had accused Catiline (*Cat.* I 15) of making numerous attempts on his life while he was both *consul designatus* and consul. He may well have been exaggerating. The point here is to get in a reference to Cicero's 'finest hour'.

      nec = *ne ... quidem:* cf. V 62.5.

5   According to Appian, Antony rewarded Popillius with 250,000 Attic drachmae. Martial rhetorically implies that Popillius was bribed in advance.

impius infando: the accumulation of condemnatory words (*nocens, demens, nefas*) reaches an alliterative climax.

6 The contrast of *tantis* with *una* leads to the scornful *tibi* – 'just for your sake'.

7 **silentia:** the plural is a poeticism found almost exclusively in epic, and usually applied to the night (see Kissel on Persius 3.81). Note its combination here with the unexpected epithet *pretiosa*; the eulogistic description of Cicero's tongue as *sacra*; and the alliteration *prosunt ... pretiosa*, which emphasises the pointlessness of the expenditure.

8 Cicero may be silent, but now everyone else will speak, and Antony's revenge will be in vain. The rhetorical exercises referred to above do indeed combine praise of Cicero with vituperation of Antony.

70

The diminutive form of the name Syriscus suggests that the man had been a favourite slave of his master, which might explain why he benefited so remarkably from his generosity (perhaps as a gift when he was freed, perhaps as a legacy). The amount is, of course, implausibly large, which adds to the effect of the poem.

1 **infusum:** 'showered upon him'. For this sense, see *OLD* s.v. 3a; Sen. *Ep.* 81.14 *divitiae in domum infusae*; Plin. *HN* XXIX 8; [Quint.] *Decl. Mai.* 12.6.
patron: a slave technically had no father, so when he was freed his former master became his *patronus* or father-substitute.

2 **plenum ... centies:** understand *centena milia sestertium* (= *sestertiorum*). The numeral came to be used colloquially as if it were a neuter substantive. Cf. Mart. I 99.1 *plenum ... vicies*.
Maximus: possibly a real person, but the name is extremely common ('less distinctive than "Smith" in English' – P. White, *Historia* 22 (1973), 300 n.16).
Syriscus: Syrus is a common slave-name (e.g. in comedy), probably no longer necessarily designating a Syrian.

3 **sit-down bars:** *popinae* were fairly crude establishments for the sale of food and drink: cf. V 44.10, and see T. Kleberg, *Hotels, Restaurants et Cabarets dans l'Antiquité Romaine* (Uppsala, 1957), 114; G. Hermansen, *Ostia: Aspects of Roman City Life* (Edmonton, 1982), 192–5. The epithet must indicate that customers ate and drank sitting down, as opposed to reclining as they would on a *triclinium*. Some inns did provide *triclinia*. The one at the sign of the elephant in the Vico del Lupanare in Pompeii had a sign boasting that it had one (*CIL* IV 807). The hostess in the *Copa* urges the guest to recline on a couch (lines 5–6, 29), and the legate at Juv. 8.171f. will be found in a *popina* at Ostia lying alongside a rum crew of fellow-drinkers. However, others did not: some excavated bars have no room for seating, while others (such as the one illustrated by Meiggs, *Roman Ostia*, plate XXIXa) have open-air stone benches. The wall-paintings from Pompeii reproduced by Kleberg (figs. 13–15) show travellers drinking while seated at small tables. The epithet *sellariola* presumably indicates this type of *popina*, which would have been of inferior status. The diminutive occurs only here (compare *ancillariolus* and *lecticariola* in XII 58), as does the adjectival use of *sellarius*.

4 **bath-establishments:** the 7th century writer Isidore links *popinae* with baths (*Etym.* XV 2.42), and cf. e.g. Mart. XII 19. Meiggs argues that the profit from food and drink must, in view of the low entrance charges, have been what made it worthwhile to run private baths (*Roman Ostia*, 417). Quintilian says that drinking in the baths (*in balneis perpotare*) is a bad habit (*Inst.* I 6.44; cf. also Sen. *Ep.* 122.6).

four: it is not easy to understand why the figure is so specific. Presumably Syriscus divided his time between four establishments.

peregit: for this sense, cf. Pers. 6.22.

6 **not even ... reclining:** the point, which unexpectedly substitutes criticism of poor taste for moral reprobation, is saved for the final word. At 'proper' meals, the Romans would recline on couches. Martial professes to be shocked that Syriscus could not even manage this degree of decency.

71

Faustinus was a wealthy friend of Martial, and is addressed or referred to by him sympathetically nineteen times between Books I and X. He had several villas, including ones at Tibur (Tivoli), Baiae, and Terracina. See I 25; V 32; 36.

The epigram recalls IV 57, where Martial says that he is too hot at Baiae at the time of the Lion, and so will join Faustinus at Tivoli.

Faustinus's name is saved up here for the fifth line, and the poem concludes with a characteristic paradox.

1 **summittit:** 'has lying below it'; see *OLD* s.v. 7.

Trebula: there were five places of this name in Italy, but it is likely that this one is the Sabine town Trebula Suffenas, on the site of the modern Ciciliano in Lazio. This is situated at a height of 619 metres, about 12 km. due west of Tivoli, and the same distance WNW of Subiaco. It is at the centre of a mountainous area, with rivers flowing in valleys to the west and north. It would obviously be even cooler than Tivoli, which is at a height of only 225m. See F. Coarelli, *Lazio* (Guide archeologiche Laterza, Rome, 1982), 117–120.

2 **the Crab:** the zodiacal sign at the time of the summer solstice.

3 **Cleonaean:** compare IV 60.2. Cleonae was a town in the Argolid near Nemea (cf. V 65.2). The epithet was used, in the same position in the line, by Lucan (IV 612 *ille Cleonaei proiecit terga leonis*). Leo is the next zodiacal sign after Cancer: it is humorously personified as a Herculean monster.

4 **Aeolian:** Aeolus was god of the winds. The meaning of this line is not clear. For the sense of *amica*, *TLL* compares Hor. *Carm.* II 6.18–19 *amicus Aulon fertili Baccho* ('Aulon which is friendly to fertile Bacchus'), and Columella *Rust.* III 1.10 *vinea ... solo sicco quam pluvioso est amicior* ('the vine is more friendly to dry than to rainy soil'). What, however, is meant by 'friendly to a wind'? The answer must depend on whether the wind specified is beneficial or not. According to the *Guida del Touring Club Italiano* to Lazio, in the hot season the SW and NW (Mistral) winds alternate with the scirocco, which predominates in September. The latter would not be welcome, but the SW wind no doubt would be, so perhaps it is best to understand the phrase as meaning that the house is friendly to *Notus* in the sense that the latter cools it pleasantly. However, it may be relevant that there are high mountains to the SW of Ciciliano. According to L.R. Taylor ('Trebula Suffenas and the Plautii Silvani', *Memoirs of the American Academy at Rome*, 24 (1956), 13), 'the cool summer climate [Martial] praises is still a matter of pride with the inhabitants'.

6   Tivoli was especially celebrated as a summer resort: cf. e.g. IV 57.9–10.

72

When Bacchus's mother Semele was destroyed by the thunderbolts of Jupiter, the foetus was placed by him in his thigh until it reached its term. In the *Metamorphoses* (IV 12), Ovid had described Bacchus as *satumque iterum solumque bimatrem* ('born a second time, and the only one to have two mothers'). He was following the author of Middle Comedy Alexis, who had called Bacchus διμάτωρ Βρόμιος (fr. 283): Alexis himself is thought to have taken the phrase from a lyric or tragic poet.

Presumably a more recent poet had actually called Jupiter Bacchus's mother: such hyperbole would be by no means untypical of Silver Latin mythological poetry.

1   **Tonantem:** 'the Thunderer' – see on V 16.5.
2   **Semelen:** the Greek accusative.
     Rufe: a very common name. As often in Martial, the vocative interrupts the flow and prepares for the final punch-word.

73

Naturally people often asked Martial to give them copies of his works (e.g. I 117; IV 72). The joking reply here is as much in the manner of Catullus as the way in which the last line repeats the first with subtle alteration. The theme recurs at VII 3.

3   **Theodorus:** the name is used for a bad poet also at XI 93, where Kay comments ' "God's gift to poetry", with unveiled sarcasm'.

74

Of Pompey's two sons, the elder, Gnaeus, was killed at Miletus in Asia Minor, by an officer of M. Antonius, while the younger, Sextus, was executed in 45 BC after the battle of Munda in Spain. For the death of their father, see V 69.

The manner of this epigram is highly rhetorical. It recalls a passage in the *Bellum Civile* of Petronius (*Sat.* 120, lines 61–66) on the burial places of the First Triumvirate (Crassus in Parthia; Pompey in 'Libya'; Julius in Rome). Lucan also makes the point that Pompey's worldwide fame is such that he needs no tomb (VIII 793–9).

Two groups of epigrams in the *Anthologia Latina* deal with the same theme as Martial (396–9 and 452–4 in Shackleton Bailey's edition; 400–403 and 454–6 in Riese's). 398 ends (lines 5–6) *divisa ruina est: uno non potuit tanta iacere solo*, and there are several other similarities (compare especially 397.2; 399; 454). The old attribution of these poems to Seneca is now regarded as implausible: it is more likely that they are borrowing from Martial.

2   Libyes: the Greek genitive. *Libya* is often used by the poets for Africa.
    if any earth: it was not certain that Pompey had even been buried.
4   ruina: with its full sense of 'collapse'.

<h1 style="text-align:center">75</h1>

The law referred to here must be the *Lex Iulia de adulteriis coercendis*, Augustus's law against adultery, which had been introduced in 18 BC or soon after (see S. Treggiari, *Roman Marriage* (Oxford, 1991), 277f.). Domitian reintroduced the law, in virtue of the censorial powers which he had assumed in 85 (see Introduction, p.), and several epigrams in Book VI relate to this. VI 7 states that not more than thirty days have passed since the law was reenacted (*renata*, line 1): it would therefore seem likely that this epigram must have been one of the last written for Book V, and VI 7 one of the first written for Book VI.

Presumably Quintus and Laelia had been having an adulterous affair, but now one (or both) has obtained a divorce, so that they can marry.

Too much has been made by some recent authors (particularly J. Garthwaite, *Prudentia* 22 (1990), 13–22) of the apparent inconsistency between Martial's praise of Domitian for reintroducing the law (VI 2; 4) and his humorous poems about people who made a farce of it (e.g. VI 7; 22; 45; 91). As Treggiari rightly comments (224 n.84), Martial is 'chiefly interested in jokes, not moralising', and NB I 4.7 *innocuos censura potest permittere lusus* ('censorship can permit harmless fun'). B.W. Jones suggests that in any case the main reason why Domitian revived the various moral laws was his desire to remedy the financial crisis by means of the fines imposed (*Domitian*, 76).

1   Laelia: the name is used twice elsewhere by Martial. At X 68 she is a Roman matron of decent birth.
    Quintus: a common *praenomen* (cf. V 21).
2   uxorem ... legitimam: for this phrase, cf. Ov. *Ars Am.* II 545.

<h1 style="text-align:center">76</h1>

A comic and unexpected use of a story from Roman history. Mithridates VI, King of Pontus, fought three wars against the Romans in the early first century BC. He had good reason to fear poisoning, since oriental rulers were frequently at risk from their own families or rivals. Pliny (*HN* XXV 6) tells how he drank poison every day, after taking the appropriate antidotes. According to Gellius (*NA* XVII 16), when finally defeated he tried in vain to commit suicide by means of poison, and had to have recourse to his sword.

Martial's irony here can be compared with that of Catullus 23, where Furius is congratulated on the blessings that result from his poverty.

2   toxica ... saeva: Martial uses this phrase of bad wine at I 18.6; X 36.4.
4   Cinna: see on V 57. Attacks on poor men are not uncommon: compare Catullus 21 and 24, in addition to 23 (see above); Mart. I 92; XI 32; XII 32. But maybe Cinna is just mean.

77

The meaning of this epigram has been much discussed, but the best explanation was provided by Erasmus (*Opera Omnia* (Amsterdam), II.1 (1993), 540 – *Adagiorum Chilias Prima* no. 463). He pointed out that oil was put into the ear for medicinal purposes, either to encourage water to flow out, or to prevent water from getting in: a man with oil in his ear would incline his head to prevent it from flowing out. He suggested that this gesture might be adopted by a man who did not want to listen to someone else, and (according to the important discussion by G.C. Kuiper in *Humanistica Lovaniensia* 39 (1990), 67–84) supported this by an oblique reference to Mart. VI 42.22–3, where the poet rebukes the man addressed with the words:

> non adtendis et aure me supina
> iam dudum quasi neglegenter audis

('you aren't paying attention, and for a long time now you have been listening to me with ear tilted back').

For this use of *supinus*, compare Mart. V 8.10, and also Plin. *HN* XX 158 *naribus supinis* (the nostrils thrust backwards to stop medicinal juice from flowing out).

The insertion of different kinds of oil into the ear for various medicinal purposes is recommended by Celsus (*Med.* VI 7) and Pliny (*HN* XXIII 73, 83, 85–6, 88, 92, 95). Doctors still prescribe the use of olive oil in order to soften wax in the ear.

Erasmus also suggested that the phrase might refer to flatterers, who as it were drip oil into the ear, but pointed out that this would require the reading *in auriculam*. Kuiper shows that some editors (including now Shackleton Bailey in his Loeb edition) have misrepresented Erasmus. He argues that, although Erasmus identified *oleum in auricula ferre* as a proverbial expression, he seems to have had doubts about this, and rightly, since, if it were a well-known expression, it would hardly have been reckoned to be 'a neat remark'.

Many other explanations have been proposed, mostly preposterous. Interpretation has not been assisted by the *lemma* (title) given to the epigram in the MSS of the β family, *ad marullum pedarisiam*. These *lemmata* are generally considered to go back to the edition made by Torquatus Gennadius in AD 401. This one is obviously corrupt, and no attempt at emendation is at all plausible.

1   **narratur ... dixisse ... dixit:** somewhat pleonastic for Martial.
     belle: strictly the diminutive of *bonus*, this word is usually ironical in Martial: compare II 7 and III 63. Here, however, it is a colloquialism.
2   **Marullus:** this quite common *cognomen* is used only here in Martial (but cf. *Marulla* VI 39; X 55; *Marullinus* IV 70.3).

78

Invitation poems are common enough. They are described by Nisbet and Hubbard (on Hor. *Carm.* I 20) as 'a minor category of Hellenistic epigram'. It was conventional that the simplicity of the meal should be emphasised. A well-known example is Hor. *Ep.* I 5: that poem also combines the element of compliment to the person addressed with humorous depreciation of the comparatively humble fare which is all that the poet can afford. However, it would be a mistake to think that what Martial is offering is an unappetising meal, even though it may lack the expensive meat or fish, the exotic sauces, the rare mushrooms, and so on, which a rich man might serve up. And, as often, the pleasant company and relaxed atmosphere will make up for any deficiencies in the menu. See Kay on XI 52, and Courtney's introduction to Juvenal 11 (which, as he points out, owes much to Mart. V 78 and X 48). On the foods served, see J. André, *L'Alimentation et la Cuisine à Rome* (Paris, 1961).

The poem is discussed by E. Gowers, *The Loaded Table* (Oxford, 1993), 250–255. Her interpretation may be found appealing by those who consider it unimaginative to take an author at his own words.

1   **domicenium:** this is apparently a word invented by Martial, used elsewhere only at XII 77.6. The Greeks had a word for it – μονοσιτεῖν. It is a satirical commonplace that having to eat at home was 'the ultimate indignity for the client' (or parasite): see Kay on Mart. XI 24.15; Juv. 1.132–4. Hence *tristi* and *laboras.*
     Toranius: addressed in the preface to Book IX as *frater carissime*, he is otherwise unknown.
     esurire: contrary to expectation for *cenare.*

3   **προπίνειν:** here 'drink before the meal' (although the word often means 'toast'). This fashion only came in under Tiberius, according to Pliny (*HN* XIV 143), who did not approve. With the *gustatio*, or hors d'oeuvre, described in lines 4–5, *mulsum* (honey-wine) was usually drunk.

4   **Cappadocian:** a type of lettuce. At XIII 14 Martial wonders why, when 'our ancestors' used to eat lettuces at the end of their meals, we eat them at the beginning.
     overpowering leeks: at XIII 18 leeks are described as *graviter olentia* ('strong-smelling'). For recipes, see Apic. III 10. Lettuces and leeks also form part of the *gustatio* at X 48.9 and at XI 52.5–6.

5   At the same meals, the *gustatio* includes, in one case, lizard-fish crowned with chopped eggs, and in the other mackerel garnished with eggs. The regular appearance of eggs as part of the *gustatio* explains the proverbial expression *ab ovo usque ad mala* ('from the egg to the apples', e.g. Hor. *Serm.* I 3.6–7). At Juv. 5.84 the poor client is served with *dimidio constrictus cammarus ovo* ('a crayfish closed in by a halved egg').
     cybium: Greek κυβίον, the flesh of the πηλαμύς (young tunny) salted in cubes (André, 113). Its cheapness is indicated by the nickname given by the Alexandrians to Vespasian, because of his meanness – Cybiosactes ('the tunny-fish packer').
     lie hid: humorous – the eggs make it hard to recognise.

6–10 The main course.
     to be held with greasy fingers: the Romans did not, of course, use forks. Slaves would bring water for hand-washing at intervals. The broccoli is served with oil, as at Hor. *Serm.* II 3.125; 6.64.

7   The colour-contrast is striking. The black earthenware dish would have been comparatively cheap, though the black colour would have been unusual in Italy: it was presumably made by firing a clay slip coloured with an iron compound (see D. Brown in *Roman Crafts*, ed. D. Strong and D. Brown (London, 1976), 87f.). The *coliculus* (diminutive of *caulis*) will have been broccoli, or something similar. For recipes, see, Apic. III 9.2–6: he despised them. They were quite expensive (André, 24). *virens* (green) presumably indicates that *nitra* (some sort of alkali) had been put into the water: Mart. XIII 17 recommends this, to prevent cabbage from going 'disgustingly pale' (cf. Juv. 5.87).

8   **cool garden:** no doubt sheltered and well-watered. The cabbage would be fresh.

9   **botellus:** diminutive of *botulus*, which is identified by André (151) as blood-pudding. Apicius gives a recipe (II 3.2), which involves stuffing an intestine with eggs, nuts, pine-nuts, onion, leek, sauce, pepper, fish-sauce, and wine. It may seem surprising that no blood is included (though André, in his edition of Apicius, argues that blood-pudding would be out of place in the refined cookery of Apicius), and no meat either, but at XIII 35 the *Lucanica* (a word still used in Italy for a type of sausage) is described as 'daughter of a Picenian sow'. It too 'crowns' snow-white *puls*. This was a kind of polenta or porridge, made from a type of wheat (*alica* or *simila*, Apic. V 1.1–4). Originally a traditional basic food (hence Plautus's *pultiphagus* for a Roman, *Most.* 828, and cf. Juv. 11.58–9), it changed character when bread supplanted it, and was mixed with meat or spices (André, 62f.; 147).
niveam again emphasises the colour-contrast, as does *rubente* in the next line, with *pallens*.

10   **bacon:** some meat at last, though hardly of a sophisticated sort. Home-cured bacon was served, along with vegetables from their garden, by Philemon and Baucis (Ov. *Met.* VIII 646–50). The combination of beans and bacon is mentioned by Horace at *Serm.* II 6.63–4 as a desirable country meal, and cf. ib. 2.117. For a recipe for *lardum* (or *laridum*) see Apic. VII 11.

11   The *mensae secundae* were the dessert.

12   **shrivelling grapes:** grapes not fully ripe at the vintage were left to be picked later, and would be sweeter. They were preserved for eating, by methods described by Pliny (*HN* XIV 16; see also André, 91). They were not dried, like raisins, but naturally shrivelled to some extent. For such grapes as part of the dessert, see Mart. I 43.3.

13   'Syrian' pears (Virg. *G.* II 88) were a variety which originated in Syria, but were grown specially at Tarentum: hence Martial's description, for which compare Columella V 10.18 *Tarentina quae Syria dicuntur.* He includes them among the best varieties, as does Pliny (*HN* XV 53). See Juv. 11.73, with Courtney's note. Pears also appear at Mart. I 43.5.

14–15   Chestnuts, offered by Tityrus along with apples and cheese at Virg. *Ecl.* 1.81, are not often mentioned by Roman writers, though Ovid suggests them as a gift for girls, along with grapes (*Ars Am.* II 267). Pliny (*HN* XV 92 f.) describes them as *vilissima* ('extremely cheap'), and thinks that the best way to eat them is roasted, and ground up. Athenaeus (54d) quotes Diphilus as saying that chestnuts are easier to digest when roasted, but less filling; boiled ones are less flatulent and more nourishing than roasted ones. See André, 85. Clausen interprets Virgil's epithet *molles* (*Ecl.* 1.81) as 'soft and mealy', and suggests that they were roasted over a slow fire like those referred to here by Martial.

16   This polite compliment is intended to compensate for what was obviously an ordinary sort of wine. A similar remark is made twice by Trimalchio. At Petr. *Sat.* 39.2 he tells his guests *hoc vinum vos oportet suave faciatis* ('it is up to you to make this wine sweet'). The wine here is not specified, but at 48.1 it comes from one of his own estates (on the borders of Terracina and Tarentum – some 220 miles apart!), and he says that he will change it if they don't like it: *vos illud oportet bonum faciatis* ('it's up to you to make it good').

17–21   After the meal, the guests drink, but the drinking may stimulate their appetites again.

20   Olives from Picenum (on the Adriatic coast) were, and still are, highly prized. Pliny (*HN* XV 16) says that this was because of their size. Olives could be eaten as part of the *gustatio* or as dessert (Mart.I 43.8; XIII 36).

21   These rather substantial foods are more surprising as snacks to accompany post-prandial drinking, but at the grand dinner which Habinnas had just attended (Petr. *Sat.* 66.4) the dessert included *cicer et lupinum* surrounded by hazel-nuts and apples. *cicer* was boiled, or sometimes fried (or rather roasted), chickpeas (a sort of pease-pudding). It was sold hot in the streets, very cheaply: see I 41.6; 103.10; André, 37–8. Lupin-seeds are referred to by Martial only here. According to Pliny, they were eaten steeped in hot water (*HN* XVIII 136). They too were a cheap food, sold in the streets (André, 39).

23–4   The promise that conversation would be frank but private was often an important feature of invitation poems. Compare Mart. X 48. 21–25, where the guests are assured that there will be no conversation of the sort that they will regret next day: they will talk about chariot-racing. Similarly at Hor. *Ep.* I 5.24–5 the author promises to make sure that no-one present will repeat anything said later, and Pliny (*Ep.* I 15.4) tells a friend: *potes apparatius cenare apud multos, nusquam hilarius, simplicius, incautius* ('you can dine more lavishly with many others, but nowhere with more cheerfulness, openness, or freedom from anxiety'). Seneca (*Ben.*III 26f.) tells two stories of men who almost got into trouble because of risky talk while under the influence of drink.

24   **vultu tuo:** see on V 6.10.

25   Similarly at XI 52.16 Martial promises his literary friend Cerialis *plus ego polliceor: nil recitabo tibi* ('I promise you more: I shall recite nothing to you'). See Kay *ad loc.*, who compares *Anth. Pal.* XI 10 (Lucillius). At III 45 and 50 Martial attacks a man who only invites people to dinner to get an audience for his awful poems. Compare also VII 51.13f.; Petr. *Sat.* 68.4–5; Plin. *Ep.* I 15.2; III 1.9; Juv. 11.180–2.

26   At *Ep.* I 15.3 Pliny teases Septicius, who failed to turn up to dinner, by saying that he must have preferred someone else's more exotic fare and *Gaditanae* ('girls from Cadiz'), and at 11. 162–76 Juvenal assures Persicus that, if he is expecting a troupe of sexy Spanish dancing-girls in his own humble home, then he is looking in the wrong place. Juvenal takes the word *prurire* from Martial (cf. XIV 203.1), and describes how the girls *ad terram tremulo descendunt* *clune* ('sink to the ground with trembling hips'). See Mart. I 41.12 with my note, quoting Richard Ford's description of nineteenth-century Spanish 'Olé' dancers; A,T. Fear, *Greece and Rome* 38 (1991), 75–9.

27 **sine fine:** there must be a play on the sexual sense of *finis* ('climax'), for which see Mart. IX 69.1; Juv. 7.241; J.N. Adams, *The Latin Sexual Vocabulary* (London, 1982), 143 n.l; 144. The Spanish girls only frustrate their guests (compare XIV 203). The phrase *sine fine prurientes* occurs also at *Priap.* 26.4.

28 **lumbos:** for this word, see Adams 48; 194.

30 **Condylus:** presumably a slave musician of Martial, and so perhaps the slave advised by him not to seek his freedom at IX 92. Music was a normal accompaniment of a meal, but more commonly took the form of singing. At IX 77 Martial defines the best dinner-party as one at which no *choraules* (see on V 56.9) is present, but that implies the presence of a chorus. Quintilian (I 10.20) describes the playing of lyres and *tibiae* as a feature of 'old Roman dinner-parties'.

κόνδυλος in Greek means 'knuckle'. It is rarely used as a name, but is obviously appropriate for a *tibia*-player.

31–2 Claudia must be a woman invited by Martial: he asks Toranius what female guest he would like him to invite. The order of guests then is: Toranius's woman-friend; Martial; Claudia; Toranius. This is the explanation of Shackleton Bailey, based on that of J.B. Greenough in *HSCP* 1 (1890), 191–2. All other interpretations are more or less nonsensical. Shackleton Bailey compares for the word *sequor* Sid. Apoll. *Epist.* I 11.10; and, for *priorem*, *superiores* in Plaut. *Most.* 42.

79

The pretentious Zoilus is so proud of his many dinner-suits that he keeps changing them on spurious grounds of health. The first couplet explains the situation, and the second gives Zoilus's justification. In the third, the teasing enquiry leads to the comically illogical conclusion.

1 **surrexti =** *surrexisti*: Martial often uses this syncopated form.

Zoilus: Martial's use of this name is interesting: see Kay on XI 12. It was a common slave name, but also recalls the much-reviled Homeric critic. There are Zoilus 'cycles' in Books II and XI, and this is one of five other appearances: 'his character as a *nouveau riche* is developed' (Kay).

2 **synthesis:** a matching suit of tunic and *pallium*, worn at dinner-parties, and especially associated with the Saturnalia (XIV 1.1). For an illustration of a reconstruction, see L.M. Wilson, *The Clothing of the Ancient Romans* (Baltimore , 1938), fig. 51. It could be coloured: Martial mentions a green one at X 29.4, and cf. II 46.4 *sic micat innumeris arcula synthesibus* ('your clothes-chest glitters with innumerable dinner-suits').

4 **laxam tenuis:** it is not easy to explain the exact sense of either epithet. *laxus*, used of parts of the body, means 'relaxed', 'loose' (*OLD*). Shackleton Bailey refers it to 'open pores'. *tenuis* is commonly used of air (' thin air'). However, the combination of the two strengthens the impression of idle effeminacy.

6   At IV 66.4 Martial quizzes a man who, in his frugal small-town life, made one
        synthesis last ten summers.

80

Martial compliments two literary friends of his by asking them to look over his book
and criticise it. Compare IV 86 (also near the end of its book). For Severus, see on
V 11. Secundus may be the Caecilius Secundus addressed at VII 84, where he has
commissioned a portrait of Martial, and is said to be serving in the army on the
Danube. Martial describes him as a 'dear friend' (*carus sodalis*). It is unlikely that
he is Pliny.

The style is mostly colloquial, but in the last lines it rises to form a grander
conclusion.

1–2 Shackleton Bailey rightly puts a comma after *dones*, so that this is taken as the
        subjunctive of polite request, and *licet* governs only *imputes*.
        si vacabis: for this conversational idiom, cf. Juv. 1.21 si *vacat ac placidi
        rationem admittitis, edam*: Hor. *Epist.* II 2.95 *si forte vacas, sequere et procul
        audi*; Plin. *Ep.* III 18.4.
        imputes: cf. V 20.13.
3   **nugas:** the word used by Catullus to refer to his poems at 1.4 – also in a
        context of humorous self-disparagement.
        exigisque: for this sense, cf. Mart. IV 82.2; Quint. I 5.19; *TLL* s.v. 1463.14f..
4   **ferias:** the word is often used of days when legal business was suspended, so
        this word and *disertus* in line 6 suggest that Severus and Secundus practised in
        the courts. Martial often claims that his poetry is particularly suited for holiday
        reading, but his friends are being asked here to do more than just enjoy it.
7   **improbi:** often used in the sense of asking for more than is one's due – see
        OLD s.v. 4.
9   **its master:** since the book 'belongs to' its author, it can be compared with a
        slave. The most celebrated example of this is Hor. *Epist.* I 20, and it is frequent
        in Ovid's *Tristia* (e.g. I 1.2). In his numerous poems addressing his books
        Martial several times plays on the idea (e.g. I 3.9; 52.6; 53.2; 66.9).
10   The idea is presumably that the book will not be afraid of ending up, not just
        dead like Sisyphus, but also having wasted its time. Sisyphus had to roll a
        stone up a hill, down which it always rolled back. For his labour in the
        proverbial sense, compare e.g. Prop. II 17.7; 20.32. The name *Sisyphi* makes a
        piquant alliterative contrast with *Severo* and *Secundi*.
11   **marble:** an exotic way of referring to Sisyphus's rock.
12–13 censoria ... lima: the *lima* as an implement of literary criticism goes back to
        Cicero (*Brut.* 93; *De Or.* I 180) and Horace (*Ars P.* 291 *limae labor*); *Serm.* I
        10.65), and it is strikingly combined with an epithet suggesting the moral
        supervision of the Roman censor. (Cf. Quint. I 4.3 for this sense.)
        momorderit is colourful both in assonance with *lima* and in its vivid sense
        (literally 'bite').

81

The idea that only those already rich benefit from the generosity of their fellows is familiar from Juvenal (e.g. 3. 208–222). It is not surprising that this poem appealed to Samuel Johnson, who used it as the motto for the number of *The Rambler* (October 19 1751) in which he deplored the neglect of merit when it was associated with poverty.

The verbal dexterity of the epigram is remarkable: the opening triplets of words correspond neatly, then comes the name, and the last line is marked by chiastic alliteration.

1 **Aemilianus:** this very common name was used by Martial also at I 50.
2 **nullis:** for this rare substantival use, compare e.g. Sen. *Ep.* 73.1 *nulli adversus illos gratiores sunt, nec inmerito: nullis enim plus praestant ...*; also Nipperdey's note on Tac. *Ann.* II 77. For the variant reading *nulli* (TDX), Heraeus compares Hor. *Sat.* I 4.73 *nec recito cuiquam nisi amicis.*

82

The theme is related to that of the previous epigram. As often, Martial is particularly disgusted by the pretentious deceitfulness of a man who boasts about the scale of his future gifts, but fails to deliver.

The construction is neat, with three questions followed by an imprecation and a dismissive insult. In the first question, the second half of the pentameter picks up the second half of the hexameter. The third question is emphasised by the indignant *rogo.*

1 **Gaurus:** the Greek name, which was rare at Rome, may be used here with reference to its meaning ('pompous'), but this is not so in the other poems where it appears (II 89; IV 67; VIII 27; IX 50). Greek names suggest freedmen.
   two hundred thousand (sesterces): this was half the property qualification for the equestrian order, and so a very large sum.
2 Meanness would be even worse than boastfulness.
4 The sense of the first three words is not clear. Shackleton Bailey punctuates *i tibi, dispereas,* and suggests that *i tibi* may be the equivalent of 'get along with you', but he admits that there are no parallels. Heraeus suggested that *tibi dispereas* was a comic inversion of *tibi vivas,* in the sense of 'live for yourself, for your own benefit': for this sense cf. Ter. *Ad.* 865 *sibi vixit*; Hor. *Epist.* I 18.107–8 *mihi vivam, quod superest aevi*; Ov. *Tr.* III 4.5 *vive tibi. disperiam si non ...* is a colloquialism of which Martial is fond ('damn me if I don't ...'): compare e.g. I 39.8.
   pusillus: at I 9 and III 62.7–8 this word is contrasted with *magnus.* The diminutive form of the word intensifies the disparagement.

83

The paradox of the lover who scorns an excessively easy conquest formed the subject of a celebrated epigram by Callimachus (*Anth. Pal.* XII 102) where the poet compared himself to a huntsman pursuing a hare. Martial's immediate Latin source is Ov. *Am.* II 19.36 *quod sequitur, fugio; quod fugit, ipse sequor* ('I run away from what follows me; I follow what runs away'). Very similar, however, is an epigram by Strato (*Anth. Pal.* XII 203):

Οὐκ ἐθέλοντα φιλεῖς με, φιλῶ δ' ἐγὼ οὐκ ἐθέλοντα.
εὔκολος ἦν φεύγω, δύσκολος ἦν ἐπάγω.

('You love me when I don't want it, but I love you when you don't want it. You are receptive if I run away, but difficult if I press you.') M. Lausberg (*Das Ein-zeldistichon* (München, 1982), 309) argues that Martial is trying to outdo Strato in brevity of expression, but Strato's priority in date remains unproven.

At *Ars Am.* III 475–8, Ovid recommends the girl to be a bit difficult. Martial reuses the theme also at I 57 and IV 42.11. This type of paradox is particularly close to his heart. It is emphasised by the chiasmus in each line.

2 **velle tuum:** the use of the infinitive as a substantive with a personal pronoun is a colloquialism. Compare e.g. Petr. *Sat.* 52.3 *meum ... intellegere*; Pers. 5.53 *velle suum cuique est*; 1.27.
Dindymus: only found as a personal name in Martial. It was the name of a mountain in Asia Minor associated with the worship of Cybele, whose eunuch priests were well-known (see on V 41.3). Martial uses it for boys, in erotic contexts, at X 42; XI 6 (see Kay's note); XII 75.4; for eunuchs at VI 39.21; XI 81.

84

For the exchange of gifts at the Saturnalia, see on V 18; for the gambling associated with the festival, see on V 30.8. The first part of the poem is appropriate for the end of the book, since Martial often links his poetry with the Saturnalia, but it serves as the prelude to a characteristic joke.

1 Naturally schools had holidays at the Saturnalia. At *Ep.* VIII 7.1, Pliny writes to Tacitus *adeo tu in scholam revocas, ego adhuc Saturnalia extendo* ('you are summoning me back to school, but I am still extending the Saturnalia').
nuts: for gambling for nuts by small boys, compare V 30.8; also XIV 19, where Martial says that gambling for nuts has often 'carried off boys' bums', usually interpreted as meaning that they have been beaten when playing for nuts has made them late for school.
The phrase *nucibus ... relictis* comes from Persius 1.10, where it indicates the ending of childhood.
2 Schoolmasters were notorious for shouting: hence Martial's bitter complaint against a neighbouring one, whose *clamor* is louder than that of the crowd in the amphitheatre, when their favourite gladiator wins, at IX 68.
3 **blando:** an appropriate epithet for an addiction.
fritillus: an onomatopoeic word. The box was grooved on the inside, to prevent against cheating, and this would increase the noise of rattling. See Balsdon, *Life and Leisure*, 387 n.107.
4 **popina:** see on V 70.3.

5   Gambling was, at least in theory, illegal except at the Saturnalia, and the aediles
       would be the magistrates with the task of enforcing the law. Compare XIV 1.3,
       where the *verna* (home-born slave) *nec timet aedilem moto spectare fritillo* ('is
       not afraid of catching sight of the aedile when shaking the dice-box'). See also
       Kay on XI 6.2, where the Saturnalia are described as days *regnator quibus
       imperat fritillus* ('on which King Dice-Box reigns'). Carter (on Suet. *Aug.* 71.1)
       argues that 'clearly public disapproval was minimal by Augustus's day', and
       suggests that the law under the Empire was 'directed rather against
       professionals and those who made a habit of gaming in public places than
       against people who liked a flutter at dinner'. Domitian shared a taste for
       gambling with Augustus and Claudius (Suet. *Dom.* 21).

       the aedile: in a comparison between virtue and pleasure, Seneca says that we
       shall find the latter *latitantem ... circa balinea et sudatoria ac loca aedilem
       metuentia ... mero atque unguento madentem* (cf. *udus*) – *Vit. Beat.* 7.3 ('hiding
       around the baths and sweating-houses and places that fear the aedile ... and
       soaked in neat wine and perfume').

       rogat: 'asks for favour', as at VIII 8.3.

       udus: compare for this sense *madidus*; also XII 70.4.

7   **smaller ones:** at VIII 71.3–4 Martial insists that the value of the gifts should
       either stay the same from year to year or increase.

8   **Galla:** a common name often used by Martial.

10–11 The first of March was the feast of the *Matronalia*, when presents were given
       to women, just as they were given to men at the Saturnalia – hence *vestra*.
       Despite the title of the feast, they were not only given to married women.

       It so happened that this day was also Martial's birthday, which explains his
       joke at X 24.3, where he says that even girls send him presents (although it is
       their day for getting them).

166

Indexes

INDEX OF NAMES

INDEX OF SUBJECTS

INDEX OF GREEK AND LATIN WORDS